Ariel Feldman
Tefillin and Mezuzot from Qumran

Beihefte zur Zeitschrift für die alttestamentliche Wissenschaft

Edited by
John Barton, Reinhard G. Kratz, Nathan MacDonald,
Sara Milstein and Markus Witte

Volume 538

Ariel Feldman

Tefillin and Mezuzot from Qumran

—

New Readings and Interpretations

DE GRUYTER

ISBN 978-3-11-072526-1
e-ISBN (PDF) 978-3-11-072537-7
e-ISBN (EPUB) 978-3-11-072543-8
ISSN 0934-2575

Library of Congress Control Number: 2021948865

Bibliographic information published by the Deutsche Nationalbibliothek
The Deutsche Nationalbibliothek lists this publication in the Deutsche Nationalbibliografie;
detailed bibliographic data are available on the Internet at http://dnb.dnb.de.

© 2022 Walter de Gruyter GmbH, Berlin/Boston
Typesetting: Meta Systems Publishing & Printservices GmbH, Wustermark
Printing and binding: CPI books GmbH, Leck

www.degruyter.com

MIX
Papier aus verantwor-
tungsvollen Quellen
FSC
www.fsc.org   FSC® C083411

Preface

I became interested in tefillin and mezuzot from the Judean Desert while writing an essay on the book of Deuteronomy in the Dead Sea Scrolls. Prior to this, I knew almost nothing about these curious objects. Having spent long hours in their company, I still feel that I know less than I should. It is, however, my hope that this study contributes to the important task of bringing these precious artifacts to the attention of those who are interested in the history of biblical texts, their early reception, and Second Temple Judaism in general. I am very grateful to Professor Reinhard Kratz and his distinguished colleagues on the editorial board of BZAW, Professors John Barton, Nathan MacDonald, Sara Milstein, and Markus Witte, for accepting this monograph for publication in their prestigious series. The staff at De Gruyter has been, as always, extremely efficient. Sophie Wagenhofer, Aaron Sanborn-Overby, Alice Meroz, and Sabina Dabrowski have generously offered the much-needed support and guidance. Dr. Marilyn Lundberg Melzian has kindly provided the permission to include here the images of 1QPhyl taken by Bruce and Kenneth Zuckerman. Atalya Fadida, Beatriz Riestra, and Orit Rosengarten of the Israel Antiquities Authority have graciously responded to my multiple requests and granted the permission to publish the images of the texts. Zachary Poppen has generously given of his time to proofread the entire manuscript. I offer my sincere thanks to them all.

The work on minute fragments written in minuscule scripts is challenging yet rewarding. I am truly blessed to have a spouse with whom I could share the challenges and joys of this project which grew out of our joint work on deciphering the Dead Sea Scrolls. It is even more gratifying to see our kids showing interest in our academic endeavors. It is to our two sons, Jonathan and Tal, that this book is dedicated.

Brite Divinity School   Fall 2021

https://doi.org/10.1515/9783110725377-201

Contents

Preface —— v

Abbreviations —— ix

Frequently Cited Sources —— xi

Introduction. Tefillin and Mezuzot from Qumran: An Unfinished Business —— 1

1   Tefillin and Mezuzot from the Judean Desert: The Artifacts —— 5

2   Tefillin and Mezuzot among Other Manuscripts of Exodus
    and Deuteronomy from the Judean Desert —— 32

3   1QPhyl (1Q13) —— 62

4   4QPhyl L (4Q139) —— 74

5   4QPhyl T (4Q147) —— 80

6   4QPhyl U (4Q148) —— 91

7   4QMez C (4Q151) —— 96

8   8QPhyl (8Q3) —— 102

Conclusion —— 141

Bibliography —— 143

List of Figures —— 151

Subject Index —— 153

Index of Ancient Sources —— 155

Contents

Abbreviations

BZAW	Beihefte zur Zeitschrift für die alttestamentliche Wissenschaft
CBET	Contributions to Biblical Exegesis and Theology
DJD	Discoveries in the Judaean Desert
DSD	*Dead Sea Discoveries*
FAT	Forschungen zum Alten Testament
FRLANT	Forschungen zur Religion und Literatur des Alten und Neuen Testaments
IEJ	*Israel Exploration Journal*
HTR	*Harvard Theological Review*
HUCA	*Hebrew Union College Annual*
JAJ	*Journal of Ancient Judaism*
JBL	*Journal of Biblical Literature*
JJS	*Journal of Jewish Studies*
JSP	*Journal for the Study of the Pseudepigrapha*
JSQ	*Jewish Studies Quarterly*
RevQ	*Revue de Qumrân*
STDJ	Studies on the Texts of the Desert of Judah
SVT	Supplements to Vetus Testamentum
TSAJ	Texte und Studien zum antiken Judentum
VT	*Vetus Testamentum*

https://doi.org/10.1515/9783110725377-202

Frequently Cited Sources

DJD 1   Dominique Barthélemy and Józef T. Milik, *Qumran Cave 1*. DJD 1. Oxford: Clarendon Press, 1955.

DJD 2   Pierre Benoit et al., *Les grottes de Murabba'at*. DJD 2, 2a. Oxford: Clarendon Press, 1961.

DJD 3   Maurice Baillet et al., *Les 'petites grottes' de Qumrân*. DJD 3, 3a. Oxford: Clarendon Press, 1962.

DJD 6   Roland de Vaux and Józef T. Milik, *Qumrân grotte 4.II: I. Archéologie, II. Tefillin, Mezuzot et Targums (4Q128–4Q157)*. DJD 6. Oxford: Clarendon Press, 1977.

DJD 9   Patrick Skehan, Eugene Ulrich, and Judith E. Sanderson, *Qumran Cave 4.IV: Palaeo-Hebrew and Greek Biblical Manuscripts*. DJD 9. Oxford: Clarendon Press, 1992.

DJD 12   Eugene Ulrich et al., *Qumran Cave 4.VII: Genesis to Numbers*. DJD 12. Oxford: Clarendon Press, 1994.

DJD 14   Eugene Ulrich et al., *Qumran Cave 4.IX: Deuteronomy, Joshua, Judges, Kings*. DJD 14. Oxford: Clarendon Press, 1995.

DJD 23   Florentino García Martínez et al., *Qumran Cave 11.II: 11Q2–18, 11Q20–31*. DJD 23. Oxford: Clarendon Press, 1998.

DJD 38   James H. Charlesworth et al., *Miscellaneous Texts from the Judaean Desert*. DJD 38. Oxford: Clarendon Press, 2000.

https://doi.org/10.1515/9783110725377-203

Introduction. Tefillin and Mezuzot from Qumran: An Unfinished Business

Tefillin and mezuzah, the two iconic Jewish ritual objects, require little introduction. Affixed to a doorpost, a small capsule of mezuzah holds inside two passages from the book of Deuteronomy, Deut 6:4–9 and 11:13–21.[1] Each of the two boxes of tefillin, also known as phylacteries, contains the same two scriptural texts, as well as Exodus 13:1–16.[2] These are customarily donned during a morning prayer: one box is attached to the forehead and the other to the arm.

These familiar practices are traditionally derived from the biblical verses placed inside mezuzah and tefillin: Exod 13:9, 16 and Deut 6:8–9; 11:18. Thus, for instance, Deut 6:8–9 commands: "Bind them as a sign on your hand and let them serve as a symbol on your forehead; inscribe them on the doorposts of your house and on your gates."[3] And yet, it is far from certain whether these and similar injunctions from Exodus and Deuteronomy were meant to be taken literally.[4] After all, the Hebrew Bible never explicitly mentions the actual practices that came to be known as tefillin and mezuzah. The early rabbis were well aware of this fact and regarded tefillin as "the classic example of a biblical law whose details are wholly 'of the Scribes'."[5]

Searching for the early evidence for the tefillin and mezuzah practices, scholars often point to the Letter of Aristeas, a Jewish work written in Greek during the second half of the second century BCE. According to some, it refers to both tefillin and mezuzah (158–159).[6] Another reference to these practices

---

1 On the origins and meaning of the term "mezuzah," see Eva-Maria Jansson, *The Message of a Mitsvah: The Mezuzah in Rabbinic Literature* (Lund: Novapress, 1999), 30–33.

2 On the various terms employed by the ancient sources to describe tefillin, see Jeffrey H. Tigay, "On the Term Phylacteries (Matt 23:5)," *HTR* 72 (1979): 45–53.

3 Unless specified, all the translations from the Hebrew Bible in this monograph are from the New Jewish Publications Society (*Tanakh*) translation.

4 See Yehudah Cohn, *Tangled Up in Text: Tefillin and the Ancient World* (Providence: Brown University, 2008), 33–53.

5 Louis Isaac Rabinowitz, "Tefillin," in *Encyclopedia Judaica*, ed. Michael Berenbaum and Fred Skolnik, 2nd edition (Detroit: Macmillan, 2007), 19:577–80 (577). One might also mention here that both Samaritans and Karaites interpret the so-called tefillin commandment metaphorically. See Nahum Sarna, *Exodus*, The JPS Torah Commentary (Philadelphia: JPS, 2003), 267. On the Samaritan and Karaite mezuzah practices, see Louis Isaac Rabinowitz, "Mezuzah," in *Encyclopedia Judaica*, ed. Michael Berenbaum and Fred Skolnik (Detroit: Macmillan, 2007), 14:156–57 (157); Reinhard Pummer, *The Samaritans: A Profile* (Grand Rapids: Eerdmans, 2016), 220.

6 See, for instance, Erich S. Gruen, "The Letter of Aristeas," in *Outside the Bible: Ancient Jewish Writings Related to Scripture*, ed. Louis H. Feldman et al. (Philadelphia: JPS, 2013), 3:2711–

https://doi.org/10.1515/9783110725377-001

might be found in the writings of Philo who lived in the first century CE Alexandria (*Spec. Laws* 4.137–142).[7] At the very latest – all seem to agree – Josephus Flavius, writing around the end of the first century CE, evokes both mezuzah and tefillin (*Ant.* 4:212–213).[8]

Precious as they are, these possible early references to mezuzah and tefillin reveal almost nothing about the objects themselves. As with many other aspects of Second Temple Judaism, it was the discovery of the Dead Sea Scrolls that rescued ancient tefillin and mezuzot from an obscurity. The findings from the Judean Desert brought to light multiple texts that have been identified as mezuzot and tefillin. Most of them come from the Caves of Qumran. Several others were found in the caves associated with the First and Second Jewish revolts against Rome. A recent study aptly describes them as the "Galapagos Islands" of the tefillin practice.[9]

Since their discovery and publication, scholarly work on tefillin and mezuzot from the Judean Desert proceeded in two directions. First, since both tefillin and mezuzot contain scriptural texts, much attention was given to comparing their readings to other textual witnesses of Exodus and Deuteronomy.[10] Second, given the existence of a considerable body of rabbinic regulations pertaining to tefillin and mezuzot, a significant effort was invested into mapping and evaluating continuities and discontinuities between the Second Temple exemplars and tefillin and mezuzot referenced in the later rabbinic texts.[11] One attempt at bringing insights gained from these two lines of inquiry into a conversation with the contemporary Hellenistic-Roman apotropaic practices is a recent monograph suggesting that tefillin originated as long-life amulets.[12]

Owing a great deal to the earlier scholarship, the present volume does not claim to be a comprehensive treatment of tefillin and mezuzot from the Judean

---

68 (2741–42). Cohn, *Tangled Up*, 80–82, however, doubts that the text implies an actual tefillin practice.

7 See, for example, Naomi G. Cohen, "On the Special Laws 1–4," in *Outside the Bible: Ancient Jewish Writings Related to Scripture*, ed. Louis H. Feldman et al. (Philadelphia: JPS, 2013), 1:1033–1133 (1106–1108); eadem, "Philo's Tefillin," *Proceedings of the World Congress of Jewish Studies: Division A: The Period of the Bible* (1985): 196–206. Cohn, *Tangled Up*, 83–86, agrees that Philo may refer here to a mezuzah, though the wording seems to imply a practice reminiscent of the late antique Samaritan custom to inscribe the Ten Commandments on stone lintels. He, however, does not think that Philo's exposition on Deut 6:6–9//11:18–20 reflects a literal interpretation of the tefillin commandment.

8 See, for instance, Jansson, *Message of a Mitsvah*, 35; Cohn, *Tangled Up*, 108.

9 Yehudah Cohn, "Were Tefillin Phylacteries?," *JJS* 59 (2008): 39–61 (40).

10 For a discussion and pertinent bibliography, see Chapter 2.

11 For an overview and relevant bibliography, see Chapter 1.

12 Cohn, *Tangled Up*, passim.

Desert. Rather, it hopes to contribute to their ongoing study by revisiting the extant editions of tefillin and mezuzot in the search for fragments that have not been adequately addressed. Such a quest may appear to be somewhat surprising, as the vast majority of tefillin and mezuzot was already published by the end of the 1970s and thus have long been available to the scholarly community. And yet, in several respects mezuzot and tefillin from the Judean Desert remain an unfinished business. Thus, multiple tefillin from Qumran remain unopened. These include the nine tefillin recently re-discovered in the depths of a storage.[13] Awaiting to be unfolded, they are not a part of this monograph. Moreover, even those tefillin and mezuzot that have been opened and published long ago have not yet revealed all their secrets.[14] A close scrutiny of their editions indicates a presence of texts that have not been fully assessed. These fall into three categories. First, there are multiple tefillin and mezuzot that contain legible fragments which their editors were unable to identify. Second, several tefillin and mezuzot feature imprints of letters that have not been deciphered. Third, there are texts which were classified as tefillin and mezuzot yet left unread.

It was the last category that drew my attention to tefillin and mezuzot in the first place. In a series of articles co-authored with Faina Feldman we have tried to decipher three texts which Józef T. Milik identified as tefillin and mezuzot but decided not to transcribe (4QPhyl T [4Q147]; 4QPhyl U [4Q148]; Mur5).[15] Our preliminary readings indicate that the wording of these three texts does not match that of the scriptural passages included either in tefillin/mezuzot from the Judean Desert or in those prescribed by the rabbis. As a follow-up to these studies, I decided to conduct a thorough investigation of the editions of tefillin and mezuzot from Qumran in the hope to find more texts that could benefit from further study. This examination led me to several fragments that belong with the other two aforementioned categories. Two such texts, 4QMez B (4Q150), where the imprints of letters reveal a lost segment of a biblical passage, and 8QMez (8Q4), containing several undeciphered fragments, have been published elsewhere.[16] My other findings are incorporated in this monograph.

---

13 Ilan Ben Zion, "Uncovered in Jerusalem, 9 Tiny Unopened Dead Sea Scrolls," *The Times of Israel*, March 12, 2014 (https://www.timesofisrael.com/nine-tiny-new-dead-sea-scrolls-come-to-light/).

14 See, for instance, a revised edition of several long-published tefillin in Anna Busa, *Die Phylakterien von Qumran (4Q128.129.135.137) aus der Heidelberger Papyrussammlung* (Heidelberg: Universitätsverlag Winter, 2015).

15 Ariel Feldman and Faina Feldman, "4Q147: An Amulet?," *DSD* 26 (2019): 1–29; eidem, "4Q148 (4QPhylactère U): Another Amulet from Qumran?," *JSJ* 50 (2019): 197–222; eidem, "Is Mur 5 a Mezuzah?," *RevQ* 32 (2019): 291–98.

16 Ariel Feldman and Tal Feldman, "4Q150 (4QMez B) and 8Q4 (8QMez) Revisited," *RevQ* 33 (2021): 121–38.

I must state from the outset that this book is not an attempt to read every partially deciphered or unidentified fragment of the published tefillin and mezuzot.[17] Instead, it focuses on those fragments where the state of preservation and the quality of the available images allowed me to say something substantially new about them.[18] Thus, this book does not claim to "finish" the "unfinished business" of tefillin and mezuzot from the Judean Desert. Nor does it pretend to be the last word on the reading of the fragments it revisits. New imaging techniques and further scrutiny of the texts will surely improve the work presented here. Nevertheless, I hope that the new readings and interpretations proposed in this volume offer a modest contribution to our understanding of both specific artifacts and the corpus in general.

To accomplish the task at hand, this study proceeds as follows. To set the stage, Chapter 1 offers a bird's-eye overview of tefillin and mezuzot from the Judean Desert, including their contents, physical and scribal features, and methods of classification. Since the majority of the new readings proposed in this book are from Exodus and Deuteronomy, to properly place these within their wider textual context, Chapter 2 briefly surveys manuscripts of Exodus and Deuteronomy from the Judean Desert. The next several chapters, Chapters 3–8, take a close look at six texts: 1QPhyl, 4QPhyl L, 4QPhyl T, 4QPhyl U, 4QMez C, and 8QPhyl. For two of these, 1QPhyl and 4QMez C, this is the first attempt at revisiting their unidentified or undeciphered fragments since their initial publication (Chapters 3, 7). In the case of 4QPhyl L, Chapter 4 offers the first transcription of the imprints of letters deposited by a segment of text that is no longer extant on the parchment. For 4QPhyl T and 4QPhyl U, two texts that Faina Feldman and I studied in detail elsewhere, Chapters 5–6 propose new physical reconstruction (4QPhyl T) and reading (4QPhyl U). The concluding remarks bring the threads together and outline several areas in which the texts addressed in this monograph contribute to the study of ancient tefillin and mezuzot.

---

17 One regrettable omission from this volume is XQPhyl 4, which Yigael Yadin was unable to decipher. See Yigael Yadin, "Tefillin (Phylacteries) from Qumran (XQPhyl 1–4)," *Eretz-Israel 9* (1969): 60–85 (75; Hebrew); idem, *Tefillin from Qumran* (Jerusalem: The Israel Exploration Society, 1969), 30–31. Unfortunately, I was unable to obtain digital images of this tefillin slip (see further note 426). I am grateful to Mrs. Hagit Maoz of the Shrine of the Book for responding to my multiple queries.

18 Thus, for instance, I do not include here a detailed study of the tefillin slips 4QPhyl D, E, and F (4Q131–133). All the three contain several badly damaged fragments that their editor, Józef T. Milik, was unable to read and identify (Milik, DJD 6:35, 56). However, a scrutiny of their images yields little results.

1 Tefillin and Mezuzot from the Judean Desert: The Artifacts

Tefillin and mezuzot from the Judean Desert constitute a relatively large corpus of artifacts.[19] The first encounter with the tiny fragments, minuscule scripts, and leather cases of varying shapes and sizes may prove to be quite bewildering. This chapter seeks to provide a brief introduction to these items. It begins with a discussion of tefillin, both texts and cases, and then turns to mezuzot.

Tefillin from the Judean Desert

The Hebrew/Aramaic noun tefillin (sg. tefillah), the precise origins of which remain obscure, appears in the texts of rabbinic Judaism.[20] Whether the artifacts studied here were called "tefillin" in late Second Temple times, the period to which they are dated, is unknown.[21] Though potentially anachronistic, the

---

19 Most of tefillin and mezuzot slips from the Judean Desert were published in the DJD series. See Dominique Barthélemy, DJD 1:72–76 (1QPhyl); Józef T. Milik, DJD 2:80–85 (MurPhyl & Mur5); Maurice Baillet, DJD 3:149–161 (8QPhyl & 8QMez); Józef T. Milik, DJD 3:178 (5QPhyl); idem, DJD 6:33–86 (4QPhyl A–U & 4QMez A–G); Florentino García Martínez and Eibert Tigchelaar, DJD 23:445–46 (11Q31; see Table 1 below); Matthew Morgenstern and Michael Segal, DJD 38:183–91 (XHev/SePhyl). A few tefillin were published elsewhere. See Yohanan Aharoni, "Expedition B," *IEJ* 11 (1960–61): 11–24 (22–23 [34ṢePhyl]); Yadin, *Tefillin from Qumran* (XQPhyl 1–4). Some of the fragments edited by Milik in DJD 6 were made available earlier by Karl Georg Kuhn, *Phylakterien Aus Der Höhle 4 von Qumran* (Heidelberg: Carl Winter, 1957). They have been recently re-edited in Busa, *Die Phylakterien von Qumran*. For a new edition of tefillin published by Aharoni, see Yonatan Adler, "Remains of Tefillin from Naḥal Ṣeʾelim (Wadi Seiyal): A Leather Case and Two Inscribed Fragments (34Se 1 A–B) with Paleographic Analysis by Ada Yardeni," *DSD* 24 (2017): 112–37. For the publication history of the tefillin cases, see discussion and pertinent bibliography in Yonatan Adler, "A Typological Distinction between Two Types of Tefillin Cases from Qumran," *Judea and Samaria Research Studies* 28 (2019): 81–99 (82–83; Hebrew).
20 On the derivation of תפילין from תפילה, "prayer," implying that this name reflects their use during prayer, see Abraham M. Habermann, "On Ancient Tefillin," *Eretz-Israel* 3 (1954): 174–77 (174; Hebrew). This etymology, however, is not without a problem, as some rabbinic sources indicate that in antiquity tefillin were worn throughout the day (b. Sukkah 28a; b. Menahot 36b). See Jeffrey H. Tigay, "Tefillin," in *Encyclopaedia Biblica* (Jerusalem: Mosad Bialik, 1982), 8:883–95 (884; Hebrew). Searching for the origins of the term, Tigay, ibid., 887, points to a text from Ugarit describing Baal as having *tply* on his head. On this text see further Jeffrey H. Tigay and Marvin H. Pope, "A Description of Baal," *Ugarit-Forschungen* 3 (1971): 117–30 (124–25).
21 Cohn, *Tangled Up*, 147, draws attention to the 3rd century BCE Aramaic papyrus from Egypt, C 3.28 Cowley 81, listing among items entrusted to a certain Jonathan twenty תפלה זי כסף. Mentioned along with "string(s) of beads" (line 105), these have been understood as silver

https://doi.org/10.1515/9783110725377-002

use of this term seems to be supported by the scholarly consensus that these objects are the forerunners of the later rabbis' tefillin.[22]

Broadly speaking, tefillin, both Second Temple artifacts and those prescribed by the later halakhah, are comprised of two main components: an inscribed leather slip (or slips) and a case in which this slip (or slips) was placed. The findings from the Judean Desert yield both the cases and the inscribed slips.[23] Each of these components deserves a closer look.

Tefillin cases.[24] A recent study counts 27 tefillin cases from the Judean Desert.[25] Some of them were found during organized excavations. Others were

---

amulets. See Bezalel Porten and Ada Yardeni, *Textbook of Aramaic Documents from Ancient Egypt: Volume 3: Literature, Accounts, Lists* (Jerusalem: Hebrew University, 1993), 260, 267.

22 The objects in question are also known as "phylacteries," a noun derived from the Greek φυλακτήριον, "means of protection, an amulet" (Andrea Becker, "Phylakterion," in *Brill's New Pauly Encyclopedia of the Ancient World*, ed. Helmuth Schneider et al. [Leiden: Brill, 2007], 11:206–207). This designation can be traced back to Matt 23:5 where, according to most scholars, φυλακτήρια describes what the rabbis call "tefillin" (see further Ariel Feldman, "On Amulets, Apotropaic Prayers, and Phylacteries: The Contribution of Three New Texts from the Judean Desert," in *Petitioners, Penitents, and Poets*, ed. Ariel Feldman and Timothy J. Sandoval, BZAW 524 [Berlin: De Gruyter, 2020], 169–98 [193–96]). Such a designation coming from a source predating rabbinic literature might appear as a more appropriate term for the Second Temple artifacts. However, it presents these objects as amulets, a view that is accepted by some (e.g., Cohn, *Tangled Up*) and rejected by others (e.g., Tigay, "On the Term Phylacteries"). In light of this, Adler concludes that the more neutral "tefillin" is preferable. Yonatan Adler, "The Distribution of Tefillin Finds among the Judean Desert Caves," in *The Caves of Qumran: Proceedings of the International Conference, Lugano 2014*, ed. Marcello Fidanzio, STDJ 118 (Leiden: Brill, 2016), 161–73 (161n1).

23 It is assumed that tefillin cases were attached to the body by means of a strap. A case photographed on Plate I in DJD 1 (#7) appears to preserve remains of such a strap. For another possible exemplar of a tefillin strap, see Milik, DJD 6:34 and Plate VI (item #14).

24 In this monograph, I adopt the term "case." Yadin, *Tefillin from Qumran*, 7 (and *passim*), prefers "capsule," which he uses as an English equivalent of the rabbinic קציצה. Yet Adler, "Typological Distinction," 82n1, observes that in the rabbinic texts קציצה often designates only the four compartments in which the four inscribed slips were placed. Cohn, *Tangled Up*, 56n2, opts for the term "housing." For him, it corresponds to the Hebrew בית (בית תפילין), while "case," he argues, implies "a more structured object than the ones found." Further on the terms employed by the rabbinic texts to describe different parts of tefillin cases see Yonatan Adler, "A Tefillin Case from the Cave of the Scrolls (Cave 34) at Naḥal Ṣeʾelim," *In the Highland's Depth, Ephraim Range and Binyamin Research Studies* 7 (2017): 145–62 (Hebrew).

25 Adler, "Typological Distinction," 82. Yehudah B. Cohn, "Reading Material Features of Qumran Tefillin and Mezuzot," in *Material Aspects of Reading in Ancient and Medieval Cultures*, ed. Anna Krauß, Jonas Leipziger, and Friederike Schücking-Jungblut, Materiale Textkulturen 26 (Berlin: De Gruyter, 2020), 89–100 (89), counts 25 cases. Here one might mention that the two tefillin slips known as MurPhyl (Mur4) were found wrapped in a piece of leather containing a text in Greek, Mur95, featuring a list of names. The folded package measured 35 × 10 mm (Milik,

discovered by the Bedouins, which renders their precise provenance uncertain.[26] Based on the available information, most of the cases came from the caves of Qumran, Wadi Murabbaʻat produced one case, and another one was found in the caves of Naḥal Ṣeʼelim.[27] These numbers are, however, subject to change when the tefillin that have been long unaccounted for are published.[28]

The tefillin cases appear to fall into two main categories: those with four compartments and those with one compartment only.[29] They are commonly understood to belong to a head and an arm tefillin respectively. This interpretation relies on a similar distinction in the rabbinic texts.[30] Among the cases with four compartments from Qumran, Yonatan Adler differentiates between two sub-categories. There are tefillin cases in which the compartments are separated by stitches made with a tendon thread.[31] These constitute the vast majority. Yet there are also three cases where the compartments are separated by a cut through the leather, in addition to the stitches. He suggests that these two sub-types reflect different interpretations of the biblical commandment.[32]

Overall, tefillin cases have a rectangular shape and are exceedingly small. Cohn observes that a typical size of a leather patch from which cases with four

---

DJD 2:80; Benoit, DJD 2:227–28). On such wrapping as reflecting a custom akin to a later rabbinic regulation, see Shelomo Goren, "The Tefillin from the Judean Desert in Light of Halakhah," in idem, *Torat Ha-Moadim* (Tel-Aviv: Abraham Zioni, 1964), 496–510 (500; Hebrew). He argues that it might have been intended to render them into one text, as required by the rabbinic halakhah for the head tefillin. See further David Rothstein, "From Bible to Murabbaʻat: Studies in the Literary, Textual and Scribal Features of Phylacteries and Mezuzot in Ancient Israel and Early Judaism" (PhD Diss., University of California, Los Angeles, 1992), 295–97.

26 See Adler, "Distribution," 162–63.

27 Adler, "Distribution," 162–63. For further discussion and breakdown of the findings by the cave, see idem, "Typological Distinction," 83. On the case from Naḥal Ṣeʼelim, see Adler, "Remains of Tefillin."

28 See note 13.

29 Among the published cases, Adler, "Typological Distinction," 83, counts 8 cases of the fist type and at least 9 of the second. Despite earlier claims, Adler, "Typological Distinction," 83n4, argues that Judean Desert yields no cases with three compartments. The two tefillin that have been classified as such in an earlier scholarship are simply damaged. Cf. Cohn, *Tangled Up*, 57–58.

30 For the relevant sources see Cohn, *Tangled Up*, 58n11. While there is an obvious danger in anachronistically applying the later rabbinic practices to Second Temple evidence, scholars suggest that in this case the halakhah of the Sages may reflect an earlier custom. Adler, "Distribution," 165; idem, "Typological Distinction," 84. Cohn, *Tangled Up*, 58–59, who rightly highlights the inherent anachronism of this approach, hypothesizes that these two kinds of cases may represent different interpretations of the tefillin ritual.

31 On the use of a tendon thread, see Yadin, *Tefillin from Qumran*, 10.

32 Adler, "Typological Distinction." He argues (ibid., 89–90) that these two kinds of cases reflect different interpretations of the enigmatic biblical טוטפת (Exod 13:16; Deut 6:8; 11:18). On this term see further Jeffrey H. Tigay, "On the Meaning of T(W)TPT," *JBL* 101 (1982): 321–31.

compartments were made is 25 × 25 mm, whereas single cell cases were typical-
ly formed from a patch measuring 35 × 10 mm.[33] As to the final product, the
available data suggest that the length of a closed tefillin case with four compartments ranges between 35 and 20 mm, while the width does not exceed 20 mm.[34]
The larger exemplars among the one-compartment cases measure 20 × 15 mm.[35]

Leather slips. As with tefillin cases, the precise number of tefillin slips from
the Judean Desert is somewhat difficult to determine. Table 1 (below) counts
some 39 slips.[36] To these one must add the recently re-discovered tefillin awaiting to be unfolded. The assessment of the slips is further complexified by two
factors. First, it is not entirely clear whether the criteria used by scholars to
differentiate between the slips of tefillin and mezuzah are adequate. In some
cases (see below) a text identified as a mezuzah could also be a tefillin and vice
versa. Second, several slips designated as tefillin yield wording that does not
match the scriptural pericopae found either in tefillin from the Judean Desert
or in those described in the rabbinic sources. One example is 4QPhyl N (4Q141)
containing verses from Deuteronomy 32. Its editor considered it to be a part of
tefillin 4QPhyl L-N (4Q139–141).[37] David Nakman, however, proposes that
4QPhyl N is not a tefillin but an amulet.[38] Moreover, there are also 4QPhyl T
(4Q147) and 4QPhyl U (4Q148) which resemble tefillin slips but contain a non-
biblical text (see Chapters 5–6). Elsewhere, Faina Feldman and I suggested that
these too could be amulets (see Chapters 5–6).[39] Indeed, according to rabbinic
sources tefillin and amulets might have looked quite alike.[40] And yet one could

---

33 Cohn, *Tangled Up*, 57–58.
34 For the pertinent data on the cases from Qumran Cave 4, see Milik, DJD 6:35. His notes
should be compared with the new measurements in Adler, "Typological Distinction," 95n31.
For the data on XQPhyl and tefillin case from Naḥal Ṣe'elim see Yadin, *Tefillin from Qumran*,
9, and Adler, "Remains of Tefillin," 115.
35 See Milik, DJD 6:35. It is not always clear whether Milik's dimensions refer to a closed case
or an open one.
36 This number does not include the fragments assigned to 11Q31 (see Table 1 below). Overall,
very few of these slips reached scholars in their original cases. These include: a. slips 4Q131–
133 found in Milik's case #1 (Cave 4); b. four slips found in Milik's case #2 (Cave 4, unrolled);
c. two or three (unspecified) slips found in Milik's case #4 (Cave 4); d. three slips in a damaged
case 5Q8 (Cave 5; unrolled); e. tefillin case purchased by Yadin with four slips, only three of
which are original to the case (XQPhyl; unknown cave). See Milik, DJD 3:178; 6:35; Yadin,
Tefillin from Qumran, 9–11, 30; and further Cohn, *Tangled Up*, 56–57.
37 Milik, DJD 6:70. This suggestion relies on the similarities in the script, which, as Milik
acknowledges, are not "très caractéristique."
38 David Nakman, "The Contents and the Order of the Biblical Sections in the Tefillin from
Qumran and Rabbinic Halakhah," *Cathedra* 112 (2004): 19–44 (35–37; Hebrew).
39 Feldman and Feldman, "4Q147"; eidem, "4Q148 (4QPhylactère U)."
40 Feldman, "On Amulets, Apotropaic Prayers, and Phylacteries," 184–85.

also argue that these aberrant texts are tefillin, just not of the type previously recognized.[41] Given this ambiguity, it seems prudent to include 4QPhyl N, 4QPhyl T, and 4QPhyl U in the following list of tefillin slips from the Judean Desert with an acknowledgment that, given all the aforementioned considerations, this list should be viewed as a provisional one.

Tab. 1: Tefillin Slips from the Judean Desert.

Caves of Qumran[42]
Cave 1

1QPhyl (1Q13; at least 1 slip [see Chapter 3]; Hellenistic-Roman[43])
    Exod 13:2–3, 7–9; Deut 5:1–9, 11–17, 21–25, 27; 10:17–18; 10:21–22; 11:1, 8–12
    In addition to these passages, several further verses from both Exodus and
    Deuteronomy are identified in Chapter 3: Exod 13:15; Deut 5:29–33; 11:4, 17–20.

Cave 4

4QPhyl A (4Q128; 1 slip; Hellenistic-Roman)
    Recto: Deut 5:1, 3, 5, 8–10, 12–14, 27–32; 6:2–3; 10:12–22; 11:1–15, 17
    Verso: Deut 11:18–21; Exod 12:43–51; 13:1–7
4QPhyl B (4Q129; 1 slip; Hellenistic-Roman)
    Recto: Deut 5:1–2, 4–11, 13–31; 6:2–3
    Verso: Exod 13:9–16
4QPhyl C (4Q130; 1 slip; Hellenistic-Roman)
    Exod 13:1–16; Deut 6:4–9; 11:13–21

---

41 In "On Amulets, Apotropaic Prayers, and Phylacteries," 184–85, I wonder whether 4QPhyl T and U, when considered along with Matt 23:5, indicate that there was no clear-cut differentiation between tefillin and amulets in late Second Temple times.

42 For other lists of scriptural passages included in tefillin, see Rothstein, "From Bible to Murabbaʿat," 501–3; Nakman, "Contents and the Order," 41–42 (partial); David Lincicum, "St. Paul's Deuteronomy: The End of the Pentateuch and the Apostle to the Gentiles in Second Temple Jewish Context" (PhD diss., University of Oxford, 2009), 220–24; Cohn, *Tangled Up*, 65–66; Armin Lange, *Handbuch der Textfunde vom Toten Meer: Band 1: Die Handschriften biblischer Bücher von Qumran und den anderen Fundorten* (Tübingen: Mohr Siebeck, 2009), 117–19; Esther Eshel, Hanan Eshel, and Armin Lange, "'Hear, O Israel' in Gold: An Ancient Amulet from Halbturn in Austria," *JAJ* 1 (2010): 43–64 (47–48); Busa, *Die Phylakterien von Qumran*, 50–51.

43 Milik, DJD 6:37, argued that the script of tefillin remained stable from the middle of the 2nd century BCE to the 1st century CE. Apparently for this reason he offered no specific dating for the tefillin slips he edited. Following Jastram, where the earlier scholarship offers no dating of a given tefillin slip, I use the tentative general dating "Hellenistic-Roman." See Nathan Jastram, "2.2.5.1 Tefillin and Mezuzot," in *Textual History of the Bible*, ed. Armin Lange (Brill, 2020), http://dx.doi.org.ezproxy.tcu.edu/10.1163/2452-4107_thb_COM_0002020501. On the order of biblical texts in this tefillin see Chapter 3.

The three slips 4QPhyl D-E-F were found in the same tefillin case:
4QPhyl D (4Q131; Hellenistic-Roman)
    Deut 11:13, 14, 16–17, 19, 21
4QPhyl E (4Q132; Hellenistic-Roman)
    Exod 13:1–2, 5–9
4QPhyl F (4Q133; Hellenistic-Roman)
    Exod 13:1–16

The three slips 4QPhyl G-H-I may belong to the same tefillin case:[44]
4QPhyl G (4Q134; Hellenistic-Roman)
    Recto: Deut 5:1–21
    Verso: Exod 13:11–12
4QPhyl H (4Q135; Hellenistic-Roman)
    Recto: Deut 5:22–33; 6:1–5
    Verso: Exod 13:14b–16
4QPhyl I (4Q136; Hellenistic-Roman)
    Recto: Deut 11:13–15, 17–19, 21; Exod 12:44–45, 47–51; 13:1, 3–10
    Verso: Deut 6:6–7

The two slips 4QPhyl J-K may belong to the same tefillin case:[45]
4QPhyl J (4Q137; Hellenistic-Roman)
    Recto: Deut 5:1–18, 20–24
    Verso: Deut 5:24–32; 6:2–3
4QPhyl K (4Q138; Hellenistic-Roman)
    Recto: Deut 10:12–22; 11:1–7
    Verso: Deut 11:7–12

The three slips 4QPhyl L-N may belong to the same tefillin case:[46]
4QPhyl L (4Q139; Hellenistic-Roman)
    Deut 5:7–9, 11–18, 21–24
4QPhyl M (4Q140; Hellenistic-Roman)
    Recto: Exod 12:44, 46, 48–50; 13:1–10
    Verso: Deut 5:33; 6:1–5
4QPhyl N (4Q141; Hellenistic-Roman)
    Deut 32:14–20, 32–33

4QPhyl O (4Q142; 1 slip; Hellenistic-Roman)
    Recto: Deut 5:1, 4–5, 8–9, 11, 14, 16
    Verso: Deut 6:7–9
4QPhyl P (4Q143; 1 slip; Hellenistic-Roman)
    Recto: Deut 10:22; 11:1–3
    Verso: Deut 11:18–20

---

44 Milik, DJD 6:58, notes their similar script.
45 Milik, DJD 6:64.
46 Milik, DJD 6:70. He, observes, however, that the similarities between their scripts are not "très caractéristique."

4QPhyl Q (4Q144; 1 slip; Hellenistic-Roman)
>Recto: Deut 11:4, 13, 15–18
>Verso: Exod 13:4–9

4QPhyl R (4Q145; 1 slip; Hellenistic-Roman)
>Recto: Exod 13:1–7
>Verso: Exod 13:7–10

4QPhyl S (4Q146; 1 slip; Hellenistic-Roman)
>Deut 11:19–21

4QPhyl T (4Q147; 1 slip? [see Chapter 5])
>The fragments may contain non-biblical text. See Chapter 5.

4QPhyl U (4Q148; 1 slip)
>The fragment may contain non-biblical text. See Chapter 6.

Cave 5

5QPhyl (5Q8)
>Three unrolled and undeciphered slips.[47]

Cave 8

8QPhyl (8Q3; 4 reconstructed slips [see Chapter 8]; 1st cent. CE[48])
>Exod 12:43–51; 13:1–16; Deut 5:1–14; 6:1–9; Deut 10:12–17, 19, 20–22; 11:1–3, 6–21
>
>In addition to these passages, several further verses from both Exodus and Deuteronomy are identified in Chapter 8, including: Deut 5:15–16, 22, 29–33.

Cave 11

11QUnidentified (11Q31; developed Herodian hand[49])
>Several undeciphered wads.[50]

Other Sites in the Judean Desert

Wadi Murabbaʿat
MurPhyl (Mur4; 2 slips; the first third of the 2nd cent. CE[51])
>Deut 11:13–21; 6:4–9

Naḥal Ṣeʾelim
34ṢePhyl (34Ṣe 1 A-B; 2 slips; 50–100 CE[52])
>Exod 13:2–16

---

47 Milik, DJD 3:178.

48 Baillet, DJD 3:149. On the order of biblical passages in these slips see Chapter 8.

49 García Martínez & Tigchelaar, DJD 23:445.

50 The undeciphered wads assigned to 11Q31 are likely to be tefillin fragments, as was suggested (*contra* García Martínez & Tigchelaar, DJD 23:445–46) by Cohn, *Tangled Up*, 58, and Adler, "Distribution," 163–64.

51 Lange, *Handbuch*, 118.

52 For the dating see the new edition by Adler, "Remains of Tefillin," 129–30.

Naḥal Ṣe'elim/Naḥal Ḥever
XḤev/SePhyl (XḤev/Se 5; 2 slips; Hellenistic-Roman)
    Exod 13:11–16; Deut 6:4–9; 11:13–21

Unknown Provenance

XQPhyl 1–3 (three slips) were found in the same tefillin case. The slip XPhyl 4 appears to originate elsewhere.[53]
XQPhyl 1 (50–1 BCE)
    Exod 12:43–51; 13:1–10; Deut 10:12–19
XQPhyl 2 (50–1 BCE)
    Deut 5:22–33; 6:1–3; 6:4–9
XQPhyl 3 (50–1 BCE)
    Deut 5:1–21; Exod 13:11–16
XQPhyl 4
    This slip, inscribed (unlike slips 1–3) on both sides, remains undeciphered.[54]

The unfolded tefillin slips come in a variety of shapes (often irregular) and sizes. For instance, the rectangular slips of XQPhyl 1–3 measure on average 27×42 mm.[55] Most of the slips are very thin. Thus, the slip XQPhyl 1 is only 0.04 mm thick.[56] The folded slips of tefillin are exceedingly small. In his list of tefillin cases from Cave 4, Milik provided measurements of the compartments in which individual folded slips were housed. The smallest compartment is 4×4 mm.[57]

Tefillin slips from the Judean Desert shed precious light on the work of the scribes who produced them.[58] Some slips are inscribed on one side only, while others are opisthographs.[59] Unlike many biblical Dead Sea Scrolls, tefillin slips

---

53 Yadin, *Tefillin from Qumran*, 12–13, suspected that XQPhyl 4 had been placed in this tefillin case in modern times.
54 For an attempt to match some of the wording of this slip with Exod 13:1–10 see Yadin, *Tefillin from Qumran*, 30–31, and note 426. As to the dating, Yadin, "Tefillin (Phylacteries) from Qumran," 75, suggested that its hand is earlier than that of XQPhyl 1–3.
55 Yadin, *Tefillin from Qumran*, 21. For 1QPhyl, Barthélemy, DJD 1:74, suggests a much wider slip, ~11 cm.
56 Yehuda Frankl suggests that this slip was made from a hide of an unborn kid. Yadin, *Tefillin from Qumran*, 43–44.
57 Milik's #5 in DJD 6:35.
58 For a more detailed discussion see, among others, Yadin, *Tefillin from Qumran*, 21–22; Emanuel Tov, *Scribal Practices and Approaches Reflected in the Texts Found in the Judean Desert*, STDJ 54 (Leiden: Brill, 2004), 256–58.
59 On opisthographs in the Dead Sea Scrolls, see George J. Brooke, "Between Scroll and Codex? Reconsidering the Qumran Opisthographs," in *On Stone and Scroll: Essays in Honour of Graham Ivor Davies*, ed. James K. Aitken et al. (Berlin: De Gruyter, 2011), 123–38.

have no dry lines to guide the writing. Scribes who wrote tefillin sought to fill the available space the best they could. As a result, they rarely left any margins and sometimes split the words between the lines, a practice known from the Qumran paleo-Hebrew scrolls. To accommodate large chunks of text on small surfaces, these scribes used tiny scripts, often less than 1 mm, and left no intervals between the words. Once the scribe finished the inscription, the slip was folded.[60] In some cases, the tiny bundles were fastened.[61] For example, XQPhyl 1–3 were tied with a hair of a goat.[62]

Classifying Tefillin Slips

The many tefillin slips from the Judean Desert can be divided into groups according to their contents. The most basic division distinguishes between slips containing non-scriptural texts (4QPhyl T; 4QPhyl U) and those featuring biblical verses. The latter group can be further broken down into two sub-groups. One of these contains biblical texts from Exod 13:1–16; Deut 6:4–9; 11:13–21. The other one yields passages from Exod 12:43–13:16; Deut 5:1–6:9; 10:12–11:21.[63] The pericopae utilized by the first sub-group of tefillin match those required by the later rabbinic halakhah.[64] Scholars proposed several sets of terms to describe

---

60 In the case of XQPhyl 1–4, the multiple stages of the folding process were carefully recorded during the unrolling. It seems that one of the guiding principles of the folding was to ensure that there were no exposed edges to avoid wear and tear. Yadin, *Tefillin from Qumran*, 15–21.
61 Yadin, *Tefillin from Qumran*, 11, observes that, unlike XQPhyl 1–3, XQPhyl 4 was not fastened.
62 Yadin, *Tefillin from Qumran*, 11.
63 This is not to say that in each and every case scholars can ascertain that a given tefillin contained all of these verses. This is merely a working assumption, since the evidence tends to be fragmentary. In fact, Milik, DJD 6:38–39, suggested that there might have been no expectation that all of the passages would be included. He argued that even the Shema could have been omitted (DJD 6:38). By the way of example, he evoked the very fragmentary 4QPhyl D-E-F found in a case in which only three compartments appear to be extant (DJD 6:35 [#1], 56). Against this view, Nakman points out that the case in question is damaged and that there was another (fourth) compartment. Milik also mentions 4QPhyl A, which appears to lack the Shema and some of Exod 12:43–13:7. Nakman, "Content and Order," 30, 32, 33, however, contests this conclusion and suggests a strategy as to how the missing verses could have been accommodated.
64 On the delineation of the four pericopae in tefillin from the Judean Desert and those of the rabbis see Yonatan Adler, "The Content and Order of the Scriptural Passages in Tefillin: A Reexamination of the Early Rabbinic Sources in Light of the Evidence from the Judean Desert," in *Halakhah in Light of Epigraphy*, ed. Albert Baumgarten et al. (Göttingen: Vandenhoeck &

these two sub-groups, such as traditional vs. non-traditional,[65] required vs. non-required,[66] abbreviated vs. extended,[67] and type 1 vs. type 2.[68] The last one, suggested by Adler, avoids the pitfall of evaluating the evidence through the lens of the later rabbinic prescriptions (traditional vs. non-traditional; required vs. non-required), as well as the implied assumptions regarding the processes that shaped the scope of the included verses (abbreviated vs. extended). These are the terms that are used throughout this monograph.

Tab. 2: Types 1 (Exod 13:1–16; Deut 6:4–9; 11:13–21) and 2 (Exod 12:43–13:16; Deut 5:1–6:9; 10:12–11:21) Tefillin Slips from Qumran.[69]

Type 1	4QPhyl C; 4QPhyl D-E-F; R; S
Type 2	1QPhyl; 4QPhyl A; B; G-M; O; P; Q; 8QPhyl;[70] XQPhyl 1–3

There is, however, a caveat to this seemingly neat bifurcation of the tefillin slips containing scriptural texts. One text does not fit in – the aforementioned 4QPhyl N featuring Deuteronomy 32. Moreover, it is worth noting that Types 1 and 2 slips have been found only at Qumran. Other sites from the Judean Desert yield Type 1 only (Mur Phyl; 34ṢePhyl; XḤev/SePhyl).[71]

In addition to the classification based on the nature and scope of the included texts, one might consider a further clustering of tefillin slips proposed by Emanuel Tov. In his two studies devoted to tefillin from the Judean Desert he

---

Ruprecht, 2010), 205–30. He concludes that the tefillin from the Judean Desert reflect the same understanding of the division of the text as the medieval Masoretic codices.

65 Rothstein, "From Bible to Murabbaʿat," *passim*.

66 Emanuel Tov, "The Tefillin from the Judean Desert and the Textual Criticism of the Hebrew Bible," in *Is There a Text in This Cave: Studies in the Textuality of the Dead Sea Scrolls in Honour of George J. Brooke*, ed. Ariel Feldman, Maria Cioată, and Charlotte Hempel, STDJ 119 (Leiden: Brill, 2017), 277–92.

67 Nakman, "Content and Order," 24.

68 Adler, "Distribution," 167.

69 The following list of Type 1 tefillin slips is a tentative one, for it relies on the absence of certain biblical verses from their extant fragments. The latter, however, are often small (e.g., 4QPhyl D and E), and there is no way to ascertain which texts they originally included.

70 8QPhyl I, if considered alone, would qualify as a Type 1 tefillin slip. On a possibility that the slips assigned to this tefillin may belong to more than one tefillin, see Chapter 8.

71 This observation assumes that XQPhyl was found in the Caves of Qumran and not elsewhere in the Judean Desert.

utilizes the following three aspects of these texts: textual profile, orthography and morphology, and affinity to rabbinic halakhah.[72]

First, Tov classifies tefillin slips according to their textual profiles. Recently he argued that Second Temple biblical texts fall into two broad categories or blocks.[73] One block includes the forerunners of the medieval Masoretic Text (henceforth: MT): the so-called proto-MT and MT-like texts. With the proto-MT belong scriptural texts deviating from the medieval Masoretic Codex Leningrad (B19^A) "by up to 2% of their content," whereas the MT-like texts vary from it "by up to 10%."[74] The second block comprises, among other texts, Qumran pre-Samaritan biblical scrolls and the Hebrew *Vorlage* of the Septuagint (henceforth: LXX). In line with this overall understanding of the late Second Temple textual landscape, Tov divides tefillin from the Judean Desert into two groups:[75]

a. Proto-MT (MurPhyl; 34ṢePhyl; 8QPhyl I) and MT-like (XḤev/SePhyl)
b. SP-LXX-independent (4QPhyl A-S; 8QPhyl II-IV; XQPhyl 1–4; and perhaps 1QPhyl)[76]

What emerges from this categorization is that there are very few tefillin slips that can be classified as forerunners of the MT and that with the exception of one, 8QPhyl I, all of them come from outside of Qumran.[77] At the same time, the majority of Qumran tefillin slips reflect scriptural texts that belong with Tov's second block which he describes as "popular" texts.[78] This seems to mirror his overall grouping of the Second Temple biblical texts.[79]

On a micro-level, one might question some of Tov's classifications.[80] First, he places the fragmentary 4QPhyl D-E-F in the SP-LXX-independent category.

---

72 Emanuel Tov, "Tefillin of Different Origin from Qumran," in *A Light for Jacob: Study in the Bible and the Dead Sea Scrolls*, ed. Yair Hoffman and Frank H. Pollak (Jerusalem: Bialik Institute, 1997), 44*–54*; idem, "Tefillin from the Judean Desert." See also Lange, *Handbuch*, 119–22.

73 Emanuel Tov, "The Development of the Text of the Torah in Two Major Text Blocks," *Textus* 26 (2016): 1–27.

74 Tov, "Tefillin from the Judean Desert," 281. See also his "'Proto-Masoretic,' 'Pre-Masoretic,' 'Semi-Masoretic,' and 'Masoretic': A Study in Terminology and Textual Theory," in idem, *Textual Developments: Collected Essays, Volume 4*, SVT 181 (Leiden: Brill, 2019), 195–213.

75 Tov, "Tefillin from the Judean Desert," 282–83.

76 Tov, "Tefillin from the Judean Desert," 282n19.

77 On 8QPhyl I, see note 70. One should mention here that in Exod 13:12 8QPhyl I has a slightly shorter text than the MT (see Chapter 8).

78 Tov, "Tefillin from the Judean Desert," 282.

79 Tov, "Development"; idem, "'Proto-Masoretic,' 'Pre-Masoretic.'"

80 Tov includes in his analysis XQPhyl 4. To the best of my knowledge, this tefillin slip remains undeciphered. As to his separate treatment of 8QPhyl I and 8QPhyl II–IV, as was suggested in note 70, it should be considered in light of the data presented in Chapter 8.

In Milik's edition, 4QPhyl E reads in Exod 13:6 שׁ[ת יֹ [מים ("s]ix d[ays"; with SamP, LXX, and several other tefillin from Qumran) against שבעת ימים ("seven days") of the MT, while 4QPhyl F has ו[הי]ו in Exod 13:16 against the MT's והיה. Adler, however, contests these readings and argues that in both instances the fragments follow the MT.[81] Admittedly, 4QPhyl E still reads a plural יד[יכ in Exod 13:9 (with SamP and several other Qumran tefillin) against the singular form in MT and LXX. Yet, Adler's corrections may tip the balance towards re-classifying 4QPhyl D-E-F as Tov's proto-MT texts. Second, Tov assigns 4QPhyl S to the SP-LXX-independent group. However, the only variant it yields is an omission of ימיכם in Deut 11:21 which could easily place it in his MT-like category.[82] Third, while Tov classifies XHev/SePhyl as an MT-like text, its editors observe that it "presents twenty-nine unique readings."[83] They note that some of these are due to scribe's carelessness and acknowledge that in several significant readings this tefillin reads with the MT against other witnesses. Still, they classify it as an independent or a non-aligned text, thus making this tefillin a candidate for Tov's SP-LXX-independent group.

On a macro-level, one wonders whether an attempt to construe texts, be it Second Temple biblical texts in general or tefillin slips in particular, as composed of two blocks suits the extant evidence well. The very need to create an intermediate category of the MT-like texts (defined by a somewhat arbitrary 10 % of variation) suggests that this approach lacks the flexibility that the evidence at hand requires.[84] As discussed in Chapter 2, an alternative method of classification, distinguishing between two scribal approaches to scriptural texts in the Second Temple period, "conservative" and "revisionist," may offer a better alternative, as it allows for placing texts on a spectrum according to the degree of scribal intervention they exhibit.[85]

---

81 Yonatan Adler, "Identifying Sectarian Characteristics in the Phylacteries from Qumran," *RevQ* 23 (2007): 79–92 (89n40). See further PAM 43.458 available at https://www.deadseascrolls.org.il/explore-the-archive/image/B-284486.

82 One omitted word out of the partially preserved 22 words yields ~5 % of variation.

83 Morgenstern & Segal, DJD 38:190. On its shorter wording of Deut 6:4, see Armin Lange, "The Shema Israel in Second Temple Judaism," *JAJ* 1 (2010): 207–14 (210).

84 Moreover, as noted in Chapter 2, the very notion of grouping Second Temple texts according to their affinities (or lack thereof) with much later textual witnesses, such as the MT, is methodologically problematic. Not only is it anachronistic, but, as Michael Segal argues, the so-called proto-MT and MT-like texts, while sharing what can be described as a conservative approach to text, hardly qualify to be a textual "family." He raises similar concerns with regards to the texts considered to be the forerunners of the LXX. Michael Segal, "The Text of the Hebrew Bible in Light of the Dead Sea Scrolls," *Materia Giudaica* 12 (2007): 5–20 (7–10, 17–18).

85 For pertinent bibliography see Chapter 2. For the notion of spectrum applied to texts in question see Sidnie White Crawford, *Rewriting Scripture in Second Temple Times* (Grand Rap-

The second feature that Tov utilizes to classify tefillin slips is their orthography and morphology. That some of Cave 4 tefillin display a conservative, MT-like orthography, whereas many others prefer a fuller one, was already noted by Milik.[86] Some of the morphological (e.g., the lengthened pronominal and verbal forms) and orthographic (e.g., the exceptionally full spelling) features exhibited in these tefillin match those identified by Tov as the markers of what he calls Qumran Scribal Practice (QSP). In his view, these features are closely associated with the sectarian community behind the Dead Sea Scrolls.[87]

Analyzing tefillin slips from the Judean Desert through this lens, Tov identifies the following groups:[88]

MT spelling (4QPhyl C-F; S; 8QPhyl I; MurPhyl; 34ṢePhyl; XḤev/SePhyl)

Conservative spelling (1QPhyl; 4QPhyl R; 8QPhyl II–IV; XQPhyl 1–3)

Qumran Scribal Practice (4QPhyl A; B; G-Q)

As with the previous rubric, one might disagree with some particularities of Tov's classification. As far as his MT spelling items are concerned, 4QPhyl C features both more defective (e.g., השבעי [Exod 13:6], ובקמך [Deut 6:7]) and fuller orthography than the MT (ועבדתה [Exod 13:5], מצאותי [Deut 11:13; cf. 4QPhyl A; B]). Also, 4QPhyl F yields a longer form, יביאכה (Exod 13:11).[89] Moreover, Tov's intermediate category – conservative spelling – is absent from his earlier study on tefillin, where he operated with only two categories: MT spelling and QSP spelling.[90] The criteria for what constitutes such a "conservative" orthography vis-à-vis MT spelling and QSP spelling are not made clear. Hence are some possible inconsistencies. 1QPhyl assigned to the conservative spelling group features at least one example of what might be perceived as a fuller

ids: Eerdmans, 2008). A similar approach was advocated by George J. Brooke, "The Rewritten Law, Prophets and Psalms: Issues for Understanding the Text of the Bible," in *The Hebrew Bible and the Judaean Desert Discoveries*, ed. Edward D. Herbert and Emanuel Tov (London: British Library, 2002), 31–40 (36). Instead of a spectrum, Brooke speaks of a "sliding scale."
86 Milik, DJD 6:36–37.
87 On QSP see, for instance, Tov, *Scribal Practices*, 261–73, 337–43. For a recent attempt at refining the statistical analysis of the Dead Sea Scrolls according to QSP see Martin Abegg, "Qumran Scribal Practice: Won Moor Thyme," in *Scribal Practice, Text and Canon in the Dead Sea Scrolls: Essays in Memory of Peter W. Flint*, ed. John J. Collins and Ananda Geyser-Fouché, STDJ 130 (Leiden: Brill, 2019), 175–204.
88 Tov, "Tefillin from the Judean Desert," 282–83.
89 Jastram, "2.2.5.1 Tefillin and Mezuzot," classifies its orthography as moderately plene.
90 Tov, "Tefillin of Different Origin from Qumran."

spelling (תעובדם [Deut 5:9]). Yet so does also 8QPhyl I (הזאות [Exod 13:5]) which Tov classifies with his MT spelling group.

On a larger scale, one wonders, once again, whether the presence of an intermediate group points in a direction suggested earlier by Eibert Tigchelaar in his assessment of Tov's QSP. Instead of two polarized groups of texts, QSP and non-QSP, he observes that the Scrolls seem to attest to a varying degree of orthographic and morphological phenomena noted by Tov. Hence is his suggestion to place the evidence on a spectrum while acknowledging that there are clusters of texts exhibiting certain features to a higher degree.[91] This in turn problematizes the implied association of tefillin reflecting the aforementioned orthographic and morphological features with sectarian circles.[92] In fact, the tendency to label some tefillin (Type 2) as Essene or sectarian and others (Type 1) as Pharisaic has been contested by several scholars.[93]

The third feature utilized by Tov to classify tefillin slips from the Judean Desert is their conformity (or lack thereof) to the rabbinic halakhah.[94] Rabbinic

---

91 Eibert Tigchelaar, "Assessing Emanuel Tov's Qumran Scribal Practice," in *The Dead Sea Scrolls: Transmission of Traditions and Production of Texts*, ed. Sarianna Metso, Hindy Najman, and Eileen Schuller, STDJ 92 (Leiden: Brill, 2010), 173–207. For an attempt to identify several such clusters among Qumran tefillin using Tov's QSP features, see Benjamin H Parker, "Fingerprinting the Scribes: Patterns of Scribal Practice in the Biblical Texts from the Judean Desert, with Special Reference to the Tefillin," in *Celebrating the Dead Sea Scrolls: A Canadian Contribution*, ed. Peter W. Flint, Jean Duhaime, and Kyung S. Baeck, Early Judaism and Its Literature 30 (Atlanta: SBL, 2011), 77–100 (82, 91). The varying degree of attestation of the QSP features in tefillin is also evident in the data presented in Martin Abegg, "Scribal Practice and the Pony in the Manure Pile," in *Reading the Bible in Ancient Traditions and Modern Editions: Studies in Memory of Peter W. Flint*, ed. Andrew B. Perrin, Kyung S. Baek, and Daniel K. Falk (Atlanta: SBL Press, 2017), 65–88 (86n14–15); idem, "Qumran Scribal Practice: Won Moor Thyme," 182–83, 202n45–46.
92 Tov acknowledges that not all sectarian texts are written in QSP, as there are seven or eight manuscripts constituting an exception (Emanuel Tov, "The Qumran Scribal Practice: The Evidence from Orthography and Morphology," *Studia Orientalia* 99 [2004]: 353–68 [355]). See further Tigchelaar, "Assessing"; Abegg, "Qumran Scribal Practice: Won Moor Thyme," 202.
93 For such a bifurcation of tefillin slips from Cave 4, see Milik, DJD 6:36, 47, 48, 51, 53, 56, 58. Earlier on, Goren, "Tefillin from the Judean Desert," 505, argued that tefillin from Qumran, unlike tefillin from Wadi Murabba'at, are sectarian (Sadducean or Essene). For a critique see Cohn, *Tangled Up*, 73–75 (and bibliography cited there); Nakman, "Content and Order," 20.
94 For an overview of tefillin and mezuzot from the Judean Desert in the context of rabbinic halakhah see Sarna, *Exodus*, 268–70; Lawrence H. Schiffman, "Phylacteries and Mezuzot," in *Encyclopedia of the Dead Sea Scrolls*, ed. Lawrence H. Schiffman and James C. VanderKam (Oxford: Oxford University Press, 2000), 2:675–77; Busa, *Die Phylakterien von Qumran*, 40–60, 90–101. The most detailed study of the topic remains that of Rothstein, "From Bible to Murabba'at."

literature yields a plethora of regulations pertaining to tefillin. Some of them match practices reflected in tefillin from the Judean Desert.[95] For instance, tefillin cases from Qumran and those prescribed in the rabbinic texts are:[96]

- of two kinds: one with a single compartment and another with four compartments[97]
- rectangular[98]
- stitched with a tendon thread[99]

As far as scribal and physical features of tefillin slips are concerned, the rabbinic tefillin and the Judean Desert ones have:

- no dry lines[100]
- a text arranged in a single column[101]
- a hair of an animal to fasten the folded slip[102]

In terms of content, Type 1 tefillin from the Judean Desert and rabbinic halakhah include the same four biblical passages: Exod 13:1–10; 13:11–16; Deut 6:4–9; 11:13–21.[103]

Surely, there are also aspects in which tefillin from the Judean Desert, particularly those from Qumran, diverge from the rabbinic regulations.[104] For tefil-

---

95 For a detailed treatment of this topic see the studies by Rothstein, Nakman, Cohn, and Adler cited below.

96 This brief discussion of the rabbinic regulations pertaining to tefillin cases relies on Adler, "Tefillin Case," 155–58.

97 See m. Sanhedrin 11:3; m. Kelim 18:8; t. Kelim, Bava Bathra 4:1 (ed. Zuckermandel, 593); Sifre Deut 35; and further Nakman, "Content and Order," 28; Cohn, *Tangled Up*, 127–28.

98 M. Megillah 4:8 prohibits round cases. Cf. y. Megillah 4:8, 75c suggesting that tefillin are to be מרובעות and b. Menahot 35a ruling that they should be in a shape of a tablet (טבלא). It is, however, unclear whether these dicta refer to the cases or to the slips. See further Yadin, *Tefillin from Qumran*, 9; Cohn, *Tangled Up*, 151–54; Adler, "Tefillin Case," 156n22.

99 B. Shabbat 28b; 108a.

100 B. Megillah 18b; b. Menahot 32b. For discussion see Rothstein, "From Bible to Murabba'at," 277–81.

101 Y. Megillah 1:9, 71c. See further Adler, "Content and Order," 213–14. On several instances of a unique layout in Qumran tefillin, see note 295.

102 B. Shabbat 28b; 108a; y. Megillah 1:9, 71c. See further Goren, "Tefillin from the Judean Desert," 500.

103 M. Menahot 3:7; Mek. de Rabbi Ishmael, Bo 18 (Exod 13:16). See further Cohn, *Tangled Up*, 124–26.

104 For attempts to explain these differences, see Schiffman, "Phylacteries and Mezuzot," 676, who suggests several scenarios, such as that the rabbinic regulations were not yet widely accepted (or observed) or that some of the tefillin slips from Qumran represent a sectarian take on the tefillin practices. Nakman, "Content and Order," 20, posits that Qumran evidence reflects an

lin cases, Adler argues that the split cases present at Qumran were rejected by the rabbis.[105] As to the slips, the most striking difference is the contents. First, three Qumran slips do not align with the texts copied in rabbinic tefillin (4QPhyl N; T; U). Second, Qumran findings feature multiple Type 2 slips which include, among other scriptural texts absent from rabbinic tefillin, the Decalogue.[106] In terms of scribal practices, unlike rabbinic tefillin in which the four scriptural passages are written in a particular order,[107] tefillin slips from Qumran do not seem to follow one preferred sequence of the biblical pericopae.[108]

Tov divides tefillin slips from the Judean Desert into two groups: those that adhere to rabbinic halakhah and those that do not. Naturally, the most prominent criterion for such a division is the contents of the slips.[109] Type 1 tefillin matches rabbinic regulations while Type 2 does not. Moreover, Tov also utilizes such scribal and physical features of tefillin as the presence of the interlinear

---

earlier halakhah. For an argument against viewing Qumran findings through the lens of the later halakhah or that of the sectarian polemic, see Cohn, "Material Aspects," 92–94.

105 Adler, "Typological Distinction," 89–90.

106 Studies dealing with this topic often cite the rabbinic tradition according to which the practice of reciting the Decalogue (along with the Shema) in the Temple (m. Tamid 5:1) was discontinued because of the *minim* (y. Berachot 1:4, 3c). It is, however, unclear whether this passage sheds any light on the inclusion/exclusion of the entire section of Deut 5:1–6:3 in tefillin from Qumran. It certainly does not explain the presence/absence of Exod 12:43–51 and Deut 10:12–11:10 (Nakman, "Content and Order," 38). Several studies note that the custom of copying the Ten Commandments in tefillin might have persisted into the Late Antiquity. See Habermann, "On Ancient Tefillin," 175; Geza Vermes, "Pre-Mishnaic Jewish Worship and the Phylacteries from the Dead Sea," *VT* 9 (1959): 65–72 (70); Heinrich Schneider, "Der Dekalog in den Phylakterien von Qumrân," *Biblische Zeitschrift* 3 (1959): 18–31 (esp. 29–30). Adler, "Typological Distinction," 75, recently pointed out that a polemic against the inclusion of the Decalogue in tefillin may be found in Sifre Deut 35.

107 For an arm tefillin, in which all the four passages are inscribed on the same piece of leather, Mek. de Rabbi Ishmael, Bo 18 (Exod 13:16), prescribes that these are to be written in their (biblical) order (כותבן כסדרן). Still, medieval authorities, Rashi and Rabbenu Tam, differed on the order of the passages. Interpreting the difficult passage from b. Menahot 34b, Rashi rules that they should be written (from right to left) in their canonical order, while Rabbenu Tam insisted that Deut 6:4–9 should follow Deut 11:13–21 (see Adler, "Content and Order"). While several scholars (e.g., Milik, DJD 2:81; Goren, "Tefillin from the Judean Desert," 501–502; Yadin, *Tefillin from Qumran*, 11–15; Schiffman, "Phylacteries and Mezuzot," 275–77; Tov, "Tefillin from the Judean Desert," 498–99) attempt to align the tefillin from the Judean Desert with these two views, Cohn argues that Rashi and Rabbenu Tam's positions are to be viewed as a product of an exegesis of the Bavli, and not as a reflection of varying practices that can be traced back to the Second Temple period. See Yehudah Cohn, "Rabbenu Tam's Tefillin: An Ancient Tradition or the Product of Medieval Exegesis?," *JSQ* 14 (2007): 319–27.

108 See further Cohn, "Rabbenu Tam's Tefillin"; Adler, "Content and Order."

109 Tov, "Tefillin from the Judean Desert," 285–86.

corrections (vs. lack thereof),[110] splitting of the words at the end of lines (vs. lack thereof),[111] writing on one side of the slip (vs. writing on both sides),[112] and the shape of a slip (regular vs. irregular).[113] The main methodological problem with this approach is its inherent anachronism. After all, that a given tefillin slip exhibits (or does not) the same scribal features as prescribed by the later rabbinic texts does not necessarily mean that this slip follows (or rejects) regulations of the early rabbis.[114] For Cohn, the significant variation in scribal practices reflected in Qumran tefillin suggests "popular practices," rather than "a proto-halakhah."[115]

---

110 Tov, "Tefillin from the Judean Desert," 290, quotes y. Meg. 1:9, 71c: "One may hang (the letter above the line) in scrolls but one may not hang (the letter above the line) in *tefillin* or *mezuzoth*. In *tefillin* and *mezuzoth* written as scrolls one may hang (the letters above the lines)" (quoted from Yadin, *Tefillin from Qumran*, 21). It is, however, unclear whether the passage completely prohibits the hanging of the letters. Thus, Goren, "Tefillin from the Judean Desert," 509, suggests that as long as the writing was not crowded, hanging was allowed. Yadin, ibid., 21 (and note 35), seems to follow suit. Rothstein, "From Bible to Murabbaʿat," 336–41, does not think that the Talmudic passage disallows a suspension of letters in tefillin and mezuzot. He acknowledges that such corrections are rare in Type 1 (his "traditional") tefillin from Qumran, yet refrains from associating this phenomenon with the aforementioned rabbinic dictum. Moreover, Tov himself notes that not all the Qumran tefillin slips with the proto-MT or MT-like profiles avoid this method of correction. He mentions 8QPhyl III as an exception (a correction of an omitted word). One can also add 8QPhyl II, 7 (see Chapter 8). Another possible exception, which prompted Goren's aforementioned opinion, is MurPhyl 7 where a letter has been added above the line. Cf. also the placement of the letters (a sort of sublinear hanging) at the end of the lines in 8QPhyl I–IV (note that 8QPhyl I contains only Type 1 passages, follows the MT, and is written in QSP); XQPhyl 1–3.
111 Tov, "Tefillin from the Judean Desert," 290, cites the late Tractate Soferim 2:1.
112 Tov, "Tefillin from the Judean Desert," 290 (he offers no rabbinic proof-text for this feature). It is unclear whether b. Eruvin 98a prohibits writing tefillin and mezuzot on both sides of the parchment. See David Nakman, "Tefillin and Mezuzot at Qumran," in *The Qumran Scrolls and Their World*, ed. Menahem Kister, Between Bible and Mishnah (Jerusalem: Yad Ben-Zvi, 2009), 2:143–55 (148; Hebrew). That Qumran tefillin show little consistency in this matter can be illustrated by two examples. 4QPhyl C listed by Tov in his group iii (below) is an opisthograph, whereas 4QPhyl N containing verses from Deuteronomy 32 (Tov's group iv) is inscribed on one side only.
113 Y. Megillah 4:8, 75c. However, as noted earlier (note 98), it is uncertain whether מרובעות here refers to the cases or to the slips. See further Yadin, *Tefillin from Qumran*, 9; Cohn, *Tangled Up*, 151–54; Adler, "Tefillin Case," 156n22. In any case, one might highlight here the irregular shape of MurPhyl, a Type 1 tefillin following the MT text and the MT orthography.
114 See Cohn, *Tangled Up*, 106.
115 Cohn, "Material Aspects," 92–93.

In his studies, Tov also attempted to bring all the aforementioned aspects of tefillin into one scheme. In an earlier paper, he aligned them to produce an overarching categorization of tefillin slips into two groups:[116]

a. Tefillin that contain the passages prescribed by the rabbis, follow the MT, and exhibit MT-like orthography and morphology[117]

b. Tefillin that contain more text than required by the rabbis, feature non-MT biblical texts, and exhibit Qumran Scribal Practice

In a later study Tov offered a classification of tefillin slips into five groups:[118]

i. Tefillin that contain the same passages as ruled by the rabbis and follow the MT text and spelling (MurPhyl; 34ṢePhyl; 8QPhyl I)

ii. Tefillin that contain the same passages as ruled by the rabbis, adopt the MT spelling, and feature a MT-like text (XḤev/SePhyl)

iii. Tefillin that contain the same passages as ruled by the rabbis, adopt a conservative orthography and morphology, and feature a SP-LXX-independent text (4QPhyl C-F; R; S)[119]

iv. Tefillin that contain more text than required by the rabbis, adopt a conservative orthography and morphology, and feature a SP-LXX-independent text (8QPhyl II-IV; XQPhyl 1–3; and possibly 1QPhyl)

v. Tefillin that contain more text than required by the rabbis, follow Qumran Scribal Practice, and feature a SP-LXX-independent text (4QPhyl A; B; G-Q)

Informed by two new intermediate categories, the MT-like textual profile and the conservative spelling, this recent classification helpfully replaces the earlier binary approach with a more nuanced one. Moreover, two intriguing observations emerge from it:

1. There are conservatively written Type 1 tefillin with a non-MT textual profile (group iii). In other words, some tefillin associated, according to Tov, with the proto-rabbinic circles used a non-MT text.

---

116 Tov, "Tefillin of Different Origin from Qumran," 282–83. Cf. Tov, *Scribal Practices*, 256–57, 270–77. For aligning two of the aforementioned criteria, non-QSP/QSP spelling and compliance/non-compliance with the rabbinic prescriptions, see also Abegg, "Scribal Practice and the Pony in the Manure Pile," 85–86.
117 Adler, "Sectarian Characteristics," 89–90, takes Tov's insights one step further and argues that 4QPhyl D-E-F and 8QPhyl I, in which all these criteria converge, are (proto-)rabbinic tefillin. For an earlier similar assessment of 4QPhyl D-E-F see Milik, DJD 6:56.
118 Tov, "Tefillin from the Judean Desert."
119 Tov, "Tefillin from the Judean Desert," 282n20, lists also XQPhyl 4, but, as was noted earlier, this tefillin slip remains undeciphered.

2. There are Type 2 tefillin slips with a non-MT textual profile that are not written in QSP (group iv).[120] This might imply, within Tov's conceptual framework, that Type 2 tefillin are not necessarily sectarian, but could have been copied and used within wider Jewish circles of the time.[121]

Tov explains #1 by suggesting that rabbinic regulations had a wider influence and by evoking the popularity of the SP-LXX-independent texts.[122] He does not seem to address #2. These "exceptions" may, however, point to a larger problem, namely that the very attempt to bring such diverse aspects of these ancient texts as their choice of scriptural pericopae, textual profile, and orthography/morphology under one roof with theories pertaining to sectarian/non-sectarian origins of certain scribal and physical features of tefillin is simply not feasible.[123]

One should note that Tov's aforementioned insights into the sociological milieu of tefillin is informed by his overall understanding of the provenance of what came to be known as the MT. It is well known that as far as biblical manuscripts are concerned, there is a stark difference between the findings at Qumran, where a variety of textual profiles is found, and other sites in the Judean Desert yielding only the proto-MT scriptural texts. As was noted earlier, this dichotomy applies also to the slips of tefillin. Those that have been found outside of Qumran all contain proto-MT texts.[124] Indeed, for Tov, the contrast between these two corpora is particularly striking in the case of the Torah, where Qumran scrolls offer multiple MT-like texts, but no proto-MT texts, except for the tefillin slip 8QPhyl I and 4QGen^b.[125] He argues that this dichotomy should not be understood diachronically, as the dates of the texts partially overlap. Hence, he proposes that the aforementioned data reflect different textual preferences. Noting that the proto-MT texts found outside of Qumran were discovered either in a synagogue setting (Masada and Ein Gedi) or at the sites associated

---

120 For a similar observation see Abegg, "Scribal Practice and the Pony in the Manure Pile," 85. Elsewhere, he also notes that there is no Type 1 tefillin slip written in QSP. Abegg, "Qumran Scribal Practice: Won Moor Thyme," 202.

121 Thus Nakman, "Content and Order," 24; idem, Nakman, "Tefillin and Mezuzot at Qumran," 152–53. At the same time, Abegg, "Qumran Scribal Practice: Won Moor Thyme," 202, argues that the non-QSP profile of a text alone cannot substantiate a claim that it is "non-sectarian."

122 Tov, "Tefillin from the Judean Desert," 286. In another study, "The Socio-Religious Setting of the (Proto-) Masoretic Text," *Textus* 27 (2018): 135–53 (141), Tov suggests that these tefillin might have been brought to Qumran from elsewhere.

123 For a critique along similar lines see Jastram, "2.2.5.1 Tefillin and Mezuzot."

124 With a possible exception of XḤev/SePhyl (see above).

125 The latter text, he notes, may originate from elsewhere in the Judean Desert. Tov, "Socio-Religious Setting," 138.

with the Bar Kokhba fighters who were closely linked to rabbinic circles, he suggests a shared "(proto-)rabbinic" or pharisaic milieu for all of them.[126] To support this theory about "a close link between the rabbis and the proto-Masoretic text," Tov evokes the bifurcation of the Qumran tefillin into two major groups (as in his earlier study), according to which tefillin that follow rabbinic regulations prefer the MT.[127]

Once again, one can hardly disagree that there is a disparity between Qumran's textual variety and the other sites' textual uniformity.[128] However, Tov's socio-historical reconstruction of the circumstances behind this phenomenon, particularly the sweeping identification of those who took refuge at Masada and other sites in the Judean Desert with proto-rabbinic circles, remains highly tentative.[129] That an association of Second Temple groups with particular scriptural texts, including tefillin, is problematic is confirmed by the same tefillin from Qumran, where, as Tov himself demonstrated, several Type 1 (i.e., Tov's proto-rabbinic) tefillin contain a non-MT text.[130]

---

126 Tov, "Socio-Religious Setting," 145. Elsewhere in this study he seems to associate rabbis with Pharisees (ibid., 147, 151, 152), a rather problematic link for several historians. See, e.g., Hayim Lapin, "The Origins and Development of the Rabbinic Movement in the Land of Israel," in *The Cambridge History of Judaism: Volume 4: The Late Roman-Rabbinic Period*, ed. Steven T. Katz (Cambridge: Cambridge University Press, 2006), 206–29 (207–12). For a critique of the attempts to link the MT to a particular Second Temple group, such as early rabbis or Pharisees, see Ian Young, "The Stabilization of the Biblical Text in the Light of Qumran and Masada: A Challenge for Conventional Qumran Chronology?," *DSD* 9 (2002): 364–90 (365–70); Armin Lange, "'They Confirmed the Reading' (y. Ta'an. 4.68a): The Textual Standardization of Jewish Scriptures in Second Temple Era," in *From Qumran to Aleppo*, ed. Armin Lange, Matthias Weigold, and József Zsengellér (Göttingen: Vandenhoeck & Ruprecht, 2009), 29–80 (esp. 80). Lange argues that the MT was used by different circles in several geographical locations.
127 Tov, "Socio-Religious Setting," 145.
128 See, especially, Young, "Stabilization."
129 See studies cited in note 126. Whether the literary texts from Wadi Murabba'at are from the First or the Second Jewish Revolt against Rome remains somewhat unclear. See Michael Owen Wise, *Language and Literacy in Roman Judaea: A Study of the Bar Kokhba Documents* (New Haven: Yale University Press, 2015), 124–26. Several scholars associate the forerunners of the MT with the priestly circles and Jerusalem Temple. See, for instance, Lange, "'They Confirmed the Reading'," 76, 80 (and the bibliography cited there); Ronald Hendel, "2.2.2 Masoretic Texts and Ancient Texts Close to MT," in *Textual History of the Bible*, ed. Armin Lange (Brill, 2020), http://dx.doi.org.ezproxy.tcu.edu/10.1163/2452-4107_thb_COM_0002020501. However, this hypothesis is hardly supported by the Second Temple sources.
130 Several alternatives to the "non-sectarian"/"sectarian" interpretation of Types 1 and 2 tefillin slips have been proposed. Thus, Adler, "Distribution," 172–173, observes that Type 1 is known from artifacts dated to the 2nd century CE, whereas Type 2 is not. This argument, however, is not without problems. Of the three non-Qumran tefillin, one – 34ŞePhyl – has been recently dated to 50–100 CE, which renders it roughly contemporaneous with 8QPhyl II-IV, the

To sum up, there is no doubt that each of the aforementioned lenses applied by Tov to the tefillin slips has a merit. The clustering of these texts according to their textual profile or orthographic/morphological features is an important exercise. Similarly, grouping the slips according to the scribal practices they exhibit is helpful. Still, in terms of clear-cut criteria for a general classification of the slips containing scriptural texts, only one seems to be available at the moment: the scope of the included pericopae, i.e., Type 1/Type 2 division. And even there, one should not forget the exception: 4QPhyl N.

Mezuzot from the Judean Desert

Unlike the term "tefillin," the noun "mezuzah" (מְזוּזָה), a "door-post," is found in the Hebrew Bible.[131] Yet, as in the case of tefillin, it is unknown whether Second Temple Jews used this appellation to describe the artifacts which the later rabbis call mezuzot.

Rabbinic mezuzot are comprised of two elements: a case and an inscribed slip.[132] The findings from the Judean Desert yield some 9 slips tentatively identified as a mezuzah.[133] Until now no contemporary mezuzah case has been found.[134]

The tentative nature of these identifications has to do with the lack of clear criteria for differentiating between a slip of tefillin and that of a mezuzah.[135] Cohn, reflecting on this issue, notes several material features that set the presumed mezuzot slips apart from those of tefillin.[136] Some of these are related to their scripts, which, unlike the scripts of tefillin described by Milik as remaining stable for over 200 years, appear to be more susceptible to changes.[137] Also, the

---

Type 2 tefillin slips from the first century CE. As to the synchronic interpretations, one could consider a possibility that different practices were tolerated within the group(s) behind the Dead Sea Scrolls and wider Jewish circles of the time (Schiffman, "Phylacteries and Mezuzot," 677; Adler, "Distribution," 172–73). If the latter is correct, then the absence of Type 2 tefillin at other sites in the Judean Desert might be purely accidental.

131 Jansson, *The Message of a Mitsvah*, 30–33.
132 Jansson, *The Message of a Mitsvah*, 39–43.
133 See Table 2 below.
134 Milik, DJD 6:35, suggests that a folded piece of a blank leather (DJD 6, Plate VI, item #15) might have been used to wrap a mezuzah.
135 Thus already Milik, DJD 6:35–37; Rothstein, "From Bible to Murabbaʿat," 200; Nakman, "Tefillin and Mezuzot at Qumran," 143.
136 Cohn, "Material Aspects." For an earlier discussion see Cohn, *Tangled Up*, 60–62.
137 See note 43.

scripts in mezuzot seem to be larger and of better quality in terms of calligraphy. Other scribal and physical aspects differentiating mezuzot from tefillin, according to Cohn, include the presence of left and right margins, greater intervals between the words, extension of the last letter in a line,[138] larger interlinear spaces, and a thicker leather.[139] Finally, one might mention that, unlike some tefillin slips from Qumran, none of the presumed mezuzah slips is an opisthograph.

In rabbinic texts slips of mezuzah are clearly distinguished from those of tefillin by their contents. A rabbinic mezuzah contains Deut 6:4–9 and 11:13–21, while tefillin includes the same two scriptural texts and Exodus 13:1–16. It turns out, that some of the Qumran texts identified as mezuzot incorporate Exod 13:1–16. This is rather puzzling, for, unlike the passages from Deuteronomy, Exodus does not mention "door-posts" at all. Also, as far as Deuteronomic verses are concerned, several Qumran mezuzot feature the same range of verses as Type 2 tefillin.[140] Hence, it comes as no surprise that some wonder whether these mezuzot are actually larger slips of tefillin or some kind of excerpted texts, not unlike those discussed in Chapter 2.[141]

For example, Milik was uncertain whether 4QPhyl S (Fig. 1), a narrow strip of leather (14 mm wide) preserving Deut 11:19–21, could rather be a mezuzah.[142] At the same time, there is a slip containing Exod 13:11–16 which was categorized as a mezuzah, 4QMez G (Fig. 2). Milik observes that its leather is thicker than is usually the case in tefillin.[143] Still, he remarks, its script resembles that of tefillin slips. Indeed, the size of the letters, a little smaller than 1 mm, is well within the range attested to in Qumran tefillin. Moreover, the foldings visible in this slip – both horizontal and vertical – are reminiscent of those found in tefillin slips.[144]

---

138 This feature is attested to in 8QMez (see Baillet, DJD 3:158).
139 Cohn, "Material Aspects," 90–91.
140 Milik, DJD 6:36.
141 Cohn, "Material Aspects," 91; idem, *Tangled Up*, 60–62.
142 Milik, DJD 6:78.
143 Milik, DJD 6:84.
144 Hence, Nakman, "Tefillin and Mezuzot at Qumran," 154, proposes that this is a slip of tefillin. Another example of a similar ambiguity is Papyrus Nash. Containing the Deuteronomic Decalogue and the Shema, this small text is folded. It has been suggested that it might have functioned as either a tefillah or a mezuzah. See Cohn, *Tangled Up*, 67–68. That Papyrus Nash's version of the Decalogue is borrowed from Deuteronomy 5, rather than from Exodus 20, has been noted by several scholars. See, recently, Emanuel Tov, "The Papyrus Nash and the Septuagint," in *A Necessary Task: Essays on Textual Criticism of the Old Testament in Memory of Stephen Pisano*, ed. Dionisio Candido and Leonardo Pessoa de Silva Pinto, Biblica 14 (Roma: Pontificia Università Gregoriana and Pontificio Istituto Biblico, 2020), 33–50 (35).

Fig. 1: 4QPhyl S (B–295563).[145]

Fig. 2: 4QMez G (PAM 43.458).[146]

---

145 https://www.deadseascrolls.org.il/explore-the-archive/image/B-295563. All the images included in this chapter are courtesy of the Leon Levy Dead Sea Scrolls Digital Library; Israel Antiquities Authority. The new infrared and full-color images are by Shai Halevi. The earlier PAM images are by Najib Anton Albina.
146 https://www.deadseascrolls.org.il/explore-the-archive/image/B-284486.

Given these considerations, the following list of mezuzah slips should be taken as a tentative one. In fact, another item listed in Table 2 requires special attention – Mur5, the only mezuzah slip found outside of Qumran. This single fragment, which was left undeciphered by its editor, has been classified both as a mezuzah and a tefillin.[147] The main argument in favor of its classification as a mezuzah was a material one – its leather seems to be too thick for a tefillin slip.[148] Recently, Faina Feldman and I have suggested a tentative transcription of this fragment. According to it, its wording does not match Type 1 or Type 2 passages.[149] In light of this one could eliminate it from the list of mezuzot from the Judean Desert. And yet, as in the case of the slips 4QPhyl T and U, its physical resemblance to a slip of a mezuzah (or a tefillah) suggests that it might be prudent not to exclude it, thus allowing for a possibility that early mezuzot might have included other texts.[150]

Tab. 3: Mezuzot Slips from the Judean Desert.

Caves of Qumran[151]
4QMez A (4Q149; 1 slip; 2nd–1st cent. BCE[152])
Deut 5:11, 13–16[153]
4QMez B (4Q150; 1 slip; mid-1st cent. CE)
Deut 5:32; 6:1–6; 10:14, 16, 18, 20, 22; 11:1–2[154]

---

147 Milik, DJD 2:85, classifies it as a mezuzah, while Hartmut Stegemann and Jürgen Becker, "Zum Text von Fragment 5 aus Wadi Murabbaʿat," *RevQ* 3 (1961): 443–48 (444), argue that this is a tefillah.

148 Milik, DJD 2:85–86.

149 Feldman and Feldman, "Is Mur 5 a Mezuzah?"

150 Cf. magical additions attested to in later mezuzot as discussed in Eva-Maria Jansson, "The Magic of the Mezuzah in Rabbinic Literature," *Nordisk Judaistik/Scandinavian Jewish Studies* 15 (1994): 51–66; idem, *The Message of a Mitsvah, passim*; Gideon Bohak, "Mezuzot with Magical Additions from the Cairo Genizah," *Dine Israel* 26–27 (2009–10): 387–403 (Hebrew).

151 For other lists of scriptural passages found in mezuzot from the Judean Desert, see the bibliography provided in note 42.

152 The paleographic dating of mezuzot slips follows their *editio princeps*. Whenever the DJD edition refrains from dating the text, I follow Jastram's general "Hellenistic-Roman" dating. Jastram, "2.2.5.1 Tefillin and Mezuzot."

153 While Milik, DJD 6:80, considers a possibility that this fragment contains Exodus version of the Decalogue, Esther Eshel, "4QDeut^n – A Text That Has Undergone Harmonistic Editing," *HUCA* 62 (1991): 117–54 (145–46), and Jastram, "2.2.5.1 Tefillin and Mezuzot," pointed out that this is a Deuteronomic Decalogue harmonized towards Exodus.

154 For the identification of Deut 5:32; 6:1–4, see Feldman and Feldman, "4Q150 (4QMez B) and 8Q4 (8QMez) Revisited."

4QMez C (4Q151; possibly 2 slips [see Chapter 7]; 50–1 BCE?)
Deut 5:27–33; 6:1, 3, 5, 7, 9; 10:12, 15–18, 20
In addition to these passages, several further verses from Deuteronomy are tentatively identified in Chapter 7.
4QMez D (4Q152; 1 slip; 1 cent. BCE)
Deut 6:5–7
4QMez E (4Q153; 1 slip; Hellenistic-Roman)
Deut 11:17–18
4QMez F (4Q154; 1 slip; 100–50 BCE)
Exod 13:1–4
4QMez G (4Q155; 1 slip; Hellenistic-Roman)
Exod 13:11–16
8QMez (8Q4; 1 slip; Herodian hand)
Deut 10:12–22; 11:1–21

Other Sites in the Judean Desert

Wadi Murabba'at
Mur5 (1 slip; Hellenistic-Roman)
The fragment may contain non-biblical text.

Classifying Mezuzot

Unlike tefillin, mezuzot from the Judean Desert received significantly less scholarly attention. In addition to the aforementioned uncertainties in differentiating between tefillin and mezuzot, their relative neglect may have to do with the fact that, in comparison to tefillin, they constitute a significantly smaller corpus and, for the most part, are rather poorly preserved. To allow for an easy comparison with tefillin, in what follows I utilize the same features of these texts that Tov used in his classification of the tefillin slips: content, textual profile, orthography/morphology, and affinity with the later rabbinic mezuzot.

Content. At first glance, it may seem that with an exception of Mur5 all mezuzah slips attest to the same two ranges of scriptural passages as Types 1 and 2 tefillin.[155] However, a closer look reveals a more complex picture. Overall, no extant slip of Qumran mezuzot contains passages from both Exodus and Deuteronomy. As far as Deuteronomy is concerned, there are several slips featuring Type 2 text (4QMez A-C; 8QMez), but no certain example of Type 1.[156] The opposite is true for the book of Exodus: all we have are Type 1 texts (4QMez F; G).

---

155 Another curious case is 4QMez C. One of its two fragments features Deuteronomy 5–6 and 10, whereas the other yields, according to its editor, a wording that does not match Exodus and Deuteronomy. See, however, an alternative proposal in Chapter 7.
156 4QMez D and E could have been of help, but they preserve very little text.

Textual profile. As tefillin slips, Qumran mezuzot display a variety of scriptural profiles. Two slips containing some of Exodus 13, 4QMez F and 4QMez G, exhibit a conservative approach to the text akin to that of the MT.[157] At the same time, 4QMez C features a shorter wording of Deut 5:32–33, while the Decalogue in 4QMez A yields a harmonization of the Sabbath commandment towards Exodus 20.[158]

Orthography and morphology. Several mezuzah slips display a preference for a defective orthography (4QMez B-E [D and E feature very little text]). One or two slips yield a slightly more *plene* spelling (4QMez C [frag. 1; very little text preserved] and G), while 4QMez A features a full spelling and prolonged morphological forms.[159]

Affinity to rabbinic halakhah. Whithout anachronistically aligning Qumran mezuzot with the later halakhic regulations, one may note that in terms of contents, unlike rabbinic mezuzot, these include Exodus 13 and Type 2 text of Deuteronomy. As far as scribal practices are concerned, there is a shared preference for writing mezuzah passages in a single column.[160] As to the differences, one could mention, among other things, the diverging customs pertaining to the guiding lines: rabbinic halakhah seems to require dry lines in a mezuzah slip, whereas Qumran evidence yields no lining at all.[161]

Concluding Remarks

It is rather curious that none of the many texts found in the Caves of Qumran, including numerous works concerned with legal matters, refers to the objects

---

157 Given Tov's aforementioned observation about the paucity of the proto-MT Torah texts among the Dead Sea Scrolls, one might suggest that these two mezuzot could be included in this category. The first one is 4QMez F. While there is very little text to assess, in Exod 13:3 it reads with the MT זכור (against SamP זכרו; cf. LXX: μνημονεύετε) and ממצרים (4QPhyl A; I; SamP; and apparently 4QExod^g have מארץ מצרים; LXX reads ἐκ γῆς Αἰγύπτου). On 4QExod^g, see Oren Ableman, "Newly Identified Pentateuchal Fragments: 4QExod^G (4Q18, Exod 12:51–13:3), 4QDeut^{K3} (4Q38B, Deut 30:13–18)," *RevQ* 30 (2018): 91–100 (93–94). The second text, 4QMez G, deviates from the MT at ~2.4%.

158 On the short wording in Deut 5:32–33 in 4QMez C see Chapter 2. For a possibility of a shorter text of Deut 5:32b–6:3a in 4QMez B see Feldman and Feldman, "4Q150 (4QMez B) and 8Q4 (8QMez) Revisited." On the reason for the Sabbath commandment in 4QMez A as borrowed from Exod 20:11 see note 391.

159 For the ranking of Qumran mezuzot according to their use (or lack of it) of Tov's QSP, see Abegg, "Qumran Scribal Practice: Won Moor Thyme," 202n45–46.

160 B. Menahot 33a. See further Rothstein, "From Bible to Murabba'at," 286–94.

161 B. Megillah 18b; b. Menahot 32b. See discussion in Rothstein, "From Bible to Murabba'at," 277–81.

and practices that rabbinic literature calls tefillin and mezuzah. This silence can be explained in several ways. On the one hand, these might have been considered non-controversial customs taken for granted by the sources.[162] On the other hand, one could argue that it reflects a period of time when they were not yet widely followed.[163] However one interprets the absence of explicit references to tefillin and mezuzot in the Scrolls, they produce the earliest known exemplars of both. When studied closely, two overall aspects noted in the earlier scholarship loom large. First, there is a notable continuity between these tefillin and mezuzot and the later rabbinic practices.[164] Second, the relatively large corpus of tefillin and mezuzot from the Judean Desert reveals a significant degree of variation, be it in the nature or scope of the included texts, the scribal approaches to the task of copying a scriptural text, the order of the biblical passages, and more.[165] These diverse artifacts resist a clear-cut classification other than a basic grouping according to their contents.

With a few possible exceptions, these ancient tefillin and mezuzot are first and foremost scriptural texts. How do they fit within the wider textual landscape of other manuscripts of Exodus and Deuteronomy found in the Judean Desert, especially at Qumran? This is the topic of the next chapter.

---

162 As Sarna, *Exodus*, 268, points out, Mishnah also yields very little on the "makeup and contents" of tefillin. He refers to Maimonides's comment (in Mishneh Torah [Tefillin, Mezuzah and Sefer Torah]) that these might have been well known to the reader and therefore required no explanation.

163 Habermann, "On Ancient Tefillin," 175, notes that according to the rabbinic sources the practice of tefillin was limited both in late antiquity (b. Menahot 47b) and medieval times.

164 Schiffman, "Phylacteries and Mezuzot."

165 Cohn, "Were Tefillin Phylacteries?," 41.

2 Tefillin and Mezuzot among Other Manuscripts of Exodus and Deuteronomy from the Judean Desert

The vast majority of the Judean Desert fragments identified as tefillin and mezuzot contain passages from Exodus and Deuteronomy. This chapter seeks to place these texts within their contemporary textual landscape. To do so, it first surveys the manuscripts of Exodus and Deuteronomy from the Judean Desert, highlighting features that will be relevant for the chapters that follow. Next, it takes a closer look at several unique readings attested to in tefillin and mezuzot from Qumran. These, too, anticipate Chapters 3–8.

The Book of Exodus in the Scrolls from the Judean Desert

Before the Discoveries in the Judean Desert

Prior to the discovery of the Dead Sea Scrolls, any attempt to reconstruct the early textual history of Exodus would have relied on a close comparison of the Masoretic Text, the Samaritan Pentateuch (henceforth: SamP) – both extant in their entirety only in medieval copies – and ancient translations, primarily the LXX.[166] Each of these three texts of Exodus has its own unique profile.

MT Exodus. When compared to the LXX, the most striking feature of the MT Exodus is its longer and differently arranged Second Tabernacle Account in Exodus 35–40. While there is no consensus on the matter, some scholars suggest that LXX preserves an earlier edition of Exodus 35–40, whereas the MT contains a text that has been expanded, harmonized, and reordered to correspond more closely with God's instructions to Moses in Exodus 25–30.[167] Another notable aspect of MT Exodus vis-à-vis LXX and SamP is the relative paucity of small-scale harmonizations.[168] Tov argues that of these three texts, the MT Exodus is the least harmonized one.

---

[166] For the fragments of MT Exodus that are earlier than the major medieval codices, see Ronald Hendel, *Steps to a New Edition of the Hebrew Bible*, Text-Critical Studies (Atlanta: SBL, 2016), 203–4.

[167] Hendel, "2.2.2 Masoretic Texts and Ancient Texts Close to MT."

[168] According to Tov, MT Exodus shares with SamP 16 harmonizations against the shorter text of LXX and 18 more with LXX against the shorter text of SamP. He suggests that there are only two unique harmonizations in the MT Exodus (Exod 5:6; 9:24). See Emanuel Tov, "Textual Harmonization in Exodus 1–24," *TC: A Journal of Biblical Textual Criticism* 22 (2017): 1–24.

https://doi.org/10.1515/9783110725377-003

SamP Exodus. One of the features distinguishing SamP Exodus from the MT and LXX is the presence of multiple large additions.[169] These can be broadly divided into two groups. First, there are passages that were expanded using materials found elsewhere in Exodus. Thus, in the Plagues Narrative, when the MT cites a divine command but does not record its execution, SamP provides a description of its fulfillment reusing the language of the command (Exod 7:18, 29; 8:19; 9:5, 19). The same technique is attested to in those cases when the command is missing – SamP provides it by "recycling" the description of its execution (Exod 10:2; 11:4).[170] With the second group belong those instances where SamP duplicates Deuteronomic Mosaic pronouncements and actions that are absent from the parallel accounts in Exodus.[171] Along with these large additions, there are also multiple small-scale harmonizations.[172] All these are widely considered to be of non-Samaritan origin. One exception to this rule might be the so-called Samaritan Tenth Commandment (Exod 20:17), a pastiche of Deuteronomic passages (Deut 11:29a; 27:2b–3a, 4a, 5–7, and 11:30) calling for a construction of an altar on Mt. Gerizim,[173] though recently scholars suggested that it, too, may belong to the pre-Samaritan layer of SamP Exodus.[174]

LXX Exodus. Overall, the LXX version of Exodus has been described as "a faithful translation of the Hebrew that is less literal than that of Numbers and

---

169 Magnar Kartveit, *The Origin of the Samaritans* (Leiden: Brill, 2009), 259–312; idem, "2.2.4.2 Exodus," in *Textual History of the Bible*, ed. Armin Lange (Brill, 2020), http://dx.doi.org.ezproxy.tcu.edu/10.1163/2452-4107_thb_COM_0002020402.

170 See also SamP Exod 6:9 (cf. 14:12); 8:1 (reusing its own wording); 11:4 (cf. 4:22–23); 27:19 (cf. 39:1); 39:21 (cf. 28:30).

171 This is the case in Exod 18:24–25 (Deut 1:9b–18), 32:10a (Deut 9:20), and 20. In Exodus 20, long expansions from Deuteronomy occur in v. 19a (Deut 5:24–27) and v. 21b (Deut 5:28b–29; 18:18–22; 5:30–31). While these duplications have been often described as harmonizations, they hardly create a smoother text. Rather, as Segal, "Text of the Hebrew Bible," 16, argues, they seem to provide a "source" for what is yet to follow.

172 Tov, "Textual Harmonization," 2. He suggests that, in addition to 18 unique harmonizations, SamP Exodus shares 32 harmonizations with the LXX against the MT and 16 with the MT against the LXX (ibid., 14).

173 Among the "non-sectarian" readings in SamP Exodus are also several instances of reordering. Thus, the regulations pertaining to the incense altar appear in SamP in Exod 26:35 (Exod 30:1–10 in MT), whereas the requirement to sprinkle blood and oil on Aaron and his sons in SamP is found in 29:28 (Exod 29:21 MT). Drew Longacre also notes the tendency to generalize the laws in chapters 21 (vv. 18, 20, 28, 29, 31–33, 35, 36) and 22 (v. 3). Drew Longacre, "A Contextualized Approach to the Hebrew Dead Sea Scrolls Containing Exodus" (PhD diss., University of Birmingham, 2014), 190.

174 See Stefan Schorch, "The So-Called Gerizim Commandment in the Samaritan Pentateuch," in *The Samaritan Pentateuch and the Dead Sea Scrolls*, ed. Michael Langlois, CBET 94 (Leuven: Peters, 2019), 77–97 (90).

Deuteronomy, but closer than LXX Genesis."[175] Still, different sections of the Greek Exodus seem to display varying approaches to the Hebrew text.[176] In Exodus 21–31 (except for 23:20–24:18), dealing with legal matters, the translator appears to follow his Hebrew *Vorlage* rather closely, while in the narrative sections (1–20; 24; 32–34) he exercises a "considerable creativity ... sometimes moving away from his Hebrew text."[177] LXX Exodus abounds with small-scale harmonizations which render it, according to Tov, the most harmonistic of the three texts.[178] Still, the main feature distinguishing the LXX Exodus from both MT and SamP is its version of the Second Tabernacle Account (MT Exodus 35–40). It is often shorter and displays a different order. For instance, it lacks the extensive section dealing with the construction of the tabernacle (MT Exod 36:9–34) and the passage concerned with the incense altar (MT Exod 37:24–28). Among various scenarios explaining these divergences are such opposing opinions as a different (earlier than the MT) Hebrew *Vorlage* and an involvement of a second translator (or a later editor).[179]

After the Discoveries in the Judean Desert

The Dead Sea Scrolls brought to light a wealth of texts illuminating the early history of Exodus.[180] These scrolls can be broadly divided into "biblical" and "non-biblical."[181] The following overview focuses on the first group alone. Still,

---

175 Alison Salvesen, "Exodus," in *T&T Clark Companion to the Septuagint*, ed. James K. Aitken (London: T&T Clark, 2015), 29–42 (30); see further Tov, "Textual Harmonization," 2–4; Larry Perkins, "2.4.1.2 Exodus," in *Textual History of the Bible*, ed. Armin Lange (Brill, 2020), http://dx.doi.org.ezproxy.tcu.edu/10.1163/2452-4107_thb_COM_0002040102.
176 Perkins, "2.4.1.2 Exodus."
177 Perkins, "2.4.1.2 Exodus."
178 Tov, "Textual Harmonization." He counts 137 cases of unique harmonizations in LXX Exodus, as well as 32 instances where LXX agrees with SamP against MT.
179 Emanuel Tov, *Textual Criticism of the Hebrew Bible*, 3rd ed. (Minneapolis: Fortress, 2012), 316–17.
180 See James R. Davila, "Exodus, Book of," in *The Encyclopedia of the Dead Sea Scrolls*, ed. Lawrence H. Schiffman and James C. VanderKam (New York: Oxford University Press, 2000), 1:277–79; Ronald Hendel, "Assessing the Text-Critical Theories of the Hebrew Bible after Qumran," in *The Oxford Handbook of the Dead Sea Scrolls*, ed. John J. Collins and Timothy H. Lim (Oxford: Oxford University Press, 2010), 281–302; Sidnie White Crawford, "Exodus in the Dead Sea Scrolls," in *The Book of Exodus: Composition, Reception, and Interpretation*, ed. Thomas Dozeman, Craig A. Evans, and Joel N. Lohr (Leiden: Brill, 2014), 305–21; Longacre, "Contextualized Approach."
181 I am aware that the widely used bifurcation of the relevant Qumran texts into "biblical" and "non-biblical" (or "scriptural" and "non-scriptural") is not only anachronistic but also problematic due to the lack of clear-cut criteria. It is adopted here for practical purposes.

it casts its net widely to include 4QReworked Pentateuch scrolls (4QRP[a-e]; 4Q158; 4Q364–367) and excerpted texts of Exodus. Some of the former resist a clear-cut classification as either biblical or rewritten bible text, while the latter can be too easily dismissed because they do not contain a running text of Exodus.[182] The list below includes all of them.[183]

Tab. 4: Manuscripts of Exodus from the Judean Desert.[184]

Caves of Qumran
Cave 1
1Q2 (1QExod; 1–50 CE[185])   Exod 16:12–16; 19:24–25; 20:1, 5–6, 25–26; 21:1–2, 4–5

182 On the classification of the 4QRP scrolls, see Molly Zahn, "Reworked Pentateuch," in *T&T Clark Encyclopedia of Second Temple Judaism*, ed. Daniel Gurtner and Loren T. Stuckenbruck (London: T&T Clark, 2019), 1:461–64, and further Michael Segal, "4QReworked Pentateuch or 4QPentateuch?," in *The Dead Sea Scrolls: Fifty Years After Their Discovery*, ed. Lawrence H. Schiffman, Emanuel Tov, and James C. VanderKam (Jerusalem: Israel Exploration Society, 2000), 391–99. For an exclusion of the excerpted texts of Exodus from a recent study of the Exodus manuscripts from Qumran, see Longacre, "Contextualized Approach," 133.
183 There are also several fragments of Exodus that are most likely modern forgeries. These include the fragments found in the following collections: the Schøyen Collection (DSS F.103 [MS 4612/2a]: Exod 3:14–15; DSS F.104 [MS 4612/2b]: Exod 5:9–14; DSS F.105 [MS 4612/2b]: Exod 16:10), the Southwestern Baptist Theological Seminary Collection (DSS F.161: Exod 23:8–10), and Museum of the Bible collection (DSS F.192: Exod 17:4–7). On these see further Eibert Tigchelaar, "A Provisional List of Unprovenanced, Twenty-First Century, Dead Sea Scrolls-Like Fragments," *DSD* 24 (2017): 173–88; Kipp Davis et al., "Nine Dubious 'Dead Sea Scrolls' Fragments from the Twenty-First Century," ibid., 189–28; Kipp Davis, "Caves of Dispute: Patterns of Correspondence and Suspicion in the Post-2002 'Dead Sea Scrolls' Fragments," ibid., 229–70; Torleif Elgvin and Michael Langlois, "Looking Back: (More) Dead Sea Scrolls Forgeries in The Schøyen Collection," *RevQ* 31 (2019): 111–33. The catalogue of the forgeries provided at "The Lying Pen of Scribes" (https://lyingpen.com/2020/08/05/post-2002-dead-sea-scrolls-like-fragments-lines-and-measurements-preliminary-list/) includes also a fragment containing Exod 12:3–5. It is listed as DSS F.151 of the Azusa Pacific University. Tigchelaar, "Unprovenanced," 180, however, records it as possibly containing Hab 2:1–3. This fragment does not appear on the APU's webpage naming the DSS fragments it owns (https://www.apu.edu/library/specialcollections/books/deadseascrolls/).
184 Table 1 relies on the editions of the texts in the DJD series, as well as on other studies cited below, including Longacre, "Contextualized Approach."
185 Unless noted otherwise, the dating of the manuscripts follows the data provided in their respective *editio princeps*. Here the dating is from Armin Lange, "2.2.1 Ancient, Late Ancient, and Early Medieval Manuscript Evidence," in *Textual History of the Bible*, ed. Armin Lange (Brill, 2020), http://dx.doi.org.ezproxy.tcu.edu/10.1163/2452-4107_thb_COM_0002020100.

Cave 2

2Q2 (2QExod[a]; Herodian)
>Exod 1:11–14; 3:4–6;[186] 7:1–4; 9:27–29; 11:3–7; 12:32–41; 21:18–20?; 26:11–13; 30:21?, 23–25; 32:32–34

2Q3 (2QExod[b]; Herodian)
>Exod 4:31; 12:26–27?; 18:21–22; 21:37; 22:1–2, 15–19; 27:17–19; 31:16–17; 19:9+34:10; 36:3–4?, 33–34?

2Q4 (2QExod[c]; 50–1 BCE[187])
>Exod 5:3–5

Cave 4

Exodus only
Hebrew:
4Q15 (4QExod[d]; late 2nd or early 1st cent. BCE)
>Exod 13:15–16; 15:1

4Q16 (4QExod[e]; middle to late 2nd cent. BCE)
>Exod 13:3–5

4Q18 (4QExod[g]; 50 BCE)
>Exod 12:51; 13:1–3;[188] 14:21–27

4Q19 (4QExod[h]; 50–1 BCE)
>Exod 6:3–6

4Q20 (4QExod[j]; early first century CE)
>Exod 7:28–29; 8:1–2

4Q21 (4QExod[k]; 50 BCE or later)
>Exod 36:9–10

4Q22 (4QpaleoExod[m]; c. 100 BCE)
>Exod 6:25–30; 7:1–19, 29; 8:1, 12–22; 9:5–16, 19–21, 35; 10:1–12, 19–28; 11:8–10; 12:1–2, 6–8, 13–15, 17–22, 31–32, 34–39; 13:3–7, 12–13; 14:3–5, 8–9, 25–26; 15:23–27; 16:1, 4–5, 7–8, 31–35; 17:1–16; 18:1–18, 20–27; 19:1, 7–17, 23–25; 20:1, 18–19; 21:5–6, 13–14, 22, 24–32; 22:3–4, 6–7, 11–13, 16, 18–30; 23:15–16, 29–31; 24:1–4, 6–11; 25:11–12, 20–29, 31–34; 26:8–15, 21–30; 27:1–3, 9–14, 18–19; 28:3–4, 8–12, 22–24, 26–28, 30–36, 38–43; 29:1–5, 20, 22–25, 31–41; 30:10, 12–18, 29–31, 34–38; 31:1–8, 13–15; 32:2–19, 25–30; 33:12–23; 34:1–3, 10–13, 15–18, 20–24, 27–28; 35:1; 36:21–24; 37:9–16[189]

Greek:
7Q1 (7QpapLXXExod; 100 BCE)
>Exod 28:4–7

---

186 On Exod 3:4–6 see Longacre, "Contextualized Approach," 102n1.

187 For the dating see Lange, "2.2.1 Ancient, Late Ancient, and Early Medieval Manuscript Evidence."

188 On the tentative identification of Exod 12:51; 13:1–3 see Ableman, "Newly Identified Pentateuchal Fragments," 93–94.

189 Further identifications were proposed by Nathan Jastram, "A Comparison of Two 'Proto-Samaritan' Texts From Qumran: 4QpaleoExod[m] and 4QNum[b]," *DSD* 5 (1998): 264–89 (Exod 20:20; 21:33; 22:10; 24:5; 28:11 [p. 283]), and Longacre, "Contextualized Approach," 115–116n3 (Exod 19:9–11; 20:20–21a; 21:32–34; 22:20; 24:9–10; 28:10–11).

Exodus along with other books of the Torah

4Q1 (4QGen-Exod[a]; 100–25 BCE)
    Exod 1:3–17, 22; 2:1–5; 3:8–16, 18–21; 4:4–9, 26–31; 5:1, 3–17; 6:4–21, 25; 7:5–
    13, 15–20; 8:20–22; 9:8?
4Q11 (4QpaleoGen-Exod[l]; 100–25 BCE)
    Exod 1:1–5?; 2:10, 22–25; 3:1–4, 17–21; 8:13–15, 19–21; 9:25–29, 33–35; 10:1–5;
    11:4–10; 12:1–12, 42–46; 14:15–24; 16:1–7, 13–14, 18–20, 23–31, 33–35; 17:1–3,
    5–11; 18:17–24; 19:24–25; 20:1–2; 22:23–24; 23:5–16; 25:7–20; 26:29–37; 27:1,
    4, 6–14; 28:33–35, 40–42; 36:34–36; 40:15?
4Q13 (4Q[Gen]-Exod[b]; 30 BCE–20 CE[190])
    Exod 1:1–6, 10–11, 16–21; 2:2–18; 3:13–22; 4:1–8; 5:3–14[191]
4Q14 (4Q[Gen]-Exod[c]; 50–25 BCE[192])
    Exod 7:17–23, 26–28; 8:1, 5–14, 16–18, 22; 9:11, 15–20, 22–25, 27–35; 10:1–5,
    7–9, 12–19, 23–24; 11:9–10; 12:12–16, 31–48; 13:18–22; 14:1–13; 15:9–21; 17:1–
    16; 18:1–12; 19:12–14
4Q17 (4QExod-Lev[f]; 250 BCE)
    Exod 38:18–22; 39:3–24; 40:8–27
4Q158 (4QRP[a]; 50–1 BCE; Herodian or slightly pre-Herodian[193])
    Gen 32:25–32; Exod 4:27–28+;[194] Gen 47:29–30?; Exod 24:4–6; Exod 6:3;
    Gen 17:7;[195] Exod 19:17–23; 20:19–21, 12–17, 21–26; 21:1–25, 32–37; 22:1–13;
    30:32–34?; text related to Exod 6:3–8 and 15:1–20.[196]
4Q364 (4QRP[b]; 75–50 BCE)
    Exod 21:14, 15, 19–22; 19:17?; 24:11–14, 18+; 25:1–2; 26:1, 33–35; 33:10–11

---

190 A tentative reconstruction of the scroll suggests that it might have also contained the book of Genesis. See Longacre, "Contextualized Approach," 110.

191 A fragment containing the text of Exod 1:10–11 was identified by Eibert Tigchelaar, "On the Unidentified Fragments of DJD XXXIII and PAM 43.680: A New Manuscript of 4QNarrative and Poetic Composition, and Fragments of 4Q13, 4Q269, 4Q525 and 4QSb(?)," *RevQ* 21 (2004): 477–85 (483).

192 According to Longacre, "Contextualized Approach," 111, a tentative reconstruction of the scroll indicates that it could have included Genesis. Further fragments of this scroll (now in Schøyen collection) were identified by Esther and Hanan Eshel as Exod 3:13–15; 5:9–14. As noted above, they are believed to be modern forgeries. Esther Eshel and Hanan Eshel, "A Preliminary Report on Seven New Fragments from Qumran," *Meghillot* 5–6 (2007): 271–78 (272–74; Hebrew).

193 John Strugnell, "Notes en marge du volume V des 'Discoveries in the Judaean Desert of Jordan'," *RevQ* 2 (1970): 163–276 (168).

194 On this unit as an exposition of Exodus employing the passage from Genesis (Jacob wrestling at Penuel) to bear on the encounter in Exod 4:24–26, see Michael Segal, "Biblical Exegesis in 4Q158: Techniques and Genre," *Textus* 19 (1998): 45–62 (47–48).

195 On the use of Genesis 17 and Exodus 6 here to identify the covenant at Sinai with two other covenants mentioned in these passages, thus clarifying the meaning of the phrase the "book of the covenant" (Exod 24:7), see Segal, "Biblical Exegesis in 4Q158," 49–51.

196 See further Molly Zahn, *Rethinking Rewritten Scripture: Composition and Exegesis in the 4QReworked Pentateuch Manuscripts*, STDJ 95 (Leiden: Brill, 2011), 246–58.

4Q365 (4QRP^c; 75–50 BCE)
  Exod 8:13–19; 9:9–12; 14:10+, 12–21; 15:16–20+,22–26; 17:3–5; 18:13–15;
  26:34–36; 28:16–20; 29:20–22; 30:37–38; 31:1+, 2, 3; 35:3–5; 36:32–38; 37:29;
  38:1–7; 39:1–19
4Q366 (4QRP^d; 75–50 BCE)
  Exod 21:35–37; 22:1–6

Other Sites in the Judean Desert

Mur1 (MurGen-Exod, Num^a; beginning of the 2nd cent. CE)
  Exod 4:27–31; 5:3; 6:5–11

The Contribution of the Exodus Manuscripts from the Judean Desert

The contribution of the aforementioned texts to the study of the book of Exodus is manifold. A glance at the scholarly attempts to classify them illuminates some of their salient features. Just like tefillin slips (see Chapter 1), Exodus manuscripts are routinely catalogued according to the readings they share (or do not share) with the MT, SamP, and LXX. One recent example of such classification is that of Armin Lange.[197] His analysis excludes several manuscripts as being either too fragmentary, non-classifiable, or rewriting Exodus.[198] For what is left, he suggests the following categorization:

Proto-MT: Mur1

Semi-Masoretic: 4QGen-Exod^a; 4QpaleoGen-Exod^l

Pre-Samaritan: 4QpaleoExod^m

Non-aligned: 2QExod^a; 4Q[Gen]-Exod^b; 4Q[Gen]-Exod^c; 4QExod-Lev^f; 4QRP^{b-d}

While this and similar classifications have been rightly criticized for privileging MT, SamP, and LXX, as well as for using these late texts to assess much earlier evidence, for our purposes it helpfully highlights the presence of a copy of Exodus containing expansions featured by the SamP.[199] Dubbed "proto-Samaritan" or "pre-Samaritan," the scroll 4QpaleoExod^m (4Q22) incorporates two-thirds of

---

197 Lange, "2.2.1 Ancient, Late Ancient, and Early Medieval Manuscript Evidence."
198 The latter is 4QPR^a (4Q158). On the classification of this scroll, see note 182.
199 See George J. Brooke, "E Pluribus Unum: Textual Variety and Definitive Interpretation in the Qumran Scrolls," in *The Dead Sea Scrolls in Their Historical Context*, ed. Timothy H. Lim et al. (Edinburgh: T&T Clark, 2000), 107–22; Segal, "Text of the Hebrew Bible."

the large additions found in the SamP Exodus.[200] These include at the very least one of the expansions attested to in the SamP Decalogue.[201]

Lange excludes from his classification two scrolls represented by a single fragment each: 4QExod^d and 4QExod^e.[202] These fragments, however, are of special interest for this study, as they appear to be excerpted texts of Exodus.[203] A single fragment, 4QExod^d juxtaposes Exod 13:15–16 with Exod 15:1.[204] As discussed in Chapter 1, Exod 13:1–16 is included in tefillin and mezuzot from the Judean Desert. As to Exodus 15, the Song of the Sea is prominent in later Jewish liturgy.[205] The second text, 4QExod^e is a remnant of a small scroll – its height is only 8.2 cm.[206] It, too, contains Exodus 13, in this case vv. 3–5. There is no way to ascertain how these two scrolls might have been used. Overall, scholars assume that excerpted texts served for study or some type of devotional or liturgical purposes.[207]

---

200 Patrick Skehan et al., DJD 9:66. The passages in question include Exod 7:18b, 29b; 8:1b, 19b; 9:5b, 19b; 10:2b; 11:3b; 18:25+; 20:19a, 21b.

201 The fragments contain some of the wording of the addition in SamP Exod 20:19a. See Patrick Skehan et al., DJD 9:101–102; Kartveit, *Origin*, 281–82.

202 For Lange, they are too fragmentary to be classified. Lange, "2.2.1 Ancient, Late Ancient, and Early Medieval Manuscript Evidence."

203 On excerpted (or abbreviated) texts see Lutz Doering, "Excerpted Texts in Second Temple Judaism: A Survey of the Evidence," in *Selecta Colligere, II: Beiträge zur Technik des sammelns und kompilierens griechischer Texte von der Antike bis zum Humanismus*, ed. Rosa M. Piccione and Matthias Perkams, Hellenica 18 (Alessandria: Ediziioni dell'Orso, 2005), 1–38; Brent Strawn, "Excerpted Manuscripts at Qumran: Their Significance for the History of the Hebrew Bible and the Socio-Religious History of the Qumran Community and Its Literature," in *The Bible and the Dead Sea Scrolls: Volume 2: The Dead Sea Scrolls and the Qumran Community*, ed. James H. Charlesworth (Waco: Baylor University Press, 2006), 107–67; idem, "Excerpted Non-Biblical Texts," in *Qumran Studies: New Approaches, New Questions*, ed. Michael Thomas and Brent Strawn (Grand Rapids: Eerdmans, 2007), 65–123; Emanuel Tov, "Excerpted and Abbreviated Biblical Texts from Qumran," in *Hebrew Bible, Greek Bible, and Qumran: Collected Essays*, ed. idem, TSAJ 121 (Tübingen: Mohr Siebeck, 2008), 27–41; Sidnie White Crawford, "The Excerpted Manuscripts from Qumran, with Special Attention to 4QReworked Pentateuch D and 4QReworked Pentateuch E," in *Scribal Practice, Text and Canon in the Dead Sea Scrolls: Essays in Memory of Peter W. Flint*, ed. John J. Collins and Ananda Geyser-Fouché, STDJ 130 (Leiden: Brill, 2019), 247–68. For a study of excerpted texts highlighting tefillin and mezuzot from the Judean Desert, see Stephen Reed, "Physical Features of Excerpted Torah Texts," in *Jewish and Christian Scripture as Artifact and Canon*, ed. Craig A. Evans and H. Daniel Zacharias (London: T&T Clark, 2009), 82–103.

204 See discussion and pertinent bibliography in Longacre, "Contextualized Approach," 103–5.

205 See, for instance, Rachel Fridman, "Searching for Holiness: The Song of the Sea in the Bible and in the Liturgy," in *Sanctification*, ed. David Birnbaum and Benjamin Blech (New York: New Paradigm Matrix, 2015), 211–22.

206 Judith Sanderson, DJD 12:129.

207 See, recently, Crawford, "Excerpted Manuscripts from Qumran," 260.

Another method of classification, developed by Eugene Ulrich, tracks the literary growth of a given biblical book. For Exodus, he notes the following texts as reflecting five successive editions thereof (from left to right):[208]

LXX Exod 35–40   MT Exod   4QpaleoExod[m]   SamP Exod   4QRP[c]

This list draws attention to the scroll 4QRP[c] (4Q365) featuring, among many other scribal phenomena, the expanded "Song of Miriam" (Exodus 15). Unlike the large additions in the pre-Samaritan 4QpaleoExod[m], which are essentially segments of text copy-pasted from other passages in Exodus and Deuteronomy, the "Song of Miriam" is a new scribal creation.[209]

Yet another method of classifying the biblical Dead Sea Scrolls situates the manuscripts within two major scribal approaches evident in these texts. These two have been described as "free" and "careful,"[210] "conservative" and "revisionist,"[211] or "exact" and "facilitating."[212] One attempt to classify the copies of Exodus along these lines (with an exclusion of the excerpted texts) yields the following result:[213]

Conservative: 1QExod; 2QExod[c]; 4QGen-Exod[a]; 4QpaleoGen-Exod[l]; 4Q[Gen]-Exod[c]; 4QExod[g]; 4QExod[h]; 4QExod[k]; 4QpaleoExod[m]; 4QRP[d]; Mur1

Revisionist: 2QExod[a]; 2QExod[b]; 4Q[Gen]-Exod[b]; 4QExod-Lev[f]; 4QExod[j]; 4QRP[a]; 4QRP[b]; 4QRP[c]

The Exodus scrolls exhibiting a "revisionist" or "facilitating" approach yield a vast array of scribal interventions.[214] These include additions, omissions, har-

---

208 Emanuel Tov and Eugene Ulrich, "1.1.1.2 Textual Theories," in *Textual History of the Bible*, ed. Armin Lange (Brill, 2020), http://dx.doi.org.ezproxy.tcu.edu/10.1163/2452-4107_thb_COM_0001010102.

209 Admittedly, it, too, reuses some of the wording found in the preceding Song of the Sea. See further Ariel Feldman, "The Song of Miriam (4Q365 6a ii + 6c 1–7) Revisited," *JBL* 132 (2013): 905–11.

210 Tov, *Textual Criticism of the Hebrew Bible*, 184–86.

211 Sidnie White Crawford, "Understanding the Textual History of the Hebrew Bible: A New Proposal," in *The Hebrew Bible in Light of the Dead Sea Scrolls*, FRLANT 239 (Göttingen: Vandenhoeck & Ruprecht, 2012), 60–69.

212 David Andrew Teeter, *Scribal Laws: Exegetical Variation in the Textual Transmission of Biblical Law in the Late Second Temple Period*, FAT 92 (Tübingen: Mohr Siebeck, 2014), 205–64.

213 Longacre, "Contextualized Approach," 174.

214 In addition to these methods, one could also mention Hendel's "hybrid" approach incorporating insights from all the aforementioned methods (Hendel, "Assessing"). Moreover, Long-

monizations, and more.[215] Anticipating the discussion of 8QPhyl in Chapter 8, I highlight here one of these strategies: rearrangement. A peculiar example of this technique appears in one of the 4QReworked Pentateuch scrolls, 4QRP[a] (4Q158). Scholars find this scroll, in which stretches of plain biblical text are intertwined with segments incorporating exegesis, particularly difficult to classify.[216] It has been even argued that 4QRP[a] combines (mistakenly) two distinct compositions: a rewritten Bible work (frags. 1–4, 14) and a pre-Samaritan Torah text (frags. 5–12).[217] Be that as it may, it is the latter fragments containing the Decalogue that are of interest for this study. As was mentioned earlier, the pre-Samaritan and SamP versions of Exodus 20 incorporate several passages from Deut 5:24–31 and 18:18–22.[218] They insert Deut 5:28–29; 18:18–22 and Deut 5:30–31 between Exod 20:21 and Exod 20:22. This seems to be the case also in 4QRP[a] 6–9 with one notable difference. The diagram adopted from Segal's study of 4QRP[a] exhibits the difference between SamP and 4Q158 as follows:[219]

Samaritan Pentateuch	4Q158 6–9
	Fragment 6
Decalogue	Not preserved
Exod 20:18–19a	Not preserved
Deut 5:24–27	Deut 5:27
Exod 20:19b–21	Exod 20:19b–21
Deut 5:28–29	Deut 5:28–29
Deut 18:18–22	Deut 18:18–22
	Fragments 7–9
	Exod 20:12–17
Deut 5:30–31	Deut 5:30–31
Exod 20:22–26	Exod 20:22–26

---

acre has recently attempted a fresh classification of the Exodus scrolls from the Judean Desert by identifying groups of scrolls that are inter-linked by what he calls "connective readings" and clusters of texts that are statistically related on the basis of agreements and disagreements (Longacre, "Contextualized Approach," 216).

215 Longacre, "Contextualized Approach," 164–65, 177–87.

216 See note 182.

217 Cana Werman, "The Two Covenants: An Interpretation of the 4Q158 Fragments," *JSP* 28 (2019): 183–213.

218 See notes 171 and 201. In addition to 4QpaleoExod[m] featuring a Deuteronomic expansion in Exod 20:19, a pre-Samaritan text of Exodus 20:21 juxtaposing Deut 5:28–29 and 18:18–19 is found also in the excerpted text known as 4QTestimonia (4Q175) 5–8.

219 Segal, "Biblical Exegesis in 4Q158," 56.

The fact that Exod 20:12–17 appears here prior to Deut 5:30–31 is puzzling. Segal suggests that this re-arrangement of the Ten Commandments reflects an understanding, implied in the wording of the Decalogue itself, that God addressed Israel directly with the first two commandments, while the remaining eight were delivered by Moses.[220] Such an interpretation of the Sinai revelation appears in several rabbinic texts and may be reflected in another text from Qumran, 4Q377.[221] Below I tentatively suggest that a similar interest in clarifying the order of communication at Sinai underlies the addition found in 4QPhyl G (Deut 5:1–2) and the rearranged text of Deuteronomy 5 in 8QPhyl 30 (Chapter 8).

The Book of Deuteronomy in the Scrolls from the Judean Desert

Before the Discoveries in the Judean Desert

As with the book of Exodus, prior to surveying the manuscripts of Deuteronomy from the Judean Desert, it seems fitting to review the three main texts of Deuteronomy that were available to scholars prior to Qumran discoveries: MT, SamP, and LXX.

   MT Deuteronomy. Among the readings setting MT Deuteronomy apart from the SamP and LXX are theologically motivated revisions found in MT Deut 27:4; 32:8, 43.[222] Thus, the reading "Ebal" in Deut 27:4 seems to supplant the earlier "Gerizim" (preserved in Vetus Latina), apparently as an anti-Samaritan polemic.[223] As to Deuteronomy 32, verses 8 and 43 appear to reflect an anti-polytheistic revision. In v. 8 the earlier "sons of God" (preserved in 4QDeutʲ and LXX) had been replaced with "sons of Israel." In a similar vein, v. 43 omits the reference to the "sons of God" and replaces "heaven" with "nations" (the earlier readings

---

220 Segal, "Biblical Exegesis in 4Q158," 56–58.

221 See Canticles Rabbah 1:2 and further James L. Kugel, *Traditions of the Bible: A Guide to the Bible as It Was at the Start of the Common Era* (Cambridge: Harvard University Press, 1998), 637–38. On 4Q377, see Ariel Feldman, "The Sinai Revelation According to 4Q377 (Apocryphal Pentateuch B)," *DSD* 18 (2011): 155–72.

222 Hendel, "2.2.2 Masoretic Texts and Ancient Texts Close to MT."

223 Stefan Schorch, "The Samaritan Version of Deuteronomy and the Origin of Deuteronomy," in *Samaria, Samarians, Samaritans: Studies on Bible, History and Linguistics*, ed. József Zsengellér, Studia Samaritana 6 (Berlin: De Gruyter, 2011), 23–37 (28). On DSS F.154 F.Deut2, presumably containing Deut 27:4–6 with Mt. Gerizim instead of Mt. Ebal, as a modern forgery see below.

are found, with variants and expansions, in 4QDeut[q] and LXX).[224] Another feature of the MT, shared to a varying degree by SamP and LXX, are small-scale harmonizations. As with MT Exodus, Tov suggests that the MT Deuteronomy is the least harmonized of the three texts.[225]

SamP Deuteronomy. While in SamP it is the book of Deuteronomy that often serves as a source of materials incorporated into other books of the Torah, in a few cases the reverse process can be observed, e.g., in Deut 2:7 (Num 20:14, 17 f.; cf. also 4QRP[b] 23a–b i 1–4); 10:6–7 (Num 33:31–37; cf. 4QRP[b] 27); and 14 (Leviticus 11).[226] Also, SamP Deuteronomy yields multiple small-scale harmonizations.[227] Furthermore, there are readings that have been long considered to be Samaritan. These are the recurring phrase "the place that God has chosen" (MT and LXX: "the place that God will choose") and the aforementioned "Gerizim" in Deut 27:4. However, it is not impossible that these are earlier readings, or, at least, readings that were current in wider Second Temple Jewish circles.[228] Recent scholarship suggests that this applies also to the so-called Samaritan Tenth Commandment (Deut 5:17).[229]

LXX Deuteronomy. The Greek translation of Deuteronomy is usually described as fairly literal yet idiomatic.[230] This suggests that when the Greek text diverges from the Hebrew, it is likely to reflect a variant Hebrew reading. One large group of such variants are small-scale harmonizations. Indeed, as with LXX Exodus, Tov suggests that LXX Deuteronomy is the most harmonized of

---

224 See, among others, Alexander Rofé, "The End of the Song of Moses (Deuteronomy 32.43)," in *Deuteronomy: Issues and Interpretation* (London: T&T Clark, 2002), 47–54.

225 According to Tov, the MT Deuteronomy shares 44 harmonizations with the SamP against the shorter text of LXX and 8 more with LXX against the shorter text of SamP. His study indicates that there are only two unique harmonizations in the MT Deuteronomy (1:35; 23:12). Emanuel Tov, "Textual Harmonizations in the Ancient Texts of Deuteronomy," in *Mishneh Toda: Studies in Deuteronomy and Its Cultural Environment in Honor of Jeffrey H. Tigay*, ed. Nili Sacher Fox, David A. Glatt-Gilad, and Michael J. Williams (Winona Lake: Eisenbrauns, 2015), 15–28.

226 Kartveit, *Origin*, 312.

227 Tov, "Textual Harmonizations in the Ancient Texts of Deuteronomy," lists 22 harmonizations that are unique to SamP, 44 that are shared with MT against the shorter LXX, and 49 that are shared with LXX against the shorter MT.

228 Schorch, "Samaritan Version of Deuteronomy," 28, 32, and the bibliography cited there.

229 For the widespread view that this is a Samaritan addition to the text of Deuteronomy, see Sidnie White Crawford, "2.4.1.5 Deuteronomy," in *Textual History of the Bible*, ed. Armin Lange (Brill, 2020), http://dx.doi.org.ezproxy.tcu.edu/10.1163/2452-4107_thb_COM_0002040105. For the possibility that this commandment belongs to the pre-Samaritan layer of SamP Deuteronomy, see note 174.

230 See Larry Perkins, "Deuteronomy," in *T&T Clark Companion to the Septuagint*, ed. James K. Aitken (London: T&T Clark, 2015), 68–85; White Crawford, "2.4.1.5 Deuteronomy."

the three texts.[231] Besides these, there are many other readings where LXX deviates from the MT and SamP. For example, LXX Deut 5:17–18 reverses the order of the commandments (as does also Papyrus Nash and LXX Exod 20:13–15), while LXX Deut 6:4 (and also Papyrus Nash) offers an extensive addition reminiscent of Deut 4:45.[232] Further instances of substantially longer text in LXX include Deut 23:18; 26:9–10; 32:43.[233]

After the Discoveries in the Judean Desert

The scrolls from the Judean Desert offer a plethora of texts illuminating the early transmission and reception of Deuteronomy.[234] As with Exodus, the following overview focuses on the biblical manuscripts of this book, including the 4QReworked Pentateuch scrolls (4QRP[a-e] [4Q158; 4Q364–367]) and the excerpted texts of Deuteronomy. All these texts are listed in the following table.[235]

---

231 Tov counts 134 instances of harmonization in LXX Deuteronomy. Of these, 99 are unique to this text and 49 are shared with SamP against the MT. See Tov, "Textual Harmonizations in the Ancient Texts of Deuteronomy."
232 Alexander Rofé, "Deuteronomy 5.28–6.1: Composition and Text in the Light of Deuteronomic Style and Three Tefillin from Qumran (4Q128, 129, 137)," in *Deuteronomy: Issues and Interpretation* (London: T&T Clark, 2002), 31; Teeter, *Scribal Laws*, 99–102; Tov, "The Papyrus Nash and the Septuagint." 42–47.
233 Teeter, *Scribal Laws*, 119–41, 159–61, offers a discussion of multiple variants in the legal sections of Deuteronomy, some of which are attested in the Qumran manuscripts of Deuteronomy.
234 On Deuteronomy in the Dead Sea Scrolls, in addition to the publications cited in this chapter, see also Julie A. Duncan, "Deuteronomy, Book of," in *Encyclopedia of the Dead Sea Scrolls*, ed. Lawrence H. Schiffman and James C. VanderKam (Oxford: Oxford University Press, 2000), 1:198–202; Sidnie White Crawford, "Reading Deuteronomy in the Second Temple Period," in *Reading the Present in the Qumran Library*, ed. Kristin De Troyer and Armin Lange (Atlanta: SBL, 2005), 127–40; Timothy H. Lim, "Deuteronomy in the Judaism of the Second Temple Period," in *Deuteronomy in the New Testament*, ed. Maarten J. J. Menken and Steve Moyise (London: T&T Clark, 2007), 6–26; Hanne von Weissenberg, "Deuteronomy at Qumran and in 4QMMT," in *All Good Things: Essays in Memory of Timo Veijola*, ed. Juha Pakkala and Marti Nissinen (Helsinki: Finnish Exegetical Society, 2008), 520–37; Ariel Feldman, "Deuteronomy in the Texts from the Judean Desert," in *Oxford Handbook of Deuteronomy*, ed. Don C. Benjamin (Oxford University Press, 2020), https://www.oxfordhandbooks.com/view/10.1093/oxfordhb/9780190273552.001.0001/oxfordhb-9780190273552-e-22.
235 There are also several fragments of Exodus that are most likely modern forgeries. These include the fragments found in the following collections: the Schøyen Collection (MS 5214/1 [4Q[?]Deut1, DSS F.108, DSS F.Deut5]: Deut 6:1–2; MS5214/2 [4Q[?]Deut2, DSS F.109, DSS F.Deut6]: Deut 32:5–9), the Southwestern Baptist Theological Seminary Collection (DSS F.163 [F.Deut3]: Deut 9:25–10:1; DSS F.164 [F.Deut4]: Deut 12:11–14), and the Azusa Pacific University Collection (DSS F.153 F.Deut1: Deut 8:2–5; DSS F.154 F.Deut2: Deut 27:4–6).

Tab. 5: Manuscripts of Deuteronomy from the Judean Desert.[236]

Caves of Qumran

Cave 1

1Q4 (1QDeut[a]; 30–1 BCE[237])
    Deut 1:22–25; 4:26, 43, 47, 49; 8:18–19; 9:7, 27–28; 11:10; 11:27–30; 12:14;
    13:1–6, 8, 13–14; 14:21, 24–25; 16:4, 6–7
1Q5 (1QDeut[b]; 50 BCE–30 CE or 30–1 BCE)[238]
    Deut 1:9, 11, 13; 8:8–9; 9:10; 11:30–31; 15:14–15; 17:16; 21:8–9; 24:5, 10–16;
    25:13–18; 28:44–48; 29:9–20; 30:19–20; 31:1–10, 12–13; 32:17–29; 33:12–19,
    21–24

Cave 2

2Q10 (2QDeut[a]; 50 BCE)
    Deut 1:7–9
2Q11 (2QDeut[b]; Herodian)
    Deut 17:12–15
2Q12 (2QDeut[c]; late Herodian)
    Deut 10:8–12

Cave 4

Deuteronomy only
Hebrew
4Q28 (4QDeut[a]; 175–150 BCE)
    Deut 23:26; 24:1–8
4Q29 (4QDeut[b]; 150–100 BCE)
    Deut 29:24–27; 30:3–14; 31:9–17, 24–30; 32:1–3; 33:29[239]
4Q30 (4QDeut[c]; 150–100 BCE)
    Deut 2:29–30; 3:25–26, 4:1, 13–17, 31–32; 7:3–4; 8:1–5; 9:11–12, 17–19, 29;
    10:1–2, 5–8; 11:3, 9–13, 18; 12:18–19, 26, 31; 13:5, 7, 11–12, 16; 15:1–4, 15–19;

236 The list of the Deuteronomic passages offered here is based on the editions of the respective texts in the DJD series. I have also included some of the new identifications proposed in subsequent scholarship (see below), notably, by Ulrich Dahmen, "Neu identifizierte Fragmente in den 'Deuteronomium'-Handschriften vom Toten Meer," *RevQ* 20 (2002): 571–81; idem, "Das Deuteronomium in Qumran," in *Das Deuteronomium*, ed. Georg Braulik, OBS 23 (Frankfurt am Main: Peter Lang, 2003), 269–310.
237 Unless noted otherwise the dating of the manuscripts follows the data provided in the DJD editions of these texts. In this case, the dating is from Lange, "2.2.1 Ancient, Late Ancient, and Early Medieval Manuscript Evidence."
238 For a discussion of the dating of the fragments assigned to this scroll and a possibility that they belong to two or even three scrolls, see Daniel Stökl Ben Ezra, "Paleographical Observations Regarding 1Q5 – One or Several Scrolls?," in *Qumran Cave 1 Revisited*, ed. Daniel K. Falk, STDJ 91 (Leiden: Brill, 2010), 245–57 (256–57).
239 Two fragments of this scroll were identified by Eibert Tigchelaar, "Minuscula Qumranica I," *RevQ* 21 (2004): 643–48 (646).

16:2–3, 6–11, 21–22; 17:1–5, 7, 15–20; 18:1; 26:19; 27:1–2, 24–26; 28:1–14, 20, 22–25, 29–30, 48–50, 61; 29:17–19; 31:16–19; 32:3

4Q31 (4QDeut^d; 125–75 BCE)

Deut 2:24–36; 3:14–29; 4:1

4Q32 (4QDeut^e; 50–25 BCE)

Deut 3:24; 7:12–16, 21–26; 8:1–7, 10–11, 15–16

4Q33 (4QDeut^f; 75–50 BCE)[240]

Deut 4:24–26; 7:22–25; 8:2–14; 9:6–7; 17:17–18; 18:6–10, 18–22; 19:13–15, 17–21; 20:1–6; 21:4–12; 22:12–19; 23:21–26; 24:2–7; 25:3–9; 26:18–19; 27:1–10

4Q34 (4QDeut^g; 25–1 BCE)

Deut 9:12–14; 23:18–20; 24:16–22; 25:1–5, 14–19; 26:1–5; 28:21–25, 27–29

4Q35 (4QDeut^h; 50–1 BCE)

Deut 1:1–17, 22–24, 29–39, 41–46; 2:1–6, 28–30; 4:31–34; 19:21?; 31:9–11; 33:8–22

4Q36 (4QDeut^i; 100–50 BCE)

Deut 4:49; 5:1; 20:9–13; 21:23; 22:1–9; 23:6–8, 12–16, 22–26; 24:1; 30:4–5

4Q37 (4QDeut^j; 50 BCE)

Deut 5:1–11, 13–15, 21–33; 6:1–3; 8:5–10; 11:6–10, 12, 13; 11:21?; Exod 12:43–44, 46–51; 13:1–5; Deut 32:7–8

4Q38 (4QDeut^{k1}; 30–1 BCE)

Deut 5:28–32; 11:6–13; 32:17–18, 22–23, 25–27

4Q38a (4QDeut^{k2}; 30–1 BCE)

Deut 19:3, 8–16; 20:6–19; 23:22–26; 24:1–3; 25:19; 26:5, 18–19; 27:1?

4Q38b (4QDeut^{k3}; 50 CE)

Deut 30:13–18[241]

4Q39 (4QDeut^l; 50 BCE)

Deut 10:12, 14–15; 28:67–68; 29:2–5; 31:12; 33:1–2; 34:4–6, 8?

4Q40 (4QDeut^m; 50–1 BCE)

Deut 3:18–22; 4:32–33; 7:18–22

4Q41 (4QDeut^n; 30–1 BCE)

Deut Deut 8:5–10; 5:1–29, 31–33; 6:1

4Q42 (4QDeut^o; 75–50 BCE)

Deut 2:8; 4:30–34; 5:1–5, 8–9; 28:15–18, 33–36, 47–52, 58–62; 29:22–25

4Q43 (4QDeut^p; 75–50 BCE)

Deut 6:4–11

4Q44 (4QDeut^q; 50–1 BCE or beginning of the 1st century CE)

Deut 32:9–10?, 37–43

4Q45 (4QpaleoDeut^r; 75–50 BCE)

Deut 1:8?; 7:2–7, 9–10, 16–25; 10:11–12; 11:28, 30–32; 12:1, 2–5, 11–12, 22; 13:19; 14:1–4, 19–22, 26–29; 15:5–6, 8–10; 19:2–3; 22:3–6; 23:7, 12–15; 28:15–18, 20; 31:29; 32:6–8, 10–11, 13–14, 33–35; 33:2–8, 29; 34:1[242]

---

240 Eshel and Eshel, "Preliminary Report," 274–75, claimed that they have identified another fragment of this scroll containing Deut 19:13–15. Tigchelaar, "Unprovenanced," 182, lists it as item #52. Its whereabouts seem to be unknown.

241 For additional recently identified fragments see Ableman, "Newly Identified Pentateuchal Fragments," 96–100.

242 For further tentative identifications see Skehan et al., DJD 9:131–52; Dahmen, "Neu identifizierte Fragmente," 571–81.

4Q46 (4QpaleoDeut^s; 250–200 BCE)
    Deut 26:14–15
4Q38c (4QDeut^t; also known as 4QDeut^r[243])
    Deut 12:31; 13:1; 14:28–29
4Q38d (4QDeut^u; 150 BCE)[244]
    Deut 24:20–22
Greek
4QLXXDeut (4Q122; 200–150 BCE)
    Deut 11:4
Deuteronomy along with other books of the Torah
4Q364 (4QRP^b; 75–50 BCE)
    Deut 1:1–6, 17–28, 32–33, 45–46; 2:8–9, 12–14; Num 20:17–18; Deut 2:30–37;
    3:1–2; 3:18–23; 9:6–7, 12–18, 22–24, 27–29; 10:1–4, 6–7?, 10–13, 22; 11:1–2, 6–
    9, 23–24; 14:24–26
4Q365 (4QRP^c; 75–50 BCE)
    Deut 19:20–21; 20:1
4Q366 (4QRP^d; 75–50 BCE)
    Deut 16:13–14; 14:14–16, 18, 20–21

Cave 5

5Q1 (5QDeut; 200–150 BCE)
    Deut 7:15–24; 8:5–20; 9:1–2[245]

Cave 6

6Q3 (6QpapDeut?)
    Deut 26:19

Cave 7

Greek
7Q6, 7Q7, 7Q9 (7QLXXDt)[246]
    Deut 16:19; 20:19; 33:22–23

Cave 11

11Q3 (11QDeut; 50 BCE)
    Deut 1:4–5; 2:28–30

---

243 On this text see Émile Puech, "Identification de nouveaux manuscrits bibliques: Deutéronome et Proverbes dans les debris de la Grotte 4," *RevQ* 20 (2003): 121–26 (123–24). Tigchelaar suggested several corrections to Puech's readings and proposed a siglum 4Q38c=4QDt^t (Puech prefers 4Q38c=4QDt^r). Tigchelaar, "Minuscula Qumranica I," 648; idem, "A Forgotten Qumran Cave 4 'Deuteronomy' Fragment (4Q38D=4QDeut^u)," *RevQ* 23 (2008): 525–28 (527).
244 Tigchelaar, "Forgotten Qumran Cave 4 'Deuteronomy' Fragment," 525–27.
245 Milik, DJD 3:169–71, notes that the fragments may also contain Deut 32:20–21 and 33:1–2.
246 Lincoln H. Blumell, "A Proposal for a New LXX Text among the Cave 7 Fragments," *RevQ* 29 (2017): 105–17; Émile Puech, "Les fragments de papyrus 7Q6 1–2, 7Q9 et 7Q7 = Pap7QLXXDt," ibid., 119–27.

Other Sites in the Judean Desert
Wadi Murabba'at
Mur2 (MurDeut; before 66 CE)
Deut 10:1–3; 11:2–3; 12:25–26; 14:29; 15:1 (or 15:2)
Naḥal Ṣe'elim/Naḥal Ḥever
XHev/Se 3 (XHev/SeDeut; 50–68 CE)
Deut 9:4–7, 21–23
Masada
Mas 1043/a–d (MasDeut; Mas 1c; early Herodian formal hand)
Deut 32:46–47; 33:17–24; 34:2–6

The Contribution of the Deuteronomy Manuscripts from the Judean Desert

As with the book of Exodus, a helpful point of entry into the discussion of the contribution of the aforementioned Deuteronomy scrolls is their recent classification by Lange.[247] His analysis excludes several manuscripts as either too fragmentary or non-classifiable. For the remaining texts, he suggests the following:

Proto-MT: 4QDeut^e; 4QDeut^g; MasDeut

Close to LXX: 4QDeut^q

Close to both MT and SamP: 4QDeut^d; 4QDeut^f; 4QDeut^i; 4QDeut^o; 5QDeut

Non-aligned: 1QDeut^b; 4QDeut^b; 4QDeut^c; 4QDeut^h; 4QDeut^{k2}; 4QDeut^j; 4QDeut^{k1}; 4QDeut^{k2}; 4QDeut^n; 4QpaleoDeut^r; 4QRP^{b-d}

The many non-aligned texts listed by Lange include three of the four excerpted Deuteronomy scrolls from Qumran:[248]

---

247 Lange, "2.2.1 Ancient, Late Ancient, and Early Medieval Manuscript Evidence."
248 Regarding the fourth excerpted scroll, 4QDeut^q, Lange, "2.2.1 Ancient, Late Ancient, and Early Medieval Manuscript Evidence," observes that it, too, has "non-aligned tendencies." In addition to these four, several other fragmentary Deuteronomy scrolls surveyed above could potentially be excerpted scrolls rather than running texts of Deuteronomy. One example is 4QDeut^p preserving the Shema and the following verses (Deut 6:4–11). It is relatively small, with a reconstructed column of 55–69 letter spaces (White Crawford, DJD 14:135). The other one is 5QDeut. The larger fragments of this scroll contain Deut 7:15–24 and 8:5–9:2. Milik observes that, once reconstructed, these verses would yield a column 135 mm wide and 100 mm high (Milik, DJD 3:169), i.e., a rather small scroll. However, for the smaller fragments containing Deut 32:20–21 and 33:1–2 he suggests twice as narrow of a column (DJD 3:169–71). Since two of the excerpted texts listed above contain Deuteronomy 32, one wonders whether the

4QDeut[j] (4Q37): Deut 5:1–11, 13–15, 21–33; 6:1–3; 8:5–10; 11:6–10, 12, 13, 21?; Exod 12:43–44, 46–51; 13:1–5; Deut 32:7–8

4QDeut[kl] (4Q38): 5:28–32; 11:6–13; 32:17–18, 22–23, 25–27

4QDeut[n] (4Q41): 8:5–10; 5:1–29, 31–33; 6:1

4QDeut[q] (4Q44): 32:9–10?, 37–43[249]

These four scrolls are relatively small. Three of them feature some of the Deuteronomic passages copied in Type 2 tefillin.[250] 4QDeut[j] also incorporates verses from Exodus 12–13, again, as do Type 2 tefillin from Qumran. Even the inclusion of Deuteronomy 32 in 4QDeut[j] and 4QDeut[q] can be linked to 4QPhyl N containing Deut 32:14–20, 32–33. These affinities led scholars to suggest that some of these scrolls functioned as tefillin[251] or served as master texts for scribes who copied them.[252] The only pericope found in two of these scrolls (4QDeut[j]; 4QDeut[n]) that is absent from the ancient tefillin (or mezuzot), both the artifacts from the Judean Desert and those described in rabbinic texts, is Deut 8:5–10. It is, however, used in the later Jewish liturgy.[253] Hence is the more general interpretation of these scrolls – without necessarily undermining the link to tefillin and mezuzot – as liturgical or devotional texts.[254]

---

second group of fragments with Deuteronomy 32 and a narrower column might have belonged to another scroll, possibly an excerpted one. This possibility is discussed by Tov, "Excerpted and Abbreviated Texts," 13, and Lange. On the excerpted Deuteronomy scrolls, see further Julie A. Duncan, "Excerpted Texts of 'Deuteronomy' at Qumran," *RevQ* 18 (1997): 43–62.

249 As White Crawford, DJD 14:137–142, observes, the physical features of this scroll indicate that it might have contained Deuteronomy 32 only, and even that chapter was not copied in its entirety (apparently up to verse 43).

250 For 4QDeut[j], Duncan, DJD 14:75, conjectures that it also included the verses from Deuteronomy 10 copied in Type 2 tefillin.

251 See Cohn, *Tangled Up*, 76–77 (tentatively), who notes that 4QDeut[j], 4QDeut[kl], and 4QDeut[n] were folded, while 4QDeut[n] features an "unusually tiny script." Similarly, Papyrus Nash, featuring the Decalogue and the Shema and exhibiting signs of folding, has been interpreted as a tefillin or a mezuzah (Cohn, ibid., 67–68).

252 Reed, "Physical Features of Excerpted Torah Texts," 103–104 (*apud* Brooke); Emanuel Tov, "The Qumran Tefillin and Their Possible Master Copies," in *On Wings of Prayer*, ed. Nuria Calduch-Benages, Michael W. Duggan, and Dalia Marx (Berlin: De Gruyter, 2019), 135–50. He suggests that 4QDeut[j] and 4QDeut[kl] might have served as master texts for 1QPhyl and 4QPhyl A; J-K.

253 On Deuteronomy 8 and grace after the meals see Moshe Weinfeld, "Grace after Meals in Qumran," *JBL* 111 (1992): 427–40.

254 On these four scrolls as special use manuscripts, see Duncan, DJD 14:75, 79. For 4QDeut[j] written in a larger script she suggests a pedagogical use (Duncan, "Excerpted Texts," 51). For 4QDeut[n] as a collection of prayers, see Eshel, "4QDeut[n]," 152 (citing m. Tamid 5:1). On liturgi-

Unlike the Exodus scrolls, Ulrich's list of scriptural books attested to in multiple literary editions does not include Deuteronomy.[255] For him, even SamP Deuteronomy does not seem to qualify as a discrete literary edition. Still, there is at least one Qumran manuscript that may come close to being a distinct edition of Deuteronomy, 4QRP^b (4Q364). Another of Lange's non-aligned texts, this scroll, preserving a considerable amount of Deuteronomy, features a wide array of scribal interventions, including a juxtaposition of Deut 2:8–14 with Num 20:17–18 (as in SamP), a unique reordering of the text (frg. 26b, e, col ii), multiple instances of longer wording (Deut 2:30–3:2; 10:6–7, 10; 11:6), and paraphrase (frag. 37).[256]

Of special interest for this study, is also another non-aligned text associated with 4QReworked Pentateuch, 4QRP^d (4Q366).[257] In frag. 4 i of this scroll a running text of Num 29:32–30:1 is followed by Deut 16:13–14. The juxtaposition of these two passages most likely has to do with the fact that both deal with the festival of Sukkoth (cf. also frag. 3 containing Num 29:14–24).[258] The fragment, however, leaves it unclear whether the base text here is Numbers or Deuteronomy. Still, a recent reading and reconstruction of the second column of this fragment by Elisha Qimron indicates that the scroll continued with Deuteronomy, not Numbers. In his view, it features a pastiche of biblical passages dealing with judges and judging. The sequence of the scriptural texts there is Deut 1:16–17, Exod 23:8, and Lev 19:15. Qimron suggests that this fragment expands on Deut 16:19. While he does not elaborate on this proposal, it appears to rely on two considerations. First, the preceding column ends with Deut 16:13–14. Second, the wording of Exod 23:8 cited in line 9 is very close to Deut 16:19.[259] If Qimron is correct, both columns of this fragment offer an example of a scribal agglomer-

---

cal scrolls in Qumran corpus, see further Daniel Falk, "Material Aspects of Prayer Manuscripts at Qumran," in *Literature or Liturgy*, ed. Clemens Leonhard and Hermut Löhr (Tübingen: Mohr Siebeck, 2014), 33–87; idem, "Liturgical Texts," in *T&T Clark Companion to the Dead Sea Scrolls*, ed. George J. Brooke and Charlotte Hempel (London: T&T Clark, 2019), 423–34.

255 See, for instance, Tov and Ulrich, "1.1.1.2 Textual Theories."

256 See discussion in Zahn, *Rethinking Rewritten Scripture*, 83, 87, 91–96, 113–15. On Deut 11:6 (frag. 30 2) see Qimron's recent reading [ואת כול אשר לקו[רח ואת כול הרכוש] (Elisha Qimron, *The Hebrew Writings from Qumran: A Composite Edition* [Tel-Aviv: published electronically, 2020], 3:113). This wording, attested to also in SamP ad loc., is borrowed from Num 16:32. It is also found in 4QPhyl A and K.

257 Crawford, "Excerpted Manuscripts," 261–63, recently argued that this is an excepted scroll. It is, however, far from clear, as the scroll is highly fragmentary.

258 Segal, "4QReworked Pentateuch or 4QPentateuch?," 397, deems it to be a harmonization akin to those found in the pre-Samaritan texts, SamP, and the Temple Scroll. One must observe, however, that SamP does not feature such a juxtaposition in either Numbers 29 or Deuteronomy 16.

259 Qimron, *Hebrew Writings from Qumran*, 3:132.

ation of thematically related verses.[260] I have already observed that in pre-Samaritan texts and SamP content-related passages from Deuteronomy are copy-pasted into Exodus. What is different in the case of 4QRP[d] frag. 4 i is that the passages in question are of a legal nature.[261] I will return to this aspect of 4QRP[d] in Chapter 8 discussing 8QPhyl which seems to exhibit a similar strategy.

How Do Tefillin and Mezuzot Fit In?

The foregoing overview of Exodus and Deuteronomy manuscripts from the Judean Desert highlights two aspects of this corpus: the presence of texts featuring a variety of scribal techniques and the inclusion of the excerpted texts. The latter feature alone should suffice to securely place tefillin and mezuzot within this corpus. After all, the vast majority of them are nothing but excerpts from Exodus and Deuteronomy. The emphasis on the diverse scribal interventions underscores this point. Multiple tefillin and mezuzot from Qumran offer a familiar array of omissions, additions, paraphrase, and harmonizations.[262] And yet, these two aspects of tefillin and mezuzot have also been interpreted differently. Thus, George Brooke, while acknowledging that tefillin are "an important group of witnesses to the transmission of the scriptural texts in the second temple period," classifies them as Rewritten Bible texts.[263] To support this classification, he notes their excerpted nature and possible liturgical use.[264] Assessing the contribution of tefillin and mezuzot to textual criticism, Nathan Jastram admits that they have some value, especially when they share readings with other

---

260 There is, of course, a danger of a circular reasoning here. Still, it seems rather unlikely to find a pastiche of these passages in the context of Numbers 30 (dealing with woman's vow), should one presume that Numbers is the base text of this fragment.
261 It has been noted that pre-Samaritan texts and SamP refrain from "harmonizing" legal sections of the Torah. See, for instance, Bernstein, "What Has Happened to the Laws?," 42.
262 For a list of major variants in tefillin and mezuzot from the Judean Desert, see Jastram, "2.2.5.1 Tefillin and Mezuzot." For a detailed discussion see George J. Brooke, "Deuteronomy 5–6 in the Phylacteries from Qumran Cave 4," in *Emanuel: Studies in the Hebrew Bible, Septuagint, and the Dead Sea Scrolls in Honour of Emanuel Tov*, ed. Shalom Paul et al., SVT 94 (Leiden: Brill, 2003), 57–70. On harmonizations in the Decalogue in tefillin and mezuzot from Qumran see further Innocent Himbaza, "Le décalogue de Papyrus Nash, Philon, 4QPhyl G, 8QPhyl 3 et 4QMez A," *RevQ* 20 (2002): 411–28.
263 Brooke, "Deuteronomy 5–6," 70.
264 Brooke, "Deuteronomy 5–6," 58, associates tefillin "with the realm of private prayer." Tov, "Development," 7, 18, also speaks of tefillin as liturgical texts. Falk, however, is uncertain as to whether tefillin qualify as such, since there is no evidence for their ritual use. See Falk, "Liturgical Texts," 426.

textual witnesses. At the same time, in his opinion, "major variants" present in tefillin and mezuzot, such as omissions, additions, and harmonizations, indicate that they "were not considered authoritative texts, but were appropriations of authoritative texts for personal use."[265] The points made by these scholars are well taken. First, in the Second Temple period, the line between scriptural texts and their rewritings appears to have been rather blurry. Second, for a textual critic, many of the unique readings found in Qumran tefillin and mezuzot are likely to be "secondary," revealing more about the reception of the biblical texts than about their "original" wording.[266] Still, liturgical or not, the nature and scope of variation in tefillin and mezuzot closely resembles those of the "revisionist" or "facilitative" manuscripts of Exodus and Deuteronomy.[267] Hence, it seems that they should be classified, first and foremost, as "ordinary biblical texts."[268] This point is finely stated by Tov:

> In the description of the textual witnesses of the Hebrew Bible *tefillin* are a stepchild, ... since they are treated as idiosyncratic biblical texts. However, in actual fact they are ordinary biblical texts, partial, but regular, since the textual data in the *tefillin* were copied from larger contexts that provide as good evidence of the Bible text as any other fragment from the Judean Desert.[269]

It is with this understanding in mind that I turn to several instances of unique readings found in tefillin and mezuzot from Qumran.[270] Once again, the choice

---

265 Jastram, "2.2.5.1 Tefillin and Mezuzot." He rightly emphasizes the fact that tefillin and mezuzot were not intended for public reading.

266 For contrasting views on the quest for the "original text" of the Hebrew Bible, see George J. Brooke, "The Qumran Scrolls and the Demise of the Distinction between Lower and Higher Criticism," in idem, *Reading the Dead Sea Scrolls: Essays in Method*, Early Judaism and Its Literature 39 (Atlanta: SBL, 2013), 1–17; Tov and Ulrich, "1.1.1.2 Textual Theories."

267 For a statistical analysis of the distribution of variant readings in the versions of the Decalogue preserved in tefillin and mezuzot and other biblical manuscripts from Qumran, see Gary D. Martin, *Multiple Originals: New Approaches to Hebrew Bible Textual Criticism*, SBL Text-Critical Studies 7 (Leiden: Brill, 2011), 228. It has been suggested that the preponderance of textual variants in tefillin and mezuzot slips is to be understood in light of the later rabbinic ruling that these are to be written from memory (b. Megillah 18b). See Lange, *Handbuch*, 121; Jastram, "2.2.5.1 Tefillin and Mezuzot." This, of course, cannot be established with any certainty. After all, several tefillin and mezuzot feature little variation from the MT.

268 Emanuel Tov, "From Popular Jewish LXX-SP Texts to Separate Sectarian Texts: Insights from the Dead Sea Scrolls," in *The Samaritan Pentateuch and the Dead Sea Scrolls*, ed. Michael Langlois, CBET 94 (Leuven: Peters, 2019), 19–40 (32).

269 Tov, "Tefillin from the Judean Desert," 277. Cf. also Martin, *Multiple Originals*, 236.

270 Each of the editors who published tefillin and mezuzot from the Judean Desert discussed (some briefly and some at length) the variant readings attested to in these texts. Of the more detailed studies on this topic, one should mention that of Brooke, "Deuteronomy 5–6."

of these examples is not accidental. Their discussion anticipates the chapters to
follow. Moreover, it seems that previous scholarship on these readings leaves
room for further clarification.

Deuteronomy 5:1–2

The first example comes from tefillin slip 4QPhyl G (4Q134). The recto of this
slip contains Deut 5:1–21. Lines 1–11 reproduced below feature verses 1–6:[271]

ויקרא¹ 1
מושה אל כול ישראל 2
ויאמר אליהם שמעה ישראל 3
את החוקים֗ [ו]א֗ת המשפטים אשר אנכי מצוכה 4
היום על ה דב֗[ר בא]֗וזניכם היום הזה ושמרתם לעשותם 5
כי אל יהוה אלהים֗ [שמ]ע֗ים א֗ת֗ם מתוך האש בהר מתוך הא֗ש 6
ואנכ֗י [אג]י֗ד֗ דב֗ר֗י בר֗י[תו הי]ו[ם הזה ולמדתם אותם את בניכם 7
ולעשו[ת]֗ם עמ[נו] ב֗חורב 3°·לוא את אבותינו כרת יהוה [8
[את הברית הז]א֗ת כי אתנו אחנו פ֗ה אלה כלנו ח֗ים היום ⁴פנים בפני֗ם 9
[דבר י֗]ה֗וה עמכם מתוך בהר האש ⁵ו{אנ}֗אנ֗ל}֗אנכי עומד בין אלהים 10
[וביני֗]כ֗ם ב֗עת ההי ולוא עליתם בה֗ר֗ לאמור ⁶אנכי יהוה אליכה 11

Between a slightly altered text of v. 1 (lines 1–5) and a remnant of v. 2 (line 8)
there appears to be an addition:

כי אל יהוה אלהים֗ [שמ]ע֗ים א֗ת֗ם מתוך האש בהר מתוך הא֗ש 6
ואנכ֗י [אג]י֗ד֗ דב֗ר֗י בר֗י[תו הי]ו[ם הזה ולמדתם אותם את בניכם 7
ולעשו[ת]֗ם עמ[נו] ב֗חורב [8

6. for you are [lis]tening to YHWH God out of the fire, on the mountain out of
   the fire.
7. And I will [an]nounce the words of his coven[ant on this da]y. And you
   shall teach them to your sons
8. [to obser]ve them wi[th us] at Horeb.

The lacuna in the beginning of line 8 makes it unclear how much of verse 2
was present on the parchment. Clearly, the phrase עמ[נו] ב֗חורב has been borrowed from it: יהוה אלהינו כרת עמנו ברית בחרב ("The Lord our God made a
covenant with us at Horeb"). However, the preceding letters restored by Milik
as ולעשו[תם ("to obser]ve them") do not match this verse. Perhaps, the frag-

ment echoes here the end of v. 1, ושמרתם לעשותם. That this addition engages v. 1 is also suggested by the phrase ולמדתם אתם ("and you shall teach them"). Absent from the wording of v. 1b in line 5, it now appears in line 7, expanded to match another "tefillin" passage, Deut 11:19 (ולמדתם אתם את בניכם).

To explain the rest of the text, Brooke suggests a harmonization towards Deut 4:12–13 (the relevant phrases are <u>underlined</u>):[272]

וידבר יהוה אליכם <u>מתוך האש</u> קול דברים אתם <u>שמעים</u> ותמונה אינכם ראים זולתי קול
<u>ויגד</u> לכם את <u>בריתו</u> אשר צוה אתכם <u>לעשות</u> עשרת הדברים ויכתבם על שני לחות אבנים

The Lord spoke to you out of the fire; you heard the sound of words but perceived no shape – nothing but a voice. He declared to you the covenant that He commanded you to observe, the Ten Commandments; and He inscribed them on two tablets of stone.

Jastram also points to Deut 5:5 and 22 (the relevant phrases are <u>underlined</u>):[273] Deut 5:22:

את הדברים האלה דבר יהוה אל כל קהלכם <u>בהר מתוך האש</u> הענן והערפל קול גדול

The Lord spoke those words – those and no more – to your whole congregation at the mountain, with a mighty voice out of the fire and the dense clouds.

Deut 5:5:

אנכי עמד בין יהוה וביניכם בעת ההוא <u>להגיד</u> לכם את דבר יהוה כי יראתם <u>מפני האש</u> ולא עליתם <u>בהר</u>

I stood between the Lord and you at that time to convey the Lord's words to you, for you were afraid of the fire and did not go up the mountain ...[274]

The resulting pastiche of Deuteronomic verses seems to highlight the fact that both God and Moses spoke to Israel at Sinai.[275] Occurring directly after Moses's call to observe the "laws and rules" (v. 1), it emphasizes their divine origin.

---

272 Brooke, "Deuteronomy 5–6," 61.

273 Jastram, "2.2.5.1 Tefillin and Mezuzot." One can also add vv. 25 (שמענו מתוך האש היום הזה) and 26 (שמע ... מתוך האש).

274 Interestingly, some of the wording that this addition might have borrowed from Deut 5:5 is missing from this verse as it appears in lines 10–11. This might be an indication of a more extensive scribal strategy encompassing not only verses 1–2 but also verse 5.

275 To the aforementioned sources one may add that the pronoun ואנכ֯י occurs (with reference to Moses) in Deut 5 (vv. 1 and 5) and that the formula היום הזה is found in Deut 5:29 (cf. also the longer היום הזה in Deut 6:2 [vs. MT's היום] in 8QPhyl II [Chapter 8]). As to the double reference to the fire in line 6, one might take the second one as an apposition elaborating on the first: not just "out of the fire," but "on the mountain out of the fire."

Moreover, this addition may reflect a concern with establishing the proper order
of the events – God's address to Israel appears to precede that of Moses. As was
noted earlier, a similar concern seems to underlie the rearranged text of Exodus 20 in 4QRPª (4Q158; see also the discussion of 8QPhyl 30 in Chapter 8).

Deuteronomy 5:32–6:2

The second example is the shorter text of Deut 5:32–6:2 attested to in four Qumran tefillin and mezuzot.[276]

1. 4QPhyl A (4Q128) recto

Milik suggests that this tefillin slip lacks Deut 5:33 and 6:1: [277]

17 [³¹·⁵ואתה פוא עמוד עמדי ואדברה אליכה את כל המצוה והחקים והמשפטים אשר תלמדם
ועשו בארץ אשר אנוכי נתן ל[ה]מה לרשתה ³²וישמֹר[תמה לעשות כאשר צוה]

18 ר[יהוה אלוהיכמה אתכמה לוא תסורו ימין ושמאל ²·⁶למען תירא את יהוה אל[וֹהֹ]כה לשמוֹ]ר
את כֹל ח[וקותו ומצאותו אשר אנוכי מצוכה]

Alexander Rofé proposes a different reading and reconstruction of these
lines.[278] In line 17, instead of Milik's וישמֹר[תמה, he reads וזאת (with "an unusual *zayin*"[279]) and restores the text as follows:

17 [³¹ואתה פוה עמוד עמדי ואדברה אליך את כל המצוה והחקים והמשפטים אשר תלמדמה ועשו
בארץ אשר אני נותן] ל[ה]מה לרשתה ¹·⁶וזאת] המצוה החקים והמשפטים]

18 [אשר צוה יהוה אלוהיכמה ללמד אתכמה לעשות בארץ אשר אתמה באים שמה לרשתה
²·⁶למען תירא את יהוה אל[וֹהֹ]כה לשמוֹ]ר את כֹל ח[וקותו ומצואתיו אשר אנוכי]

In Rofé's text, it is verses 32 and 33 that are absent. His reading וזאת, however,
is difficult. As can be seen on Fig. 3, the letter next to *vav/yod* seems to be
consistent with a *shin*.[280]

---

276 For tefillin slips in which the text of this passage corresponds to that of the MT, see
4QPhyl H (on this text see below), 4QPhyl M, XQPhyl 2, and perhaps 1QPhyl (see Chapter 3).
277 Milik, DJD 6:49 (with my tentative reconstruction). Cf. the recent transcription by Busa,
Die Phylakterien von Qumran, 83. On her reading of line 17 see note 280 below. In line 18 she
differs from Milik slightly: אל[וֹהֹ]יכה לשמוֹ]ר את כֹל חֹוקֹוֹתֹו.
278 Rofé, "Deuteronomy 5.28–6.1," 34.
279 Rofé, "Deuteronomy 5.28–6.1," 34.
280 Busa, *Die Phylakterien von Qumran*, 83, also reads here a *shin*: וש]מרתמה. For the preceding traces she suggests לה]מֹה לרשתה.

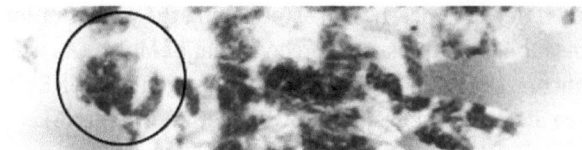

Fig. 3: 4Qphyl A recto line 17 (PAM 43.454 brightened and sharpened).[281]

2. 4QPhyl B (4Q129) recto

According to Milik, in this tefillin slip Deut 5:32b, 33, and 6:1a are missing, perhaps due to a homoioteleuton (אתכמה/אתכמה in 5:32a and 6:1a):[282]

16 [שמעתי את קול דברי העם הזה אשר דברו אליכה היטיבו כל אשר דברו ²⁹מי יתן והיה לבבם
זה להמ]ה ליראה אותי ולשמור את כול מצאותי כול הימים למעׁן

17 [ייטב להמה ולבניהמה לעלם ³⁰לך אמר להמה שובו לכם לאהליכמה ³¹ואתה פוה עמוד עמדי
ואדברה אלי]הׄכ את כוֹל הׄמצוה החקים והמשפטים אשר תלמדמׄ

18 [ועשו בארץ אשר אנכי נתן להם לרשתה ³²ושמרתם לעשות כאשר צוה יהוה אלוהיכמה
אתכמה ^{6:1}לעשות]בׁארץ אׁשר אתמה באים שמה לרשתה ^{6:2}ולמען

19 [תירא את יהוה אלוהיכה לשמור את כול חוקתיו ומצותיו אשר אנכי מצוכה אתה ובנכה ובן
בנכה כול ימי חייכה ולמ]עׁן יארכון ימֹיׄבֹה ^{6:3}ושׁמׁעׁתׁהׁ ישׁראל ושמרׄתה

Once again, Rofé proposes a different reconstruction.[283] He suggests that vv. 32 and 33 are absent. Instead of v. 32b, he restores the lacuna in line 18 with 6:1a:[284]

16 היטיבו כל אשר דברו ²⁹מי יתן והיה לבבם זה להמ]ה ליראה אותי ולשמור את כול מצאותי כול
הימים למעׁן [ייטב להמה ולבניהמה לעולם ³⁰לכה אמור להמה שובו לכמה

17 לאהליכם ³¹ואתה פוה עמוד עמדי ואדברה אלי]הׄכ את כוֹל הׄמצוה החוקים והמשפטים אשר
תלמדמה [ועשו בארץ אשר אנכי נתן להם לרשתה ^{6:1}וזאת המצוה החוקים והמשפטים

18 אשר צוה יהוה אלוהיכמה ללמד אתכמה לעשות]בׁארץ אׁשר אתמה באים שמה לרשתה
^{6:2}ולמען

Both reconstructions are materially possible.

---

281 https://www.deadseascrolls.org.il/explore-the-archive/image/B-284482. Courtesy of the Leon Levy Dead Sea Scrolls Digital Library; Israel Antiquities Authority, photo: Najib Anton Albina.

282 Milik, DJD 6:52 (with my tentative reconstruction). Unlike Milik, Busa, *Die Phylakterien von Qumran*, 86, reads מצותי in line 16, אליכ[ה in line 17, and reconstructs [שמה] in line 18.

283 Rofé, "Deuteronomy 5.28–6.1," 35.

284 His reconstruction ignores the fact that this slip preserves the left edge of the writing block.

3. 4QPhyl J (4Q137) verso

For Milik, this tefillin slip preserves Deut 5:32 and 6:2b, while 5:33 and 6:1, 2a are missing:[285]

56 [³⁰לאוהליכמה] ¹³ⁱ[ו]אתה פ[ו]ה ע[ו]מודה עמדי ואדברה אליכה את כול המצו[ה]
57 [והחוקים והמ[שפֹט]ים] אשר תלמדמה ועשו בארץ אשר אנוכי נותן להמ[ה לרש]
58 תה ³²[ו]שמרתמה לעשות כא[שר צוה יהוה אלוה]יכ[מה אתכמֹהֹ ל[°°
59 ²[אשר אנוכי מצוכֹה היום אתה ובנכה ובן בנכה כול [ימי ח]ייכה ול]מען יארכון]
60 ימיכה ³[ו]שמעתה ישראל ושמרתה לעש[ותמה אש]רֹ יטב ל[]כה ואשר]
61 תרבון מואדה כאשר דבר יהוה אלוהֹיֹ א[בותיכה לתת לכה ארץ זבת]
62 חלב ודבש

Rofé, however, reconstructs line 58 as if it contained Deut 6:1, and not 5:32:

58 [¹:⁶וזאת המצוה החוקים והמשפטים א]שר צוה יהוה אלוהי[כ]מה אתכמֹהֹ ל[עשות בארץ]
59 ²[אשר אנוכי מצוכה היום אתה ובנכה ובן נכה כול [ימי ח]ייכה ול]מען יארכון]

Not only is his reconstruction slightly longer, but it also depends on two assumptions. First, he reads and restores the last extant word in line 58 as ל[עשות [בארץ. The traces of ink are difficult to read. Karl Kuhn, followed by Anna Busa, suggests ל[ו]א] [תסורו, while Milik proposes (in a note) [ור מצאותו]לֹשֹמֹ.[286] Second, to make the wording of line 58 match Deut 6:1, Rofé assumes two omissions: אשר אתם עברים שמה לרשתה למען תירא את יהוה אלהיך ללמד in v. 1 and לשמר את כל חקתיו ומצותיו אשר in vv. 1–2 (by homoioteleuton). He suggests that these are intentional abbreviations, since the scribe had little space left at the bottom of the fragment.[287] This argument, however, is difficult, because for lines 60–62 this scribe simply turned the slip upside down and continued his work. In other words, the lack of space was hardly an issue.[288]

4. 4QMez C (4Q151) 1

Milik observes that the meager remains of this mezuzah indicate an omission of some of the wording of Deut 5:32–33 (see Chapter 7). In his opinion, this

---

285 Milik, DJD 6:66. The reconstructed text follows Busa, *Die Phylakterien von Qumran*, 89. Her reading of these lines is fairly close to that of Milik. In line 60 she has יֹטב. Milik reads here a single *yod*.

286 Kuhn, *Phylakterien Aus Der Höhle 4 von Qumran*, 8; Milik, DJD 6:64; Busa, *Die Phylakterien von Qumran*, 89.

287 Rofé, "Deuteronomy 5.28–6.1," 35.

288 Overall, Rofé argues that tefillin by their nature would not skip over biblical passages they are meant to reproduce ("Deuteronomy 5.28–6.1," 36n26). This is, however, an anachro-

might be another case of a homoioteleuton (צוה יהוה אלהיכם אתכם occurs in both verses):[289]

3 מֹ[צ]ותי כל הימים למען ייטב להם ולבניהם לעלם [30]לך אמר להם שובו לכם לאהליכם[31]ואתה פה]

4 [עמד עמדי ואדברה אליך את כל המצוה והחקים והמשפטים אשר תלמדם ועשו בארץ אשר]

5 אֹנֹכֹי [נתן להם לרשתה[32]ושמרתם לעשות כאשר צוה יהוה אלהיכם אתכם[33]למען תחיון וטוב לכם]

6 והֹאֹרֹ[כתם ימים בארץ אשר תירשון[1]וזאת המצוה החקים והמשפטים אשר צוה יהוה אלהיכם]

7 ללמד אֹתֹ[כם לעשות בארץ אשר אתם עברים שמה לרשתה[2]למען תירא את יהוה אלהיך לשמר את כל]

Several solutions have been offered to explain these four texts. Thus, Rofé argues that Deut 5:32–33 is a secondary Deuteronomistic transitional formula. For him, the aforementioned texts are evidence that a shorter text of Deuteronomy 5 was known in Second Temple times. The foregoing discussion, however, suggests that:

- to support Rofé theory, 4QPhyl A requires a doubtful emendation of the text,
- 4QPhyl B offers no unequivocal support to his hypothesis, as the text lends itself to several reconstructions,
- 4QPhyl J supports Rofé's proposal only if two otherwise unattested omissions are assumed,
- 4QMez C, which Rofé does not mention, contains some of the wording he considers secondary.

For Brooke, these instances of a shorter text are examples of an intentional abbreviation. The scribes preferred the more specific language of Deut 6:1–2 to a more general one of the preceding verses. He observes, "It is not simply that one should walk in the way of all that God has commanded, but there are particular 'commandments, statutes and ordinances' which must be put into practice."[290] While this is an intriguing possibility, one of the four slips, 4QPhyl J (as read and restored by Milik and Kuhn), omits the relevant wording of Deut 6:1–2a.

Cohn also argues for an intentional omission. He believes that several tefillin skip over divine promises related to the length of days (v. 33).[291] In addition

---

nistic assumption, viewing ancient tefillin through the lens of the later rabbinic regulations. For a critique along these lines, see Cohn, *Tangled Up*, 78.

289 Milik, DJD 6:82 (with my tentative reconstruction).

290 Brooke, "Deuteronomy 5–6," 64–65. Jastram, "2.2.5.1 Tefillin and Mezuzot," also raises a possibility of abbreviation.

291 Cohn, *Tangled Up*, 77–78, 94–95,

to the aforementioned texts, he lists the following instances of a shorter text supporting his view:

- 4QPhyl H: Deut 6:2 lacks ‏ימיך‎ ‏למען יארכן ימיך‎ (5:33 however is intact).
- 8QPhyl II: Deut 6:2 omits ‏ימיך‎ ‏כל ימי חייך ולמען יארכן ימיך‎, while 6:3 lacks ‏אשר ייטב לך ואשר תרבון מאד‎.[292]

For Cohn, tefillin originated as a long-life amulet. Hence, in his opinion, these omissions serve an apotropaic purpose:[293]

> If *tefillin* practice were supposed to achieve the same outcome (that is, length of days on the land, as promised by Deut 11:21) then some scribes might have felt it best to omit other verses on this subject so as to avoid highlighting to God – or perhaps to *tefillin* practitioners – the stringent obligations they included.[294]

This argument, however, is not without problems, as Deut 6:2b, rehearsing the link between the observance of the commandments and the length of days, is retained in all the aforementioned tefillin and mezuzah slips.[295]

Overall, two observations emerge from these fragmentary texts. First, while all the four slips feature a shorter text of Deut 5:32–6:2, they do not seem to yield one pattern of omission. Second, the missing sections offer little clues about the possible motivation for their exclusion, with the exception of scribal errors proposed by Milik for two of these texts (4QPhyl B and 4QMez C). Given the highly formulaic nature of the passage in question, scribal lapses could indeed be the most economical explanation. In fact, another tefillin slip, unnoticed by the aforementioned scholars, demonstrates how one scribe omitted a long stretch of this text and then corrected himself.

---

292 Cohn, *Tangled Up*, 77. He also cites the omission of Deut 11:8 in 8QPhyl IV (ibid., 77–78). One should note that 8QPhyl IV abounds with omissions and Cohn's examples need to be considered in light of their larger context (see Chapter 8). Still, the reference to the length of days appears in 8QPhyl IV, 15 (cf. also line 14).

293 Cohn, *Tangled Up*, 93.

294 Cohn, *Tangled Up*, 94.

295 Cohn, *Tangled Up*, 78–79, 94–95, finds further support for his argument in the peculiar layout of Deut 5:29–6:3 in 4QPhyl J. To accommodate the text, the scribe had to turn the slip twice. Cohn suggests a sympathetic/magical reason for this double inversion of the passages found in vv. 29–6:3. For him, it reflects "a wish for inversion/omission of the relevant conditions for achieving long life" (ibid., 95). To this writer scribal miscalculations of the available space appear to be a much simpler explanation.

4QPhyl H (4Q135) recto[296]

31ואתה פה עמוד עמדי ואדברה אליכה את כול   7

[המ[צ[ו]ה את כול חוקים ומשפט[י]ם אש[ר תלמד[ם] ועש[ו באר]ץ א[ש]ר אתם עברים שמה   8
לרשתה ולמען תירא את נותן להם לרשתה 32וישמֹרֹתֹם

[לעשות כאש[ר צוה יֹה[וה אלה]יֹכם אתכמֹ [לוא ת[סֹרוֹ [ooo]   ימֹ[ין ושמאל 33בכול הדרך   9
אשר צוה יהוה אלהיכם תלכון ולמֹען תֹ[חיון וטוב ל[כֹם

[והארכתם ימים [בא]רֹ[ץ אשר תירשון 6:1וזאת המצ]וה והחֹקֹים וֹהמש[פטים אשר צוה יה]וֹה   10
אלהיכם אתכם ללמד ל[ע]לֹשֹות בארץ אשר אתם עֹברים שמֹ[ה לרשתה 6:2למען]

Line 8 contains an unusual sequence:

5:31[המ[צ[ו]ה את כול חוקים וֹמשפטֹ[י]ם אש[ר תלמדֹ[ם] ועש[ו בארץ א[ש]ר 6:1bאתם
עברים שמֹה לרשתה 6:2ולמען תירא את 5:31bנותן להם לרשתה 32וישמֹרֹתֹם

5:31[comm]and[m]ent – all laws and rul[es – tha]t you shall teach [them], so that they may observ[e in the land th]at 6:1byou are about to cross into and occupy, 6:2so that you may revere 5:31b**giving them to possess.** 32Be careful, then,

The beginning of the line is from Deut 5:31. The underlined phrase אתם עברים שמֹה לרשתה ולמען תירא את occurs in Deut 6:1b–2a. The collocation נותן להם לרשתה set in bold type is from Deut 5:31b. The most plausible explanation for this sequence is that the eye of the scribe skipped from verse 31 to 6:1b via homoioteleuton:

5:31ואתה פה עמד עמדי ואדברה אליך את כל המצוה והחקים והמפשטים אשר תלמדם
ועשו **בארץ אשר** אנכי נתן להם לרשתה ... 6:1וזאת המצוה והחקים והמשפטים אשר צוה
יהוה אלהיכם ללמד אתכם לעשות **בארץ אשר** אתם עברים שמה לרשתה 6:2למען תירא
את יהוה אלהיך ...

Having inscribed the first words of 6:2, ולֹמען תירא את, the scribe recognized his mistake. Without cancelling what he had mistakenly copied, he completed the missing part of v. 31, נותן להם לרשתה, and continued with v. 32. (The pronoun אנכי of v. 31 has been lost in this attempt to rectify the mistake.) This self-corrected omission does not match any of the omissions described so far, including the two suspected cases of homoioteleuton, 4QPhyl B and 4QMez C. Thus, 4QPhyl H furnishes further support for a suggestion that the shorter text of Deut 5:32–6:2 in all the four aforementioned texts is a result of some kind of scribal lapse, for which the repetitive language of this section offers a fertile ground. And yet, since one cannot simply extrapolate from one text to another, both a scribal mistake and an intentional abbreviation remain two viable solu-

---

296 Milik, DJD 6:61.

tions for 4QPhyl A and J. Interestingly, as will be demonstrated in Chapter 8, 8QPhyl II features a text of Deut 5:32–6:2 where an omission is only one of its several textual phenomena which encompass also Deut 5:29, 31 and Deut 6:3.[297]

Concluding Remarks

This chapter places the vast majority of the published tefillin and mezuzot securely within the broader corpus of the Exodus and Deuteronomy manuscripts from the Judean Desert. As excerpted biblical texts exhibiting a familiar array of scribal interventions they are, to use Tov's words, a "microcosm" of the contemporary biblical manuscripts.[298] The foregoing discussion, especially the last section delving into the intricacies of reading and reconstructing tefillin and mezuzot, serves as a fitting starting point for Chapters 3–8 which revisit fragments that have not been fully identified or deciphered. It is to these texts that I turn now.

---

297 In Feldman and Feldman, "4Q150 (4QMez) and 8Q4 (8QMez) Revisited," 129, we have suggested that the uneven lines in the reconstructed text of Deut 5:32–6:3 (based on the newly-deciphered imprints of letters) may indicate a shorter wording.
298 Tov, "Tefillin from the Judean Desert," 288.

3 1QPhyl (1Q13)

1QPhyl (1Q13) was unfolded and deciphered by Dominique Barthélemy.[299] The image #0 included on the Plate XIV in DJD 1 captures the tiny bundle (13 × 12 mm) "en grandeur rélle" before it was unrolled.[300] Gerald Lankester Harding observes in his introduction to DJD 1 that though several single-compartment tefillin cases "of the type worn on the arm" were found in Cave 1, "none of them would seem to be large enough to hold" this bundle.[301] His classification of 1QPhyl as a self-standing tefillin, supported by Milik, is most likely based on the fact that it contains a wide array of Type 2 passages: Exodus 13 (vv. 2–3, 7–9), Deuteronomy 5 (vv. 1–9, 11–17, 21–25, 27), Deuteronomy 10 (vv. 17–18, 21–22), and Deuteronomy 11 (vv. 1, 8–12).[302] The fragments are inscribed on one side only. Barthélemy describes the leather as extremely thin, "de l'ordre du dixième de millimeter."[303] He seems to have assumed that 1QPhyl contained several slips.[304] One such reconstructed slip containing Deuteronomy 5 could have been 11 cm wide.[305]

1QPhyl is preserved at the Department of Antiquities of Jordan. In addition to the early PAM photographs of this tefillin, there are also more recent images (including infrared and full-color ones) taken by Bruce and Kenneth Zuckerman in 1988.[306] These photographs indicate that already in 1988 1QPhyl was in a

---

299 Dominque Barthélemy, DJD 1:72–76. Throughout the years, scholars dealt with 1QPhyl only briefly. One recent example is Tov, "The Qumran Tefillin and Their Possible Master Copies," 145–46, who suggests that 1QPhyl was copied from a master text similar to that found in 4QDeut^j, as the sequence of the passages in the two (with an exclusion of Deut 8:5–10 absent from 1QPhyl) is identical.
300 Barthélemy, DJD 1:72.
301 G. Lankester Harding, DJD 1:7. This is true also regarding the tefillin cases from Cave 4. The largest tefillin compartment listed by Milik in DJD 6:35 is 10 × 8 mm (#11). Hence, Cohn's conclusion is that 1QPhyl is "too large for any of the housings observed" (Cohn, "Material Aspects," 93).
302 Milik, DJD 2:81.
303 Barthélemy, DJD 1:72.
304 See his remarks on Deut 11:13–21 in DJD 1:74. Cohn, "Material Aspects," 91, makes a similar suggestion. Cf. Goren's remarks about two slips of Mur4 that have been found wrapped together in note 25.
305 Barthélemy, DJD 1:74.
306 They are available at the InscriptiFact Digital Image Library (http://www.inscriptifact.com/). I am grateful to Dr. Marilyn Lundberg Melzian for her assistance in obtaining a permission to reproduce some of these images here. They have been taken by Bruce and Kenneth Zuckerman, West Semitic Research, in collaboration with Princeton Theological Seminary. Courtesy the Department of Antiquities, Jordan.

https://doi.org/10.1515/9783110725377-004

poor condition.[307] Still, they helpfully complement the data available on the earlier PAM photographs. For instance, the full-color images demonstrate that multiple fragments of 1QPhyl are wads containing several layers of leather. Also, these photographs allow for measuring the size of the letters and the intervals between the lines with more precision. Thus, the size of the non-final letters in this tefillin fluctuates between 0.9 and 1.2 mm, while the final letters and the *lameds* range between 1.3 and 1.6 mm. The intervals between the lines are relatively large for a tefillin slip – 2.5–3.5 mm.

Of the 58 fragments included in the DJD edition of 1QPhyl, Barthélemy was able to identify 31 fragments as belonging to scriptural passages inscribed in Type 2 tefillin. He labeled the remaining 27 (frags. 32–58) as unidentified and suggested that their contents indicate that "ce phylactère devait contenir encore un certain nombre de passages qui n'ont pas été retenus par la tradition juive."[308] This observation was later echoed by Cohn who suggested that 1QPhyl, along with 8QPhyl (see Chapter 8), may have contained passages that go beyond the familiar verses from Deuteronomy 5–6, 10–11, and Exodus 12–13.[309]

Upon further inspection, Barthélemy's "unidentified fragments" appear to fall into several groups. First, there are decipherable fragments in which too little is preserved to yield a meaningful text (frags. 33, 34, 39 [a wad], 41 [a wad], 43 [a wad], 46, 47, 48, 51–56). Second, there are fragments containing generic language which can be linked to multiple biblical verses, including those found in Types 1 and 2 tefillin (e.g., frags. 40 reading ‏וﬤﬨ‏°°[and 58 featuring a phrase]‏וﬢ﬩ﬤ ﬡ‏°[; so also frags. 42, 45, 58 [a wad]). Third, there are several fragments where a revision of Barthélemy's readings leads to their placement within Type 2 pericopae. This third group, which can be further divided into fragments containing Deuteronomy 5, Deuteronomy 11, and Exodus 13, is the main focus of this chapter.[310]

---

307 On these images, some of the fragments present on the plate XIV in DJD 1 appear to be missing, while several others are damaged. Multiple shreds of leather visible in the glass cases housing these thin and brittle fragments reveal an ongoing process of deterioration.
308 Barthélemy, DJD 1:75.
309 Cohn, *Tangled Up*, 72.
310 Since the scribe of 1QPhyl left very few spaces between the words, to assist the reader, additional intervals have been introduced in the transcriptions offered below.

"Unidentified Fragments" Containing Deuteronomy 5

Frag. 32 (= Deut 5:29–31)

DSS_J5926A_R_Td	DJD Edition	Revised Text
	]הו[1	ו]היה לב[בם 1
	]שׂ◦שימל[2	לה[מ שובו ל[כם 2
	]◦צ◦[3	באר[ץ א[שר 3

Notes to Readings

Line 1 לב[בם. The trace at the end of the line can be a vertical stroke of a *bet* (cf. *bet* in שובו in line 2).

Line 2 לה[מ. Given the assumed context of this fragment, the first letter in this line could be read as an upper left corner of a final *mem*. שובו. What Barthélemy reads as a final *mem* appears to be two letters, a *bet* and a *vav*.

Line 3 באר[ץ א[שר. Instead of Barthélemy's medial *tsade*, this large *tsade*, descending below the imaginary base of the line, seems to be a final one. On both old and new images, there are no traces of a letter preceding the *tsade*. The next letter is apparently an *aleph*; its horn and diagonal stroke are well visible on the images.

Frag. 32: Reconstruction with MT Deut 5:29–31

1 [מי יתן ו]היה לב[בם זה להם לירא אתי ולשמר את כל מצותי כל הימים למען ייטב להם
ולבניהם לעלם לך]

2 [אמר לה]מ שובו ל[כם לאהליכם ואתה פה עמד עמדי ואדברה אליך את כל המצוה והחקים
והמשפטים אשר תלמדם]

3 [ועשו באר[ץ א[שר אנכי נתן להם לרשתה

The reconstructed lines 1 and 2 contain 69 and 73 letter-spaces respectively. Barthélemy's reconstructed text of Deut 5:1–22 yield lines of 95 letter-spaces on average, while the reconstructed lines of Deut 5:23–27 average 80 letter-spaces. If the identification proposed here is correct, it would imply that the scribe kept narrowing down his lines as he moved along copying Deuteronomy 5.

Frag. 50 (= Deut 5:31–32)

The small frag. 50 appears to be missing from the extant images of 1QPhyl. The reading עמדﹼי proposed by Barthélemy and supported by the photograph provided on the DJD Plate XIV matches Deut 5:31. In line with this assumption, it is suggested to read the first letter in line 1 as a *dalet* (the editor offers no reading here) and the second letter in line 2 as a medial *mem* (Barthélemy tentatively reads a *resh*).

1 עמ[ﹾד עמדﹼי]
2 ו[שﻣﹾ]רת

Frags. 32 + 50: Reconstruction with MT Deut 5:29–32

This fragment can be placed along with frag. 32 to produce the following reconstruction of Deut 5:29–32:

1 [מי יתן ו]היה לבﹾ[בם זה להם לירא אתי ולשמר את כל מצותי כל הימים למען ייטב להם ולבניהם לעלם לך]

2 [אמר לה]ﻣﹾ שובו ל[כם לאהליכם ואתה פה עם]ﹾד עמדﹼי] ואדברה אליך את כל המצוה והחקים והמשפטים אשר תלמדם]

3 [ועשו באר]ץ אﹾ[שר אנכי נתן להם לרשתה ו]שﻣﹾ[רת לעשות כאשר צוה יהוה אלהיכם אתכם [

Frag. 35, lines 1–2 (= Deut 5:33)

Frag. 35 is a wad comprised of several layers of leather. Barthélemy numbered the text visible on its other side as frag. 22. The full-color image DSS_J5926A_R_Td suggests that lines 1–2 and 3 are inscribed on different layers. On this photograph one can see the fine line (set in black on the enlarged image below) delineating their respective layers. Barthélemy read [ﹾמﹾל°[in line 3.

DJD Edition

1 [כל°]
2 [טובל°]

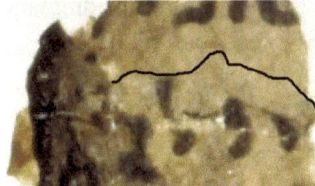

Revised Text

1 [בﹾכﹾל ה]דרך
2 ו[טוב לﹾך]

Notes to Readings

Line 1]°בֹּכֹל[. In the beginning of the line there are traces of a roof and a base, as in a *bet*. The vertical stroke at the end of the line can belong to multiple letters. Here it is read as a *he*, in line with the presumed biblical context of this fragment.

Line 2]טוב לֹךֹ[. The last letter appears to be a final one, as indicated by a vertical stroke descending below the imaginary base line. Perhaps this is a final *kaph*.

Frags. 32 + 50 + 35: Reconstruction with MT Deut 5:29–33

This fragment (set in bold type below) can be placed along with frags. 32 and 50 to produce the following reconstruction of Deut 5:29–33:

1 [מִי יתן ו]היה לבֹּ[בם זה להם לירא אתי ולשמר את כל מצותי כל הימים למען ייטב להם
ולבניהם לעלם לך]

2 [אמר לה]םֹ שובו ל[כם לאהליכם ואתה פה עמ]ֹד עמדֹי[ואדברה אליך את כל המצוה והחקים
והמשפטים אשר תלמדם]

3 [ועשו באר]ץֹ אֹ[שר אנכי נתן להם לרשתה ו]שמֹ[רת לעשות כאשר צוה יהוה אלהיכם אתכם
לא תסורו ימין]

4 [ושמאל]**בֹכל הֹ**[דרך אשר צוה יהוה אלהיכם אתכם תלדו למען]

5 [תחיון ו]**טוב לֹךֹ** והארכתם ימים בארץ אשר תרשון   [

The reconstructed line 4 contains 40 letter-spaces. This confirms what has already been observed with reference to the reconstructed frag. 32, i.e., that the scribe narrowed down his writing block as he neared the end of Deuteronomy 5. This narrowing of the lines may follow the shape of the slip.[311]

If the proposed identification of frag. 35 is correct, Deut 5:33 as preserved in 1QPhyl reads לֹךֹ (thus also LXX) against the MT's plural לכם (as do also 4QPhyl H and M; SamP; V; S; T). As discussed in Chapter 2, several tefillin and mezuzot from Qumran (4QPhyl A; B; J; 4QMez C) feature a shorter text of Deut 5:32–6:2. The foregoing reading and reconstruction suggest that overall 1QPhyl followed a text akin to the MT.

---

311 Barthélemy observes that the extant text of Deut 10:17–18; 10:21–11:1, 8–11 also yields lines ranging between 35 and 40 letter-spaces, with Deut 11:12, the end of a pericope (?), being split between three short lines (17 letter-spaces).

"Unidentified Fragments" Containing Deuteronomy 11

Frag 38, lines 1–3 (= Deut 11:4)

Frag. 38 is a wad containing several layers of text. On the recent images a part of the layer containing Barthélemy's line 1 flaked off. Also, the full-color image DSS_J5926C_R_Td suggests that Barthélemy's lines 1–2 and 3 are inscribed on two different layers of text. The black line drawn on the full-color image reproduced below indicates where the new layer begins. Hence, Barthélemy's line 3 is not included in the transcription offered below.

PAM 40.466[312]	DSS_J5926C_R_Td	DJD Edition	Revised Text
			]°[1
		]יֿשׁרֹוֹגֿ[1	וֹ]סֹוֹסיו ל[2
		]דפֿמֿ[2	]דפֿמֿ[בר 3
		]חֿ°יֿ[3	

Notes to Readings

Line 1. PAM 40.466 contains a vertical stroke of a final letter.

    Line 2 ל[סֹוֹסיו. According to PAM 40.466, the letter that Barthélemy read as a *shin* has an upper horizontal stroke and is consistent with a *samekh*. The following letter appears to be a *vav/yod*. In light of these readings and given the presumed context of this text, it is suggested to read the two vertical traces in the beginning of the line as a left vertical stroke of a *samekh* and a *vav*.]וֹ. The vertical stroke in the end of the line can be variously construed, with a *vav/yod* being a likely option. There is no trace of *gimel*'s left stroke and therefore Barthélemy's reading seems unlikely.

312 https://www.deadseascrolls.org.il/explore-the-archive/image/B-277279. All the PAM images included in this chapter are courtesy of the Leon Levy Dead Sea Scrolls Digital Library; Israel Antiquities Authority, photo: Najib Anton Albina.

Frag 38: Reconstruction with MT Deut 11:4

2 [ל]סֹוסיו וֹ[לרכבו אשר הציף את מי ים סוף על פניהם]
3 [בר]דפֹם[אחריכם ואבדם יהוה עד היום הזה ואשר עשה]

The reconstruction yields a line of 35 letters, matching the lengths of lines proposed by the editor for other fragments containing Deuteronomy 11 in which reconstructed lines range between 35 and 40 letters.

Frag. 49 (= Deut 11:4)

PAM 40.466	DJD Edition	Revised Text
	[תמיומסרֹ]	]ׄ°[1
		ף[וס םי ימ ת]א 2
		]°°[ ]°°[3

Notes to Readings

Lines 1 and 3. There are traces of letters in both lines 1 and 3.

Line 2 ף[וס םי ימ ת]א. The last letter can be easily construed as a *vav/yod* and not a *resh*.

Frags. 49 + 38: Reconstruction with MT Deut 11:4

2 [ל]סֹוסיו וֹ[לרכבו אשר הציף א]ת מי ים סו[ף על פניהם]
3 [בר]דפם[אחריכם ואבדם יהוה ע]דׄ הׄ[י]וֹׄם[הזה ואשר]

Frag. 36 (= Deut 11:17–20?)

The fragment is a wad containing several layers of leather. The text visible on the other side appears in the DJD edition as frag. 37.

PAM 40.466	DSS_J5926C_R_Td	DJD Edition	Revised Text
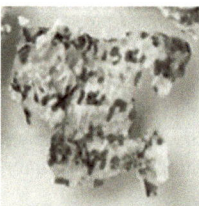		[הׄשׄמוהבׄ]° 1	[הׄשׄמים וׄ] 1
		[קׄשואׄ]°° 2	[וׄקשרׄ]°° 2
		[יהוֹהׄ...] 3	[°°]ריֹ°°[3

Notes to Readings

Line 1 הֹשׁמִים[. Barthélemy reads the last letter in this word as a *he*. However, its shape is rather consistent with a final *mem*. On PAM 40.466 a hole seems to conceal its bottom horizontal stroke. The recent images lack most of the left part of this letter.]ו. The following letter is a *vav*, and not a *bet*, as can be seen on the recent images. It is followed by a trace of another letter (or more), but it is unclear whether these traces belong to the same layer of leather.

Line 2]°°רׁשׁקו[. The trace of a vertical stroke next to the *shin* can be easily construed as a *resh* with a missing roof. Whether the following vertical traces belong to this layer of text is uncertain. The full-color image reproduced above suggests that at least some of them are inscribed on a remnant of another layer of leather.

Line 3]דׁי°°[. What the DJD edition reads as a *he* might also be a *yod* and a final *kaph*. The long vertical stroke seems to support the possibility that there is a final letter here. In the beginning of the line there appears to be a letter resembling a *dalet* or a *resh*. There are also traces of letters in the end of the line. In both cases, it is unclear whether these belong to the same layer as יׁ.

Frag. 36: Reconstruction with MT Deut 11:17–20

It seems possible that frag. 36 contains Deut 11:17–20. The following reconstruction tentatively reads the illegible traces in lines 2–3 to match the wording of the biblical passage:

1   [הֹשׁמִים ו]לא יהיה מטר והאדמה לא תתן את יבולה ואבדתם מהרה מעל הארץ הטבה
אשר יהוה נתן לכם ושמתם את דברי אלה על לבבכם ועל]

2 [נפשכם]וקׁשׁרֹתֹֹם] אתם לאות על ידכם והיו לטטפת בין עיניכם ולמדתם אתם את בניכם לדבר
בם בשבתך בביתך ובלכתך בדרך ובשכבך ובקומך וכתבתם על]

3] מזוזות ב]יׁתׁיך

This reconstruction of line 2 produces a line of some 104 letter-spaces. As was mentioned earlier, the reconstructed text of Deut 10:17–18 and 11:8–11 yields lines of 35–40 letter-spaces, while in Deut 11:12 the lines appear to be half of this length. Hence, it seems that, if the proposed identification of frag. 36 is correct, Deut 11:13–21 was copied on another slip of leather.[313] As was noted earlier, Barthélemy's reconstructed text of Deut 5:1–22 features lines averaging 95 letter-spaces.

---

313 This was already surmised by Barthélemy in the DJD edition (DJD 1:74).

"Unidentified Fragments" Containing Exodus 13

Frag 57 (= Exod 13:7)

PAM 40.470[314]	DJD Edition	Revised Text
	[לֹגבלבֹ°]	1 בכ[ל גבלכֹּם]
		2]°[

Notes to Readings

Line 1]גבלכֹּם. The penultimate letter, a vertical stroke with a base, can be read either as a medial *kaph* or a *bet*. The following base stroke could belong to a final *mem*.

   Line 2]°[. On PAM 40.470 there is a trace of at least one letter belonging to line 2.

Frags. 30 + 31 + 57: Reconstruction with MT Exod 13:7

In line with the proposed reading, frag. 57 can be placed alongside Barthélemy's reconstructed text of Exod 13:7 in frags. 30 and 31:

מצות יאכל את שבעת הימים ולא יראה]לך חמ[ץ ול[א] יראה לך]שׂאֹר בכל **גבלכֹּם**[

While the MT reads in this verse גבלך, 1QPhyl appears to have גבלכֹּם (for a 2nd masc. pl. suffix cf. Tg. Neof.; S; V).

Frag. 44 (= Exod 13:15?)

This fragment is present on the early PAM 40.466 photograph, yet appears to be absent from the 1988 images of 1QPhyl. Barthélemy proposed that it might contain Exod 13:15. If he is correct, instead of the MT's על כן אני זבח, this tefillin reads על [כן ואנֹֹי זֹ]ובח, perhaps as a scribal error. In line 3 the editor suggests [ידֹֹי], yet the extant trace of a horizontal stroke fits better the MT's יד הֹ[ויציאנו.

---

314 https://www.deadseascrolls.org.il/explore-the-archive/image/B-277283.

PAM 40.466

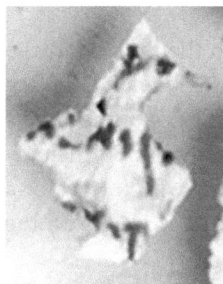

1   [°°°]
2   על [כן ואנ֯י ז]֯ובח
3   בחז[ק יד ה֯]וציאנו

Frag. 44: Reconstruction with MT Exod 13:15–16

2   [על]כן ואנ֯י ז]֯ובח ליהוה כל פטר רחם הזכרים וכל בכור בני אפדה והיה לאות על ידך
    ולטוטפת בין עיניך כי]
3   [בחז]ק יד ה֯]וציאנו יהוה ממצרים

"Unidentified Fragments" Containing a Recurring Biblical Phraseology

Frag. 37

Frag. 37 is a wad containing at least two layers of leather. The text visible on the other side appears in the DJD edition as frag. 36. The poor condition of the images does not allow to determine whether all that can be seen on both old and new photographs of frag. 37 belongs to one and the same layer of text. Still, the images suggest that Barthélemy's reading of line 1 can be revised to yield a phrase יה[ו]ה אלה֯י֯[ך/נו/כם found multiple times in Type 2 passages (e.g., **הראנו יהוה אלהינו** in Deut 5:24).

DSS_J5926C_V_Pd   **PAM 40.462**[315]   **DJD Edition**   **Revised Text**

DJD Edition:
1   [כי֯זהשאל°]
2   [°לה֯ם]

Revised Text:
1   [°ו יה]ו[ה אלה֯י֯]
2   [°ל°ם]

Notes to Readings

Line 1 ‏י°[‏. The second letter in this line is a *vav/yod*. As to the first letter, the vertical stroke curving to the left at the bottom can be a medial *nun* or a left leg of a *tav*. Barthélemy's medial *kaph* is unlikely, as there is no trace of the *kaph*'s roof. ‏יה[ו]ה‏. A *yod* and a *he* are clearly seen on the images. What Barthélemy read as a *shin* appears to be a *he*. ‏אלהי[‏. The vertical stroke with a trace of a roof next to a *lamed* is consistent with a *he*. The following *yod* is visible on the new image.

    Line 2 ‏]°ל°ם[‏. Barthélemy reads the letter next to the *lamed* as a *he*. Its shape, however, does not match that of the two *he* letters in line 1. I was unable to offer a plausible reading here.

Discussion

The newly-proposed readings of Barthélemy's "unidentified fragments" of 1QPhyl illuminate several aspects of this tefillin. First, there is the question of scope. The editor was uncertain whether 1QPhyl included Exod 13:11–16 and Deut 11:13–21. The foregoing discussion did not furnish an unequivocal evidence for the presence of the former, though frag. 44 lends some support to it, but confirmed the inclusion of the latter (frag. 36). This still leaves the problem of the glaring absence of the Shema and the preceding verses (Deut 6:1–9). The passage from Exod 12:43–51, found in other Type 2 Qumran tefillin, is also missing. It is not entirely impossible that all these texts were originally present in 1QPhyl but are either concealed in the multi-layered fragments-wads awaiting to be disentangled or have been lost during the process of unfolding. In fact, Barthélemy observes in his introduction to 1QPhyl that "Les couches extérieures noircies, collées et cassantes ont dû être sacrifiées pour dégager de l'intérieur un certain nombre de fragments ..."[316] Second, the revised transcriptions of the unidentified fragments reveal new variant readings. Barthélemy's edition suggests that the wording of Deuteronomy attested to in 1QPhyl diverges only slightly from the MT, whereas whatever little is preserved of Exodus fully agrees with it. This study adds yet another variant to his list of diverging readings in Deuteronomy, Deut 5:33 (frag. 35), and points to at least one variant

---

316 Barthélemy, DJD 1:72. Alternatively, one could suggest that these pericopae were not included in this tefillin. Milik, DJD 6:38–39, argued that several tefillin from Qumran do not include all the Type 1 passages. He noted the absence of the Shema from 4QPhyl A and 4QPhyl D-E-F. For a different interpretation of the evidence, see note 63.

in 1QPhyl's text of Exodus, Exod 13:7 (frag. 57; see also frag. 44). Third, this re-evaluation of the unidentified fragments of 1QPhyl suggests that in all those cases where a meaningful reading can be obtained, these fragments can be linked to the Exodus and Deuteronomy passages utilized in other tefillin from Qumran.

4 4QPhyl L (4Q139)

4QPhyl L is a single fragment (26 × 13 mm) containing some of Deut 5:7–24.[317] It is inscribed on one side only. Milik argues that originally 4QPhyl L was a rectangular piece of leather and suggests that lines 11–14 preserve the right edge of this slip. The interlinear spaces in this fragment range between 1.5 and 1.8 mm. The height of the non-final letters fluctuates between 0.6 and 1 mm and that of the final ones between 1.4 and 1.8 mm. This scribe appears to have used final letters (final *kaph* [with a few exceptions] and *tsade*) in a medial position.

There are horizontal and vertical creases visible on both recto and verso of 4QPhyl L. They indicate that the fragment was folded. The encircled area on Fig. 4 appears to be darker than that of the rest of the fragment. A comparison to 4QPhyl U suggests that this is probably the outside layer of the folded bundle.[318]

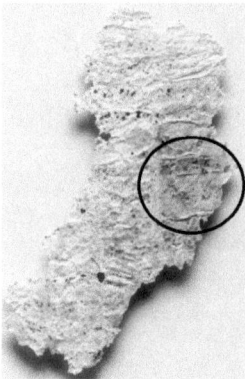

Fig. 4: 4QPhyl L verso (PAM 43.455).[319]

The vertical creases to the left of the encircled area are ~3 mm apart. The horizontal ones are more difficult to measure. The gaps between those above the encircled area seem to increase from top to bottom, from 2 mm to either 3 or 4 mm in the darkened area. The distance to the next folding appears to be

---

317 Milik, DJD 6:70.
318 See Feldman and Feldman, "4Q148 (4QPhylactère U)," 206.
319 https://www.deadseascrolls.org.il/explore-the-archive/image/B-284483. All the PAM images included in this chapter are courtesy of the Leon Levy Dead Sea Scrolls Digital Library; Israel Antiquities Authority, photo: Najib Anton Albina.

https://doi.org/10.1515/9783110725377-005

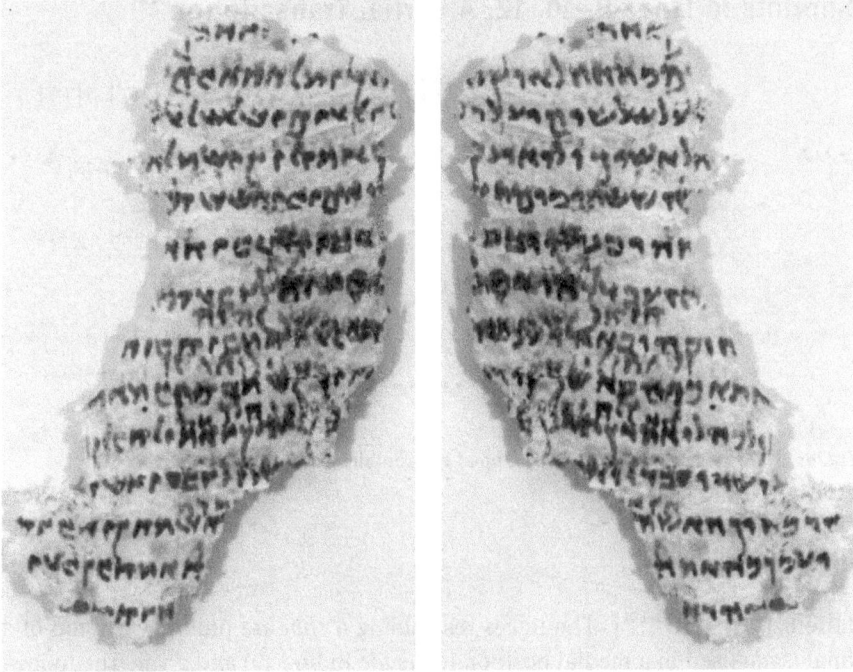

Fig. 5: 4QPhyl L recto. Left: PAM 42.828 (flipped horizontally); right: PAM 42.828.[320]

slightly narrower, ~2.5 mm. This suggests that the fragment might have been folded horizontally both from the top downwards and from the bottom upwards.

The recto of 4QPhyl L features multiple imprints of letters between the lines (Fig. 5). These imprints are found in a relatively well-defined area delineated on the right by a vertical folding line. Milik ignored these imprints.[321] This chapter offers the first attempt at their deciphering.

---

320 https://www.deadseascrolls.org.il/explore-the-archive/image/B-284795.

321 For a similar attempt to decipher imprints of letters in Qumran mezuzah 4QMez B, see Feldman and Feldman, "4Q150 (4QMez B) and 8Q4 (8QMez) Revisited."

Imprints in Lines 8–10, 12: A Partial Transcription[322]

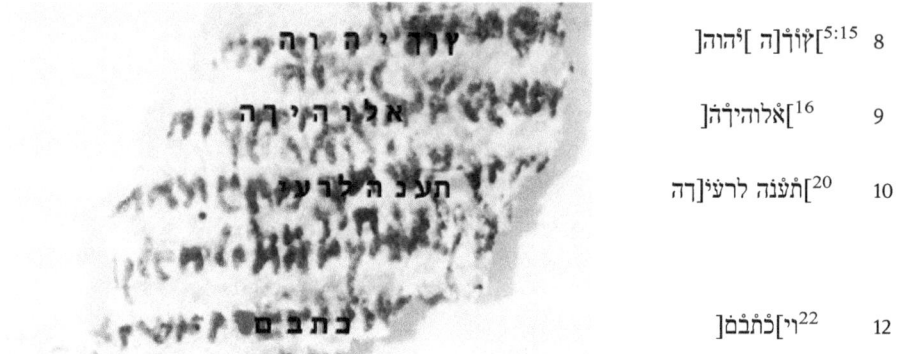

8   [יהוה]ֹ[י ה][ד]ֹוֹֹ[5:15]

9   [אֹלוהיֹֹדֹֹה][16]

10   ה[ד]ֹֹעיֹֹלר הנֹֹֹֹעֹֹת[20]

12   [מֹֹֹבֹֹֹֹתֹֹכ]יֹֹו[22]

Fig. 6: 4QPhyl L verso (PAM 42.828, flipped horizontally and brightened).

Notes to Readings[323]

Line 8 [ֹ[ד]ֹוֹֹ[ה][י ה]יהוה]. The traces resembling a *shin* are probably the top of a final *tsade* used in a medial position (cf. *tsade* in line 10) and a *vav*. The following long vertical stroke is apparently a final *kaph*. The *yod* of]ֹיהוה[seems to conflate with the vertical stroke of the *kaph* in עבדֹֹֹֹֹדֹֹֹֹֹה in line 7.

Line 9 [אֹלוהיֹֹדֹֹה]. All three strokes of an *aleph* are visible. *Lamed*, *vav*, and *he* are rather well preserved. Faint traces of a final (?) *kaph* are visible next to the *yod*. The right vertical stroke of a *he* seems to follow.

---

322 This transcription does not claim to be a comprehensive record of all the imprints found in this fragment. The scribe did not leave spaces between the words. Below they are added to assist the reader.
323 All the images included in this section are based on the digitally brightened PAM 42.828.

Line 10 תֹּעֲנֶה לרֵעֲיֹ[דה]. Only a trace of the *tav*'s left leg is visible on the image. It is partially concealed by the *lamed* of ולוֹא [תנאף (line 10) and a *resh* of כאשר (line 9). The *ayin* and medial *nun* follow. The *lamed* and *resh* are well preserved. Of the *ayin* of לרֵעֲיֹ[דה only the top is visible. A short vertical stroke of a *yod* merges with the *aleph* of the first לוֹא in line 10.

Line 12 וי[כתֹּבֹּם]. A trace of a roof as in a *bet* or a medial/final *kaph* is visible on the image. Another roof, presumably of a *tav*, follows. A vertical stroke with a roof, perhaps a *bet*, comes next. A round letter reminiscent of a final *mem* concludes the word.

Reconstructing 4QPhyl L with the MT Deut 5:7–24

The foregoing attempt at reading the imprints of letters found in the interlinear spaces between lines 7–12 suggests that these imprints belong with the now lost text found in these very lines. Milik read the fragment as follows:[324]

---

324 I have slightly altered Milik's reading in the DJD edition to reflect the use of the final forms in the non-final positions in this fragment.

[ ]יהיה לכה אלוהי[ם אחריﬦ עﬥ]ל פני לוא תעשה 1
[ ] במ[י]ﬦ מתחת לארץ לו[א]^325 2
[ ]ועל שלשים ועל רב[ﬠ]ים לשונאי 3
[ ]אלוה[י]ﬧ̇דﬣ לאשו די לוא ינק[ﬣ]ה 4
[ ]אלוהי[ﬥﬦ]כﬣ ששת ימים תע[ﬠ]בוד 5
[ ]א[ﬨ]תﬣ ובנﬧדﬣ ובתﬧﬢﬣ] 6
[ ]י[יִשּׁ]ﬡ̇וﬧﬣ עבדﬧﬢﬤﬧﬥ ואמתﬧﬢﬨ]ﬤﬥ כמוכה 7
[ ]חזקה ובאזרוע נטי[ﬣ]ה 8
[ ]וﬡ̇ת אמרﬣ כאשר ﬨﬢﬧﬤ]ﬥ 9
נו[ﬨﬤ]ﬨﬤ̇ן לכה לוא תרצﬡﬢח ולוא [תנאף 10
ﬠ̇י̇כﬣ שדו עבדו ואﬥﬦﬨﬥﬤ̇ﬨ̇ן] 11
הר מתוך האש ה[ן 12
ועמﬧﬤﬧﬦה את ה[קוﬥ 13
הﬥﬤﬠﬣ̇נﬤ̇ הראﬡﬦﬨ]נו 14

Fig. 7: 4QPhyl L verso (PAM 42.828).

Together with the newly-deciphered imprints, this tefillin slip, schematically reconstructed with the MT, reads (the imprints are set **in a bold type**):[326]

[^7^יהיה לכה אלוהי]ם אחריﬦ עﬥ]ל פני ^8^לוא תעשה לכה פסל כל תמונה אשר בשמים ואשר [בארﬧ] 1

[מתחת ואשר במ[י]ﬦ מתחת לארץ ^9^לו[א]א תשתחוה להם ולוא תעבדם כי אנכי יהוה אלהיכה אל קנא פוקד עון] 2

[אבות על בנים]ועל שלשים ועל רב[ﬠ]ים לשונאי ^10^ועשה חסד לאלפים לאהבי ולשמרי מצותו [לוא תשא את^11^] 3

[שם יהוה אלוה]י]ﬧ̇דﬣ לאשו די לוא ינק[ﬣ]ה יהוה את אשר ישא את שמו לאשו ^12^שמור את יום השבת לקדשו כאשר צו] 4

[כה יהוה אלוהי]ﬥﬦ]כﬣ ^13^ששת ימים תע[ﬠ]בוד ועשית כל מלאכתכה ^14^ויום השביעי שבת ליהוה אלוהיכה לא תעשה] 5

[כל מלאכה א[ﬨ]תﬣ ובנﬧדﬣ ובתﬧﬢﬣ] ועבדכה ואמתכה ושורכה וחמרכה וכל בהמתכה וגרכה אשר [בשﬠ] 6

[רייִשּׁﬡ למען י[יִשּׁ]ﬡ̇וﬧﬣ עבדﬧﬢﬤﬧﬥ ואמתﬧﬢﬨ]ﬤﬥ כמוכה ^15^וזכרת כי עבד היית בארץ מצרים ויצאכה יהוה אלוהיכה] 7

[משם ביד]חזקה ובאזרוע נטי[ﬣ]ה על כן [צ̲ﬡﬢﬤ̲ד|ﬥ|ה] [̲יﬣﬠ̲הוה] אלוהיכה לעשות את יום השבת ^16^כבד [את] 8

---

325 Milik read here ל[א. In lines 4 and 10 this fragment has a longer form לוא. The trace of an ink at the end of the line can be interpreted as a slightly slanted vertical stroke of a *vav*.
326 The choice of the MT text here is mostly pragmatic. One might also consider restoring this fragment with other more or less complete texts of Deuteronomy 5 from Qumran, such as 4QDeut^n^ and several tefillin (e.g., 4QPhyl G; J). SamP differs quite significantly from the MT in this passage. Its readings, however, are not supported by the fragment.

9 [אביכה]וֹאת אמרה כאשר צוְדֹה] יהוה [אֱלוֹהֶידָֹה] למען יארכן ימיכה ולמען ייטב לכה על
   האדמה אשר יה[

10 [וה נו]תֹן לכה 17לוא תרצח 18ולוא [תנאף 19ולוא תגנב 20ולוא] תֹעֲנֶה לרֹעִי]דֹה עד שאו
    21ולוא תחמד אשת רעיכה 21ולא תתאוה בית ר[

11 שֹׂדֹכה שדו עבדו ואמֹתֹו] שורו וחמרו וכל אשר לרעיכה 22את הדברים האלה דבר יהוה את כל
    קהלכמה ב[

12 הר מתוך האש ה[ענן והערפל קול גדול ולוא יסף וי]כֹתֹבֹם] על שני לחת אבנים ויתנם אלי
    23ויהי כש[ש

13 ועמֹרֹמה את ה]קֹול מתוך החשך וההר בער באש ותקרבון אלי כל ראשי שבטיכמה וזקניכמה
    24ותאמרו[

14 הֹנֹה הראֹ]נו יהוה אלהינו את כבדו ואת גדלו

The length of the lines in the reconstructed text fluctuates some, from 60 letter-spaces in line 1, to 71 in line 4, to 59 in line 8, to 78 in line 10, to 66 in line 12. These fluctuations may reflect the shape of the piece of leather the scribe had utilized. At the same time, they may suggest a presence of variant readings. Especially interesting is the positioning of the newly-deciphered imprints in lines 10 and 12. They appear to be further to the left than the words read in lines 8–9. If the proposed readings are correct, this may indicate that either the underlined spaces in lines 8 and 9 contained a longer text or that the underlined spaces in lines 10 and 12 featured a shorter wording. The Septuagint and Papyrus Nash order the three short injunctions not to murder, not to commit adultery, and not to steal differently than the MT (and most of other ancient textual witnesses).[327] This would not, however, resolve the positioning of ולוא [תֹעֲנֶה לרֹעִי]דֹה in line 10.

Though what exactly happened in these lines remains unknown, the newly-deciphered imprints in line 10 yield two variant readings. In Deut 5:16 (line 10) where the MT has ברעך, the fragment reads לרֹעִי]דֹה. While a plural form with a *yod*, matching the following בית ר[עֹיֹכה (the MT has רעך בית), occurs elsewhere (ברעיך [4QDeut^n]; ברעיכה [4QPhyl B]; ברעיֹך [4QPhyl G]), the use of the preposition -ל is unattested in other Hebrew textual witnesses of this verse (for the construction ל -ענ"ה, see Ezek 14:4, 7; 1QH^a 12:19). These two readings can be added to Milik's list of variants in this fragment.

---

327 Tov, "The Papyrus Nash and the Septuagint," 38.

5 4QPhyl T (4Q147)

While Milik included the "pratiquement indéchiffrable" 4Q147 in his DJD 6 edition of tefillin and mezuzot from Cave 4, he left it undeciphered.[328] Most likely, he classified this text as tefillin – 4QPhyl T – because it was written in a tiny script and folded. The DJD plate XXIV, representing the final stage of Milik's work on 4QPhyl T, has 12 fragments. However, the final count remains uncertain, as some of the fragments are multi-layered wads (frags. 2, 4, 12),[329] while others belong to a different text (frags. 11–12).[330] The largest fragment, frag. 1, is 30 mm wide and 15 mm high. The other fragments are much smaller. The size of the letters in 4QPhyl T ranges between 0.6–0.9 mm. The *lameds* appear to be 1 mm high, whereas the final letters fluctuate between 1.1 and 1.3 mm. The distance between the lines in frags. 1 and 2 varies between 0.9 mm and 1.4 mm. The text is written in what Milik described as a "semi-cursive, extrêment réduite" hand with very few intervals between the words.[331] In multiple spots the ink spread out, obscuring the shapes of the letters.

Recently, Faina Feldman and I have published a preliminary transcription of 4Q147. It indicates that 4QPhyl T does not contain the scriptural texts included in tefillin and mezuzot from the Judean Desert. Since it evokes angelic names (frag. 2) and deals with such themes as abundance of sustenance, protection, healing, and blessing (frag. 1), we suggested that it might be an apotropaic text, an amulet.[332] Without rehearsing our earlier work, this chapter expands on it in three ways. First, it presents a new physical reconstruction of 4QPhyl T. Second, it offers an insight into the method used to fold it. Third, it raises the question as to whether 4QPhyl T might have contained Deut 11:18–21.

PAM 42.604 and Its Implications for the Reconstruction of 4Q147

In the preliminary edition, we have suggested that Milik's frags. 1 and 2 represent two discreet texts. Three factors seemed to point in this direction. First, the

---

328 Milik, DJD 6:37, 79.

329 The new image of 4Q147 prepared under the auspices of The Leon Levy Dead Sea Scrolls Digital Library (henceforth: LLDSSDL), B-496168, numbers the fragments differently than Milik. See https://www.deadseascrolls.org.il/explore-the-archive/image/B-496168.

330 Feldman and Feldman, "4Q147," 2–3, 21–24.

331 Milik, DJD 6:79.

332 Feldman and Feldman, "4Q147."

https://doi.org/10.1515/9783110725377-006

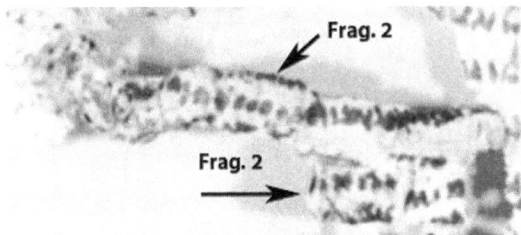

Fig. 8: Frags. 1 and 2 (PAM 42.604).[333]

hand in frag. 2 appears to be slightly less cursive than in frag. 1. Second, frags. 1 and 2 have been recovered from two separate wads. Third, the contents of frag. 2, evoking angelic names and functions, set it apart from frag. 1.[334]

Recently, an early PAM image of 4QPhyl T came to my attention.[335] This photograph, PAM 42.604, indicates that frags. 1 and 2 were found folded together (Fig. 8).[336] This, of course, does not necessarily mean that the two fragments belong to one and the same slip. As we have seen in Chapter 3, the folded tefillin 1QPhyl appears to have been comprised of several leather slips. Still, a possibility that frags. 1 and 2 constitute one and the same piece of leather merits further investigation.[337]

Indeed, this assumption fits well with two later PAM images, PAM 42.828 and 42.829, depicting an early stage in the process of unfolding. On these photographs, frags. 1 and 2 are placed beside each other, and the shape of the semi-folded frag. 2 resembles that of the corresponding bottom corner of the semi-folded frag. 1.

---

333 https://www.deadseascrolls.org.il/explore-the-archive/image/B-284015. All the PAM images included in this chapter are courtesy of the Leon Levy Dead Sea Scrolls Digital Library; Israel Antiquities Authority, photo: Najib Anton Albina.

334 Feldman and Feldman, "4Q147," 2–3.

335 The currently available printed and online resources do not list this image as associated with 4Q147. See Emanuel Tov, *Revised Lists of the Texts from the Judaean Desert* (Leiden: Brill, 2009), 33; LLDSSDL: https://www.deadseascrolls.org.il/explore-the-archive/manuscript/4Q147-1?locale=en_US).

336 This photograph also supports our earlier suggestion that Milik's frag. 12 (Feldman & Feldman: frags. 12, 12a, and 12b) does not belong to 4Q147. On PAM 42.604 it appears without any connection to 4Q147.

337 Unfortunately, I was unable to locate a PAM image capturing the very same setup as on PAM 42.604, but from the verso. Such an image could have shed additional light on the positioning of fragment 2 vis-à-vis fragment 1.

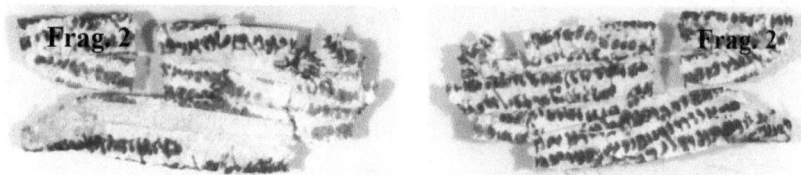

Fig. 9: PAM 42.829 (left) and PAM 42.828 (right).[338]

Fig. 10: Joining semi-folded frags. 1 and 2 (PAM 42.829).

Again, this in itself does not prove that frag. 2 was originally joined to frag. 1. In fact, Milik might have placed frag. 2 at some distance from frag. 1 for a good reason. An attempt at a digital reconstruction depicted on Fig. 10 indicates that their edges do not match.[339]

To explain this, one may hypothesize that the edges were damaged after the fragments came apart. On Fig. 8, the edge of frag. 2 is partially exposed. How much text (if at all) was lost as a result of such presumed wear and tear is difficult to determine.

If one is willing to entertain this hypothesis, the next step towards reconstruction will be to match segments of text numbered 1–5 on the image below (Fig. 11) with the unfolded fragments as presented on DJD Plate XXIV.

Segment 1: To properly identify this segment, we need to trace Milik's work on frag. 2 one step further. According to PAM 43.456; 43.457 and Plate XXIV, when he unfolded frag. 2, instead of assigning a separate number to each of the two resulting scraps, he designated the entire assemblage as frag. 2. In the preliminary edition we numbered them as frags. 2 and 2a (see Fig. 12).

338 https://www.deadseascrolls.org.il/explore-the-archive/image/B-284796; https://www.deadseascrolls.org.il/explore-the-archive/image/B-284795.
339 The same result is obtained using PAM 42.828.

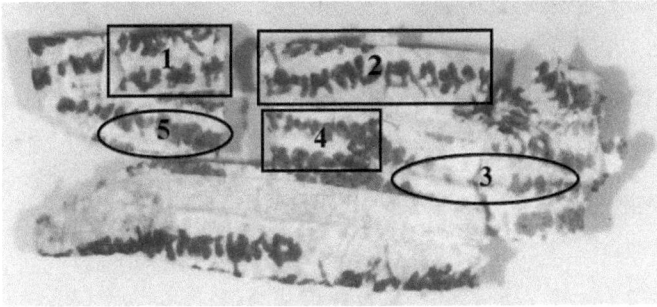

Fig. 11: Frags. 1 and 2 (PAM 42.829).

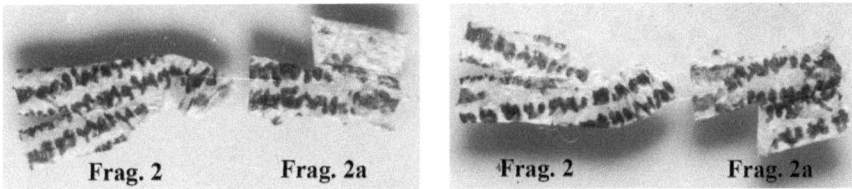

Fig. 12: Left: Frags. 2 and 2a recto (PAM 43.456); right: Frags. 2 and 2a verso (PAM 43.457).[340]

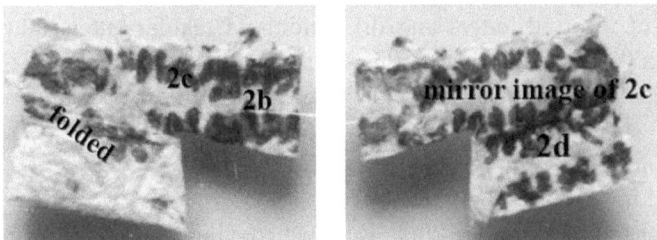

Fig. 13: Left: Frag. 2a recto (PAM 43.456); right: Frag. 2a verso (PAM 43.457).

A close inspection of frag. 2a indicates that it is a wad. There are several layers of text visible on both recto and verso (Fig. 13).

As far as the recto is concerned (Fig. 13, left), a comparison between the images suggests that the section designated 2b does not belong to the same

---

340 https://www.deadseascrolls.org.il/explore-the-archive/image/B-284484; https://www.dead seascrolls.org.il/explore-the-archive/image/B-284485.

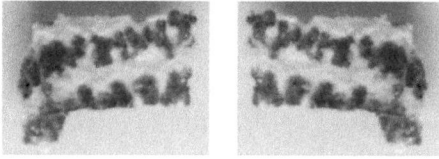

Fig. 14: Frag. 6. Left: recto (PAM 43.456); right: verso (PAM 43.457).

Fig. 15: Placing frag. 6 (PAM 43.456).

layer as section 2c. As to the verso (Fig. 13, right), the top line contains reversed letters corresponding to section 2c on the recto. Presumably the ink of 2c seeped through the thin leather here. The second line of the recto appears to be comprised of (a) tops of reversed letters and (b) bottoms of regular letters. The former belongs with the top line, whereas the latter with the bottom line, designated in the preliminary edition as frag. 2d.[341] Segment 1 on Fig. 11 matches frag. 2d.

Segment 2: Frag. 1, line 12.

Segment 3: Verso of frag. 1, lines 3 and 4.

Segment 4: Verso of frag. 6 (Fig. 14). While we have commented on frag. 6 in the preliminary edition, we failed to notice that PAM 42.829 suggests that this fragment belongs in the beginning of lines 3 and 4 of frag. 1 (segment 3 on Fig. 11), as indicated on Fig. 15.

The small scrap at the back of frag. 6 fits well, though not perfectly, with the contours of frag. 1. The relationship between the two pieces constituting

---

341 In the preliminary edition we assumed that 2d is, in fact, two layers (2d and 2e). Slightly above the bottom line there appears to be a break line (see the full-color image). However, this line may as well be a mark of a depression in the leather. In the reconstruction proposed below I follow the latter interpretation.

Fig. 16: A digital unfolding of frag. 2 (PAM 43.456; 43.457).

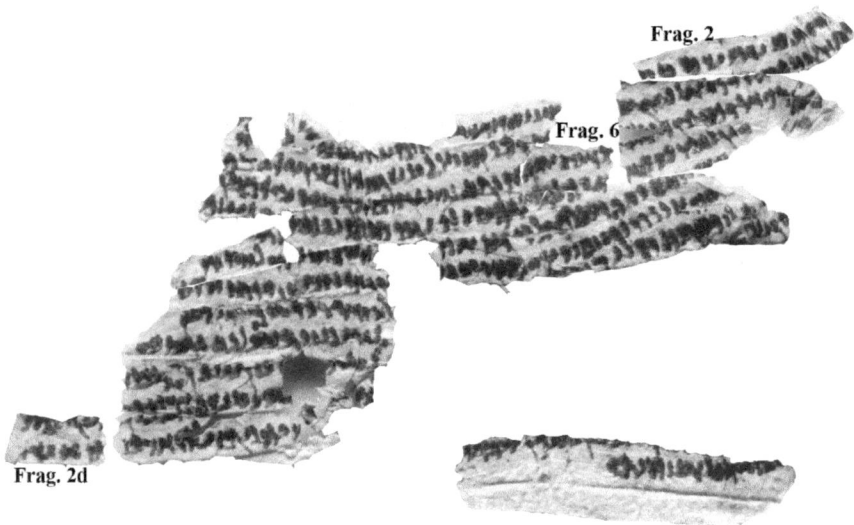

Fig. 17: Frags. 1, 2, 2d, and 6 (PAM 43.456; 43.457).

frag. 6 are unclear. They may belong to different layers of text. Yet, it is also possible that the larger piece is a continuation of the smaller one. In what follows I assume the latter option.

Segment 5: Recto of the digitally unfolded frag. 2, lines 4–6 (Fig. 16).

The foregoing discussion leads to the tentative placement of the aforementioned segments of text vis-à-vis frag. 1 as suggested on Fig. 17.[342]

---

342 For the reconstruction of frag. 1 see Feldman and Feldman, "4Q147," 4–6.

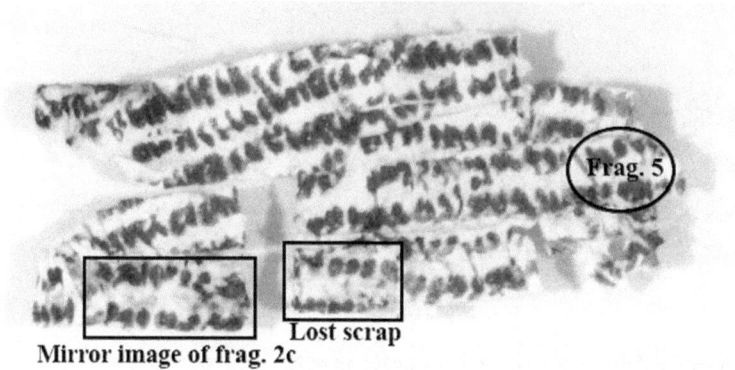

Mirror image of frag. 2c · Lost scrap

Fig. 18: Frag. 5 (PAM 48.828).

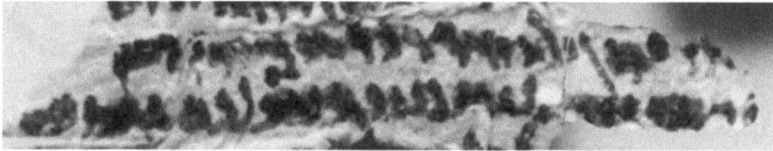

Fig. 19: Joining Frag. 5 in the beginning of lines 8–9 of Frag. 1 (PAM 43.456).

Fig. 20: Lost scraps? (PAM 48.828).

Two further details can be added to this reconstruction. First, on PAM 48.828 one can see frag. 5 situated above the beginning of lines 8 and 9 in frag. 1 (Fig. 18). Assuming that it broke off and slipped leftwards, this fragment can be tentatively placed as demonstrated on Fig. 19.[343]

Second, on Fig. 18 there are two pieces containing reversed letters. One of them has been discussed above – a verso of frag. 2c. The other one cannot be identified with any of the fragments extant on Milik's Plate XXIV. In the preliminary edition we suggested that it might have been lost. These two segments seem to belong together. Fig. 20 levels the two scraps, brings them slightly closer, and flips them horizontally.

I could not ascertain where this (predominantly illegible) text might have belonged in the reconstructed text as shown on Fig. 17.

---

343 I was unable to offer a plausible reading of a few letters preserved in frag. 5 within the presumed context of lines 8 and 9.

The Folding of 4QPhyl T

The foregoing new reconstruction of 4QPhyl T sheds light on the method in which 4QPhyl T was folded. Earlier on, I have discussed the position of frag. 6 vis-à-vis frag. 1. A comparison between PAM 48.828 and PAM 48.829 indicates that on these images this fragment is located right under the section containing the end of lines 7–8 (encircled on Fig. 21).

In order for this to happen, frag. 1 should have been:
1. Folded horizontally between lines 4 and 5, with the text facing outside.
2. Folded vertically.

While it is difficult to trace the next stages of folding with any certainty, the piece was clearly folded several times horizontally, possibly from bottom to top. The creases caused by this horizontal folding are easily detected on the images (Fig. 23).

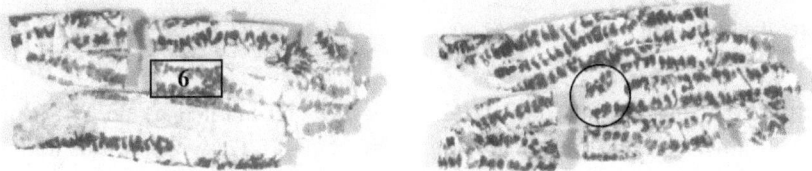

Fig. 21: PAM 42.829 (left; flipped vertically) and PAM 42.828 (right).

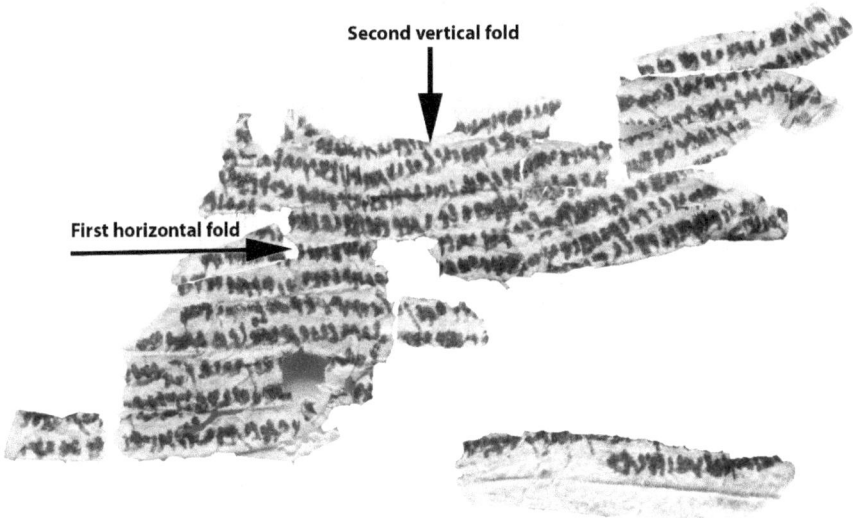

Fig. 22: Folding 4QPhyl T (PAM 43.456; 43.457).

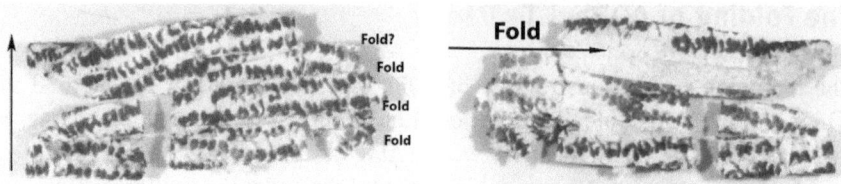

Fig. 23: Horizontal folding (left: PAM 42.828 flipped vertically; right: PAM 42.829).

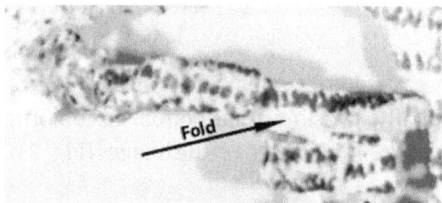

Fig. 24: The last horizontal fold (PAM 42.604).

It is possible that the last horizontal fold is the one marked by an arrow on Fig. 23 (right). On the earliest available image of 4Q147, PAM 42.604, this fold is undone (Fig. 24).

Does 4QPhyl T Cite Deuteronomy 11?

The deciphering of 4QPhyl T is a challenging task, and much in our preliminary reading of this text remains tentative. Further disentangling and unfolding of the sections that remain fully or partially folded may shed further light on its contents.[344] The newly-proposed reconstruction of 4QPhyl T is another step in this direction. The preliminary edition suggests that frag. 1, lines 3–4, alludes to Psalm 36:8–9, 11, whereas frag. 2, line 4 evokes the name of Raphael ("Raphael will frighten them"). If the aforementioned placement of frag. 2 is correct, it situates the reference to Raphael in the same line with the allusion to Ps 36:9.

Moreover, the foregoing reconstruction places frag. 2d in frag. 1, lines 11–12. The second line of frag. 2d reads ‏ה‎[.‏אשר‎][345] This sequence of letters occurs

---

344 For a discussion of segments of texts that require further attention by the curators see Feldman and Feldman, "4Q147."

345 Though the preliminary edition suggests that the first letter is an *aleph* (slanted to the left), a *he* seems to be a more likely reading.

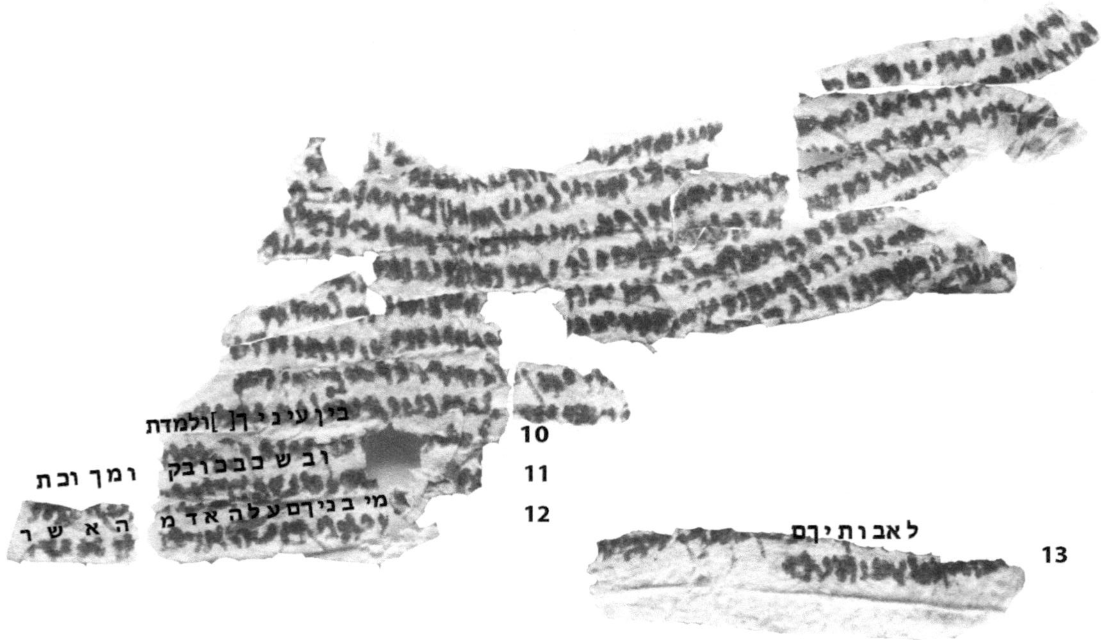

Fig. 25: Reading Deut 11:18–21 in the newly-reconstructed Frag. 1 (PAM 43.456; 43.457).

in one of the Type 1 tefillin passages. Deut 11:21 reads: ‏עַל הָאֲדָמָה **אֲשֶׁר** נִשְׁבַּע‎. Hence is the question whether 4QPhyl T might have cited Deuteronomy 11. Fig. 25 represents an attempt to construe the wording found in the composite text of lines 10–13 as containing Deut 11:18–21.

The matching text from Deut 11:18–21 can be schematically presented as follows (set in **bold** and underlined):

‏[18]‏וְשַׂמְתֶּם אֶת דְּבָרַי אֵלֶּה עַל לְבַבְכֶם וְעַל נַפְשְׁכֶם וּקְשַׁרְתֶּם אֹתָם לְאוֹת עַל יֶדְכֶם וְהָיוּ לְטוֹטָפֹת **בֵּין עֵינֵיכֶם**‎ ‏[19]‏ וְ<u>לִמַּדְתֶּם</u> אֹתָם אֶת בְּנֵיכֶם לְדַבֵּר בָּם בְּשִׁבְתְּךָ בְּבֵיתֶךָ וּבְלֶכְתְּךָ בַדֶּרֶךְ **וּבְשָׁכְבְּךָ וּבְקוּמֶךָ**‎ ‏[20]<u>וּכְתַבְתָּם</u> עַל מְזוּזוֹת בֵּיתֶךָ וּבִשְׁעָרֶיךָ‎ ‏[21]‏לְמַעַן יִרְבּוּ יְמֵיכֶם וִ<u>**ימֵי בְּנֵיכֶם עַל הָאֲדָמָה אֲשֶׁר**</u> נִשְׁבַּע יְהוָה <u>לַאֲבֹתֵיכֶם</u> לָתֵת לָהֶם כִּימֵי הַשָּׁמַיִם עַל הָאָרֶץ‎

The transcription of lines 10–13 as presented on Fig. 25 differs dramatically from the one proposed in our preliminary edition. Such diverse readings of the same traces are possible due to the fact that many of the semi-cursive letters found in these lines are open for multiple interpretations. Still, it is important to point out that in several cases the foregoing attempt to match the traces visible on the fragments with the text of Deuteronomy 11 is highly questionable. For example, in line 11 a large *qof* (below, right) is assumed to allow for the biblical ‏ובקומך‎, though the traces of ink seem to favor two letters. Similarly, in line 12 what I read as a *bet* of ‏בניכם‎ (below, middle) is more likely to be two letters. Also, the *kaph* in ‏לאבותיכם‎ (below, left) in line 13 does not match other *kaphs* (final or medial) in this text.

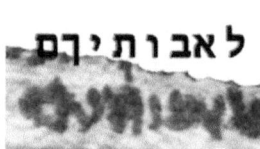

Finally, I was unable to align the text found in the beginning of line 10 or in the preceding lines with the wording of Deuteronomy 11.

In sum, this paleographic exercise underscores the challenges involved in reading 4QPhyl T. While our preliminary transcription offers the first attempt to decipher this text, it certainly remains a work in progress. Nevertheless, it seems that at least for now the overall conclusion that 4QPhyl T (either in its entirety or partially) does not match Types 1 and 2 pericopae remains intact.

6 4QPhyl U (4Q148)

As with 4QPhyl T, Milik published 4Q148 without a transcription.[346] Though he designated it 4QPhyl U, elsewhere he surmised that it might as well be a slip of a mezuzah.[347] 4Q148 is a partially folded single fragment.[348] It is approximately 16.5 mm high and 24.5 mm wide.[349] An opisthograph, each of its two sides is written by a different hand. On the fully-inscribed side – the recto – the letters' height ranges from 0.6 to 0.9 mm, with the final and *lamed* letters at 2 mm and 1.3 mm respectively. Interlinear spaces are somewhat irregular and, given the presence of multiple imprints of letters, difficult to measure. Thus, the distance between lines 10 and 11 fluctuates between 1.1 and 1.5 mm. As to the verso, its three lines are inscribed at 90° in relation to the recto. The size of the letters fluctuates between 0.6 and 1.2 mm with an exception of a *lamed* (1.4 mm) and final letters (2.4 mm). The space between lines 1 and 2 decreases from 3.3 to 1.9 mm from right to left. The single word in line 3 is 1.9 mm below line 2.

On the verso there are two dark rectangles clearly defined by the creases caused by the folding. These rectangles are the outside layers of the folded package. The symmetrical depressions found in both rectangles might have been left by a fastening thread. The sequence of folding of 4QPhyl U can be tentatively determined by following the pattern of imprints visible on both sides of the fragment.[350] The fully folded bundle was only 3 × 5 mm. A package of this size could easily fit several of the extant tefillin cases from the Judean Desert.[351]

Faina Feldman and I recently published a preliminary transcription of this text.[352] In it, we suggest that the few legible words on the recto indicate an otherwise unknown literary text, while the verso contains a legal note, perhaps a will. The following brief discussion attempts to accomplish two things. First,

---

346 Milik, DJD 6:79.
347 Milik, DJD 6:36.
348 On the images PAM 43.456; 43.457 and plate XXV in DJD 6 two fragments are associated with 4Q148. As was demonstrated in Feldman and Feldman, "4Q148 (4QPhylactère U)," 199–200, sometime during the handling process a small triangular piece was detached from the large fragment, leaving behind an easily detectable cavity matching its size and shape. At some later point, it was mistakenly attached at the top of the larger fragment, and thus it appears on the recent images of 4Q148 available at LLDSSDL, such as B-498570 (https://www.deadseascrolls.org.il/explore-the-archive/image/B-498570).
349 When fully unfolded, the width of the fragment would be ~45 mm (at max).
350 For a detailed discussion of the imprints and folding, see Feldman and Feldman, "4Q148 (4QPhylactère U)," 201–5.
351 See, for instance, the data provided by Milik, DJD 6:35 (cases #1, 4, 6–13).
352 Feldman and Feldman, "4Q148 (4QPhylactère U)."

https://doi.org/10.1515/9783110725377-007

it offers a new reading of the name of the beneficiaries mentioned in the second line of the legal note found on the verso. Second, as in the case of 4QPhyl T (Chapter 5), it revisits the question of whether the extant text of the recto can be construed as one of the passages included in other tefillin and mezuzot from Qumran.

Revisiting the Transcription of the Verso

The preliminary edition reads in line 2 בֹֿנֹ̇יׄ°°°שׁ. After further scrutiny of the images, I would like to propose that 4QPhyl U has here בֹֿנֹ̇יׄ חֹֿנֹ̇יׄ, "sons of Hanani."[353] The name Hanani, a form of Hananiah, is attested to in the Hebrew Bible (e.g., Ezra 10:20; Neh 1:2; 1 Chr 25:4; cf. also יהוא בן חנני in 1 Kgs 16:1, 7; 2 Chr 19:2; 20:34) and in non-biblical sources.[354]

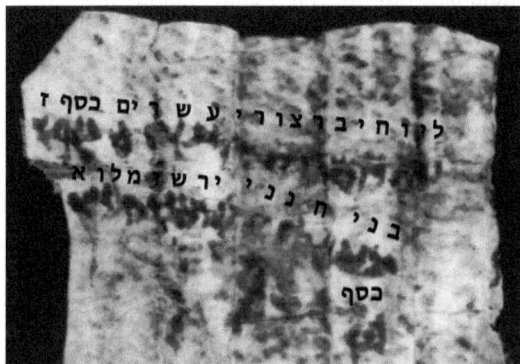

Upper margin

1 לׄיׄוֹֿחׄ בֹֿ צֹֿורׄיׄ עשרׄים כֹֿסֹֿף ז[

2 בֹֿנֹ̇יׄ חֹֿנֹ̇יׄ ירשו מלוֹא]

3 כֹֿסֹֿף

Fig. 26: 4QPhyl U verso (new infrared image).[355]

Notes to Readings

Line 2 חֹֿנֹ̇יׄ. The roof and the right leg of a *khet* are clearly visible on the new infrared image. The left leg is less clear on the image. Yet its upper tip is present.

---

353 In the transcription offered below intervals have been introduced to assist the reader.

354 Tal Ilan, *Lexicon of Jewish Names in Late Antiquity: Part I: Palestine 330 BCE–200 CE*, TSAJ 91 (Tübingen: Mohr Siebeck, 2002), 1:103–108 and #80 on p. 105.

355 All the images included in this chapter are courtesy of the Leon Levy Dead Sea Scrolls Digital Library; Israel Antiquities Authority. The new infrared and full-color images are by Shai Halevi. The earlier PAM images are by Najib Anton Albina. As this book is submitted for publication, the new infrared image of the verso has not yet been uploaded to the LLDSSDL website.

The following two letters appear to be consistent with two medial *nun* letters. The fourth letter is a *vav/yod*.

Translation

1. To Yoḥai son of Ṣuri twenty silver *z*[
2. sons of Hanani will inherit all[
3. silver

This new reading helps elucidate the names of the beneficiaries listed in this legal note. They are "Yoḥai son of Ṣuri" and "sons of Hanani." The preliminary edition suggests that the letter *zayin* in the end of line 1 might be an abbreviation for *zuzin*, a currency often used in the legal texts from the Judean Desert, and wonders whether the verso may preserve this legal document in its entirety.[356] Similarly uncertain is which of the two sides of 4QPhyl U was inscribed first. One curious possibility is that in order to inscribe the legal note, the folded literary text was unrolled and then folded (and fastened) again.[357]

Revisiting the Transcription of the Recto

In the preliminary edition we suggested that the recto of 4QPhyl U contains an unidentified literary text.[358] Indeed, such phrases as "and they will bless" (line 2), "misdeed" (line 6), and "forgive" (line 11) seem to confirm that, unlike the text inscribed on the verso, the recto is not a legal document. One may wonder, however, whether the poorly preserved traces of letters on the recto might be construed to match Type 1 or 2 texts. In what follows I attempt to read lines 2, 6, 10–11 as if they contained the wording of Deuteronomy 5.

---

356 Feldman and Feldman, "4Q148 (4QPhylactère U)," 209–12.
357 Feldman and Feldman, "4Q148 (4QPhylactère U)," 212–13.
358 Feldman and Feldman, "4Q148 (4QPhylactère U)," 207–208. The transcription offered below introduces intervals to assist the reader.

2 אֲשֶׁר בַּשָּׁמַ֫יִם מִ֫]

6 עָוֹן

10 אֱלֹהֶ֫יךָ נָתַן לָ֫ךְ לֹא תִּרְצָח
11 לֹא תַּעֲנֶ֫ה

Fig. 27: 4QPhyl U recto (PAM 43.456).

These tentative readings match the following verses from Deuteronomy 5:

Deut 5:8	2 אֲשֶׁר בַּשָּׁמַ֫יִם מִ֫]
Deut 5:9	6 עָוֹן
Deut 5:16–17	10 אֱלֹהֶ֫יךָ נָתַן לָ֫ךְ לֹא תִּרְצָח
Deut 5:20	11 לֹא תַּעֲנֶ֫ה

As with 4QPhyl T, such a reading of 4QPhyl U is based on a series of paleo-graphic assumptions which need to be made explicit.[359]

Line 2 אֲשֶׁר. This reading assumes that the letter preceding the letter *shin* is an *aleph* distorted by the folding of the leather. Second, it reads the diagonal stroke next to the *shin* as a *resh* lacking a roof. Both readings are highly doubtful.

Line 10 לֹא לָ֫ךְ. The image reproduced here has been enhanced by digitally placing the imprints of the letters (found elsewhere on the recto) on their extant traces. Both the final *kaph* of לָ֫ךְ and the *aleph* of לֹא are highly tentative.

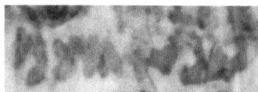

---

359 All the images utilized in the following section are based on PAM 43.456.

Line 11. לֹא תֵּעֲנֶֹה. Once again, the image enhanced by digitally merging the letters with their imprints seems to allow the viewer to construe the letters as matching the proposed reading, yet other readings could be ventured as well.

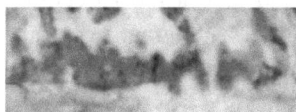

One could probably also squeeze ולֹא תגנב in the beginning of line 11, assuming that the *tav* is partially damaged due to the tear in the leather and that a *bet* of תגנב merges with the *vav* of ולֹא (תענה), as shown in Fig. 28.

Fig. 28: 4QPhyl U recto line 11 (PAM 43.456).

Still, the preceding letters do not lend themselves easily for a reading with the wording of the Decalogue.

This attempt to read the verso of 4QPhyl U as a running text of Deuteronomy 5 poses further challenges. First, the gap of several lines between line 2 containing Deut 5:8 and line 6 featuring Deut 5:9 is difficult to explain. Second, this reading implies that 4QPhyl U did not contain the entire Decalogue. The *vacat* in the end of line 11 followed by a bottom margin indicates that Deut 5:21 ("You shall not covet …") was not a part of this text.

To conclude, the foregoing experiment in reading the recto of 4QPhyl U with Deuteronomy 5 produces mixed results. Admittedly, the transcription of the recto suggested in the preliminary edition is a tentative one. Hence, while it seems prudent to allow it to stand, one might want to delay the final verdict on the nature of the recto until the fragment is fully unfolded.

7 4QMez C (4Q151)

4QMez C (4Q151) edited by Milik is comprised of two fragments.[360] These two long and narrow strips of leather, dated to the second half of the 1st century BCE, measure 82 × 25 mm (frag. 1) and 70 × 20 mm (frag. 2).[361] Frag. 1 contains verses from Deuteronomy 5, 6, and 10. For frag. 2 Milik was unable to propose a plausible reading.[362] Still, based on their paleographic and physical features, he concluded that the two fragments originate in the same mezuzah.[363] This chapter revisits frag. 2 and its affinities with frag. 1.

Frags. 1 and 2: Scribal and Physical Features

Unlike frag. 1, frag. 2 yields very few complete letters. Moreover, the identification of some of them is uncertain (see below). These factors seem to preclude any firm verdict on the kinship of their respective scripts.[364] As to other scribal features, the width of the right margin in frag. 2 ranges between 11.5 and 14 mm, whereas that of frag. 1 is slightly narrower, 11.3–12 mm. These are by far the widest margins attested to in any of the Qumran fragments identified as mezuzot (cf. 4QMez F [right margin]; 8QMez [left magin]). The height of the fully-preserved letters in frag. 2 is 2 mm, with a *lamed* at 2.7 mm. In frag. 1 the letters are often smaller, fluctuating between 1.2 mm and 2 mm, with *lameds* at 2.7–3.4 mm and a final *koph* at 3 mm. The interlinear spaces in frag. 2 are difficult to determine, with a partial exception of lines 1 and 2: 3.5–4 mm. In frag. 1 the lines appear to be slightly more crowded: 2.8–3 mm.

---

360 Milik, DJD 6:82–83.

361 Milik, DJD 6:82–83, offers different measurements: 85 × 25 mm (frag. 1) and 58 × 19 mm (frag. 2).

362 Frag. 2 is comprised of four scraps that have been joined together. The new full-color image of the verso of frag. 2 demonstrates that the joints between the scraps have been secured by an adhesive tape. The joint between scraps 2 and 3 (counting from the top) appears to be the most problematic one of the three, as the shapes of the edges do not exactly match, presumably as a result of deterioration. I am very grateful to Ms. Beatriz Riestra of the IAA who arranged for the re-imaging of 4QMez C and provided me with the new photographs.

363 Milik, DJD 6:83.

364 One might note that the single complete *lamed* preserved in frag. 2 (line 5) appears to be executed differently than the *lamed* letters extant in frag. 1. It has a relatively wide and distinct horizontal stroke vis-à-vis the narrow wavy *lameds* in frag. 1. Its top is slightly widened, possibly by a small "flag" descending from right to left. In frag. 2, some of the *lameds* have a wavy top (line 7) or a top that loops backwards (the second *lamed* in line 14).

https://doi.org/10.1515/9783110725377-008

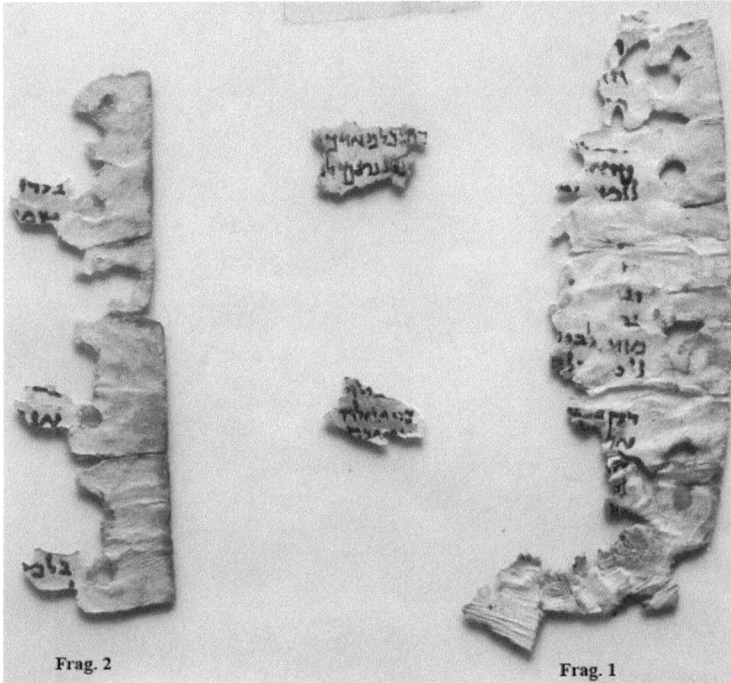

Fig. 29: Mez C (PAM 43.460).[365]

As far as physical peculiarities of the two fragments are concerned, frag. 1 has a few notable features. Its right margin is cracked in multiple places. There are also deep creases and holes in the margins. These cracks, creases, and holes shed light on the method in which this fragment was rolled or folded. The following tentative reconstruction takes the holes in the margins as its main guide (Fig. 30).

Proceeding from the top downwards, the first folding (or revolution) at Crack A aligns holes #1 and #2. The second folding (or revolution) at crease #1 matches these two holes with hole #3. The third folding (or revolution) at crease #2 aligns holes #1–3 with hole #4. Crease #3 indicates that there might have been yet another horizontal folding. The remaining mutilated bottom part of the fragment (placed in a rectangle on Fig. 30) appears to be the outside layer of the folded (or rolled) text.

---

365 https://www.deadseascrolls.org.il/explore-the-archive/image/B-284488. All the images included in this chapter are courtesy of the Leon Levy Dead Sea Scrolls Digital Library; Israel Antiquities Authority, photo: Najib Anton Albina. The two small fragments visible between frags. 1 and 2 are not a part of 4QMez C.

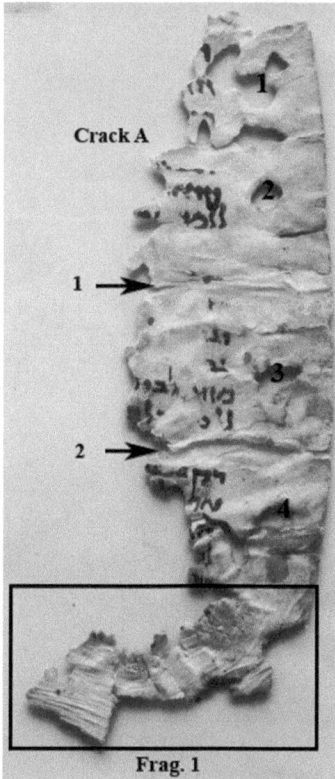

Fig. 30: Frag. 1 (PAM 43.460).

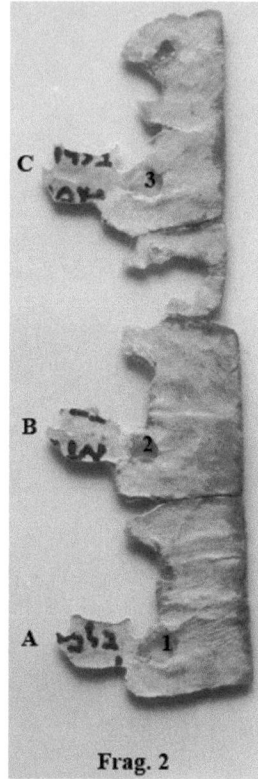

Fig. 31: Frag. 2 (PAM 43.460).

This method of folding creates a small package or a scroll. In the latter case the cracks and the creases are likely to be a result of squeezing.

Frag. 2 also features horizontal cracks, creases, and holes. Its pattern of damage differs from that of frag. 1 – it has three protruding segments (A–C on Fig. 31). Their similar shapes (note especially the concave tops of A and C) indicate that they were placed one above the other in a rolled (or folded) text. The following method of rolling or folding from the bottom upwards relies on these protrusions and holes. At the first revolution (or folding), the bottom edge is rolled upwards to align with crack #1. At the next revolution (or folding) segments A and B, as well as holes #1 and #2, are aligned. The verso of segment A should be facing the recto of segment B. At the third, somewhat looser, revolution (or folding), sections A–B are aligned with C and holes #1–2 are matched with hole #3. If the final product was a scroll, the cracks and creases are likely to be a result of a pressure.

Milik did not elaborate on his assumption that frags. 1 and 2 belong to one and the same mezuzah. Did he envision them as coming from one slip of leather? If so, this seems rather unlikely. Since the bottom of frag. 1 is severely damaged, it is rather implausible that frag. 2 might have followed beneath it. Yet its placement above frag. 1 is also improbable. Frag. 2 was rolled from the bottom up, whereas frag. 1 seems to have been folded from the top down. That the fragments may have come from different slips seems to be further supported by their distinct patterns of damage.

The Contents of Frag. 2

This brings me to the contents of frags. 1 and 2. In frag. 1, Milik was able to identify the broken text of Deut 5:27–33; 6:1, 3, 5, 7, 9; 10:12, 15–18, 20 (on its presumed shorter reading in Deut 5:32–33 see Chapter 2). The extant wording of frag. 2, however, is puzzling. Milik's transcription thereof does not match the biblical texts found in other mezuzot (and tefillin) from the Judean Desert:[366]

$$\begin{array}{r}]°בֹלֹדֹ \quad 1 \\ ]°שׁמ \quad 2 \\ ]?כ?ב \quad 3 \\ אנֹכֹ]י \text{ or }]°אנ \quad 4 \\ ]°מ בֹל \quad 5 \\ ]ל \quad 6 \end{array}$$

In two details Milik's reading calls for a revision:[367]

Line 2]°שׁמו. The short vertical stroke crossing the right arm of the *shin* appears to be a self-standing letter, a *vav/yod*, rather than an ornamental addition to the *shin* (as Milik seems to have assumed). The third letter could also be read as a medial *pe*.

---

366 While Milik numbered the remains of the text as lines 1 through 6, the three pairs of lines found in segments A (lines 5–6), B (lines 3–4), and C (lines 1–2) are separated from each other by large gaps (Fig. 31).
367 All the images provided here are from PAM 43.460.

Line 5 ‏בלמ׳ל[‏. Milik tentatively suggested that the last letter is a *shin* or an *ayin*. Yet its shape and elevated position seem to suit better a *lamed*.

These two minor revisions hardly solve the enigma of frag. 2. All one can say about it is that this fragment contains a first-person address (line 4). More could be gained, however, if we were willing to assume that the first letter in line 5 is not a *bet*, but a medial *kaph*. Kaph letters with a base protruding to the right are attested elsewhere in the texts from the Judean Desert.[368] In fact, it seems that frag. 1 also features a medial *kaph* in which the base slightly extends to the right beyond the meeting point with the vertical stroke (line 11: ‏ובכ]ל‏).

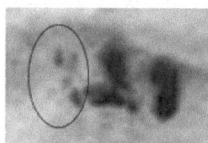

If such a reading is accepted, the letters in lines 2, 4, and 5 can be construed to match the wording of Deuteronomy 5:

Deuteronomy 5	Frag. 2
	‏בלד׳°[‏ 1
‏¹ויקרא משה אל כל ישראל ויאמר אלהם שמע ישראל ... ולמדתם אתם **ושמרתם** לעשתם‏	‏ושמר׳[תם‏ 2
	‏°°[‏ 3
‏⁵, ⁶, ⁹**אנכי**‏	‏אנכ]י‏ 4
‏¹³⁻¹⁴ועשית כל **מאלכתך** ... לא תעשה כל **מלאכה**‏	‏כל מל[אכה‏ 5
	‏ל[‏ 6

On this reading, line 1 does not have a parallel text in Deuteronomy 5. It is, of course, not impossible that my transcription of this line is incorrect. For in-

---

368 Ada Yardeni labeled them "a bet-like form." See Ada Yardeni, *Textbook of Aramaic, Hebrew and Nabataean Documentary Texts from the Judaean Desert and Related Materials* (Jerusalem: The Ben-Zion Dinur Center for Research in Jewish History, 2000), 2:188.

stance, the second letter might be a *yod* (cf. the curved *yod* in frag. 1, line 13, reproduced here [PAM 43.460, brightened]). The vertical stroke of the forth letter may belong to a *khet*.

Such a reading would yield a phrase בִּיֹֽד חֹ[זקה found in two passages included in mezuzot and tefillin, Exod 13:9 and Deut 5:15. With this in mind, one could hypothesize that line 1 reproduces the last words of Exod 13:16, **כי בחזק יד** הוציאנו יהוה ממצרים (MT), harmonizing the rare phrase בחזק יד towards the much more frequent biblical locution ביד חזקה. Such a hypothesis, however, would imply that line 1 was quite long, as it presumably contained not only much of Deut 5:1 but also Exod 13:16.

Do Frags. 1 and 2 Belong Together?

When all the data about frags. 1 and 2, such as scripts, scribal practices, methods of folding, and contents, are considered together, two observations emerge. First, the newly-proposed tentative reading of frag. 2 suggests that four out of its five legible words can be matched with the wording of Deuteronomy 5. This lends some support to Milik's initial proposal that this fragment belongs to a mezuzah, though a tefillin slip (cf. 1QPhyl with its large intervals between the lines [Chapter 3]) or an excerpted Deuteronomy scroll (see Chapter 2) are also possible. Second, the scribal and physical features of frags. 1 and 2 seem to indicate that the two fragments do not belong to the same slip of leather. Their different patterns of damage and methods of folding are among the stronger arguments in favor of viewing them as discrete texts. Could they have been used in tandem in antiquity? After all, they may preserve complementing sections of Deuteronomy 5. While this is not entirely impossible, it seems more likely that they have been grouped together by modern scholars due to similarities in their scripts and physical features.

8 8QPhyl (8Q3)

The 77 fragments of 8QPhyl (8Q3) were edited by Maurice Baillet in DJD 3.[369] Since he received the fragments unfolded, it is unknown how many tefillin slips they represent. Baillet assumed that there are several of them, and that all of them belong to one tefillin.[370] The fragments are inscribed on one side only. The vast majority of them feature letters that are less than 1 mm high (with final letters and *lameds* as tall as 1.4 mm). Three fragments, frags. 75, 76, and apparently 77, contain larger letters (~2.2 mm in frag. 75).[371] The interlinear spaces in 8QPhyl are about 1 mm. Baillet dated the script to the first century CE.

Baillet grouped 29 out of 77 fragments presented on the DJD plates XXXII–XXXIII into four groups (I–IV) which he considered to represent the four slips of this tefillin. Group I contains Exod 13:1–10, 11–16; Deut 6:4–9; 11:13–21. These are the four biblical pericopae (Type 1) which the later rabbinic halakhah prescribes for a tefillin. Groups II–IV include some of the Type 2 verses from Exodus and Deuteronomy (Exod 12:43–51; Deut 5:1–6:3; 10:12–11:12). This distribution of the passages led Yigael Yadin to suggest that 8QPhyl preserves remains of two tefillin. Group I is what the later rabbis call an "arm tefillin," while Groups II–IV belong to a "head tefillin."[372] In a subsequent publication Baillet rejected Yadin's proposal.[373] He argued that all of the fragments of 8QPhyl were penned by the same scribe and that Groups II–IV complement Group I. For

---

369 Maurice Baillet, DJD 3 (Textes):149–57; 3a (Planches): Plates XXXII–XXXIII. Baillet's edition of 8QPhyl remains the only detailed study of this text. Subsequent scholarship discussed (albeit briefly) 8QPhyl's contribution to the textual criticism. See, for instance, Himbaza, "Le décalogue," 425–26; Jastram, "2.2.5.1 Tefillin and Mezuzot"; Tov, "Tefillin from the Judean Desert." For studies discussing 8QPhyl through the lens of rabbinic halakhah, see below.
370 Baillet, DJD 3:150; idem, "Nouveaux phylactères de Qumran (XQ Phyl 1–4): à propos d'une édition récente," *RevQ* 7 (1970): 403–15 (414).
371 Baillet suggested that these belong to some sort of a heading or a title. However, no such heading has so far been identified in any of the tefillin and mezuzot from the Judean Desert.
372 Yadin, *Tefillin from Qumran*, 15n28, 33n44, 34. He is followed by Nakman, "Content and Order," 30; Adler, "Content and Order," 222n58. Yadin, ibid., 15, made yet another suggestion regarding the putative "arm tefillin" represented by Group I. He proposed that its order of the four passages, particularly the peculiar parallel placement of Deut 11:13–21 and Deut 6:4–9 (see below), reflects an attempt to reconcile two ancient views on sequencing biblical pericopae in tefillin known since the medieval times as those of Rashi and Rabbenu Tam. As discussed in Chapter 1, Cohn argues that Qumran tefillin do not follow any particular order of biblical texts. Moreover, the passage from b. Menahot 34b which Rashi and Rabbenu Tam disagreed on seems to envision a tefillin with four compartments. This is, obviously, not the case with 8QPhyl I. See Cohn, "Rabbenu Tam's Tefillin," 322–23. Note also the reservations expressed by Rothstein, "From Bible to Murabbaʿat," 373 and n197.
373 Baillet, "Nouveaux phylactères de Qumran," 414.

https://doi.org/10.1515/9783110725377-009

him, Groups I–IV were likely placed in a four-compartment tefillin case, two specimens of which had been found in Cave 8 (along with one single-compartment case).[374] Baillet's critique notwithstanding, Nakman accepts Yadin's interpretation, but with a small caveat. In his opinion, while Group I and Groups II–III represent an "arm" and a "head" tefillin respectively, Group IV is too fragmentary to identify.[375] Following on Yadin's insight, Adler argues that Group I, compliant with the later rabbinic halakhah, is one of the two "pharisaic" tefillin (along with 4QPhyl D-E-F) found at Qumran. In addition to its restrictive selection of the biblical passages, he notes Group I's conservative orthography and close adherence to the proto-Masoretic text. The latter feature sets Group I apart from Groups II–IV, which, though written in a "traditional orthography," display a "non-Masoretic textual character."[376]

This study offers a new reading of a few portions of text that Baillet struggled to match with the biblical verses included in other tefillin from Qumran. These segments of texts are found within his Groups II and IV, as well as in the "unidentified" frags. 30–77.[377] However, before these can be addressed, a brief overview of Groups I and III is necessary.

Groups I and III

Group I. Based on their physical features and contents, Baillet placed frags. 1–11 together to form a single slip of tefillin. He designated this 39 lines' long assemblage as Group I. Since its top and bottom margins are preserved intact, he estimated that this putative slip must have been some 5 cm high.

As was noted earlier, Group I contains four scriptural passages: Exod 13:1–10, 11–16; Deut 6:4–9; and 11:13–21. A blank line separates Exod 13:1–10 from 13:11–16, while another blank line sets the latter apart from the two passages from Deuteronomy.[378] Deut 6:4–9 and 11:13–21 are inscribed in a rather unique

---

374 DJD 3 (Planches), Plate VIII.
375 Nakman, "Content and Order," 24, 25n24, 30.
376 Adler, "Sectarian Characteristics," 88–89; Adler, "Content and Order," 222. Tov, "Tefillin from the Judean Desert," 286, also treats Baillet's Group I and Groups II–IV separately. In his classification, the former belongs with the Proto-MT and MT-like texts, whereas the latter reflects his SP-LXX-independent text (see Chapter 1).
377 The several spots in Group III where Baillet was unable to suggest plausible reconstructions for the lacunae fall outside of the scope of this study.
378 Here the Exodus passage precedes those from Deuteronomy. Many tefillin from Qumran reproduce the Deuteronomy texts first (cf. Group III here). Cohn, "Material Aspects," 92, notes that this is the case in eight out of twelve instances where both Exodus and Deuteronomy are preserved. See also Brooke, "Deuteronomy 5–6," 66–67

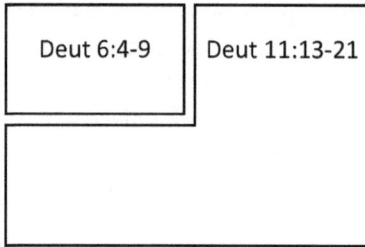

Fig. 32: The placement of Deut 6:4–9 and 11:13–21 in Group I.

(in comparison to other tefillin from the Judean Desert) fashion.[379] The text of Deut 6:4–9 is shaped into a half-line long rectangle and copied on the left side of the slip.[380] Deut 11:13–21 appears on the right side. The impression is almost as if the two passages are inscribed in two columns. However, the longer passage from Deuteronomy 11 extends below Deuteronomy 6, as shown on Fig. 32.

In addition to a peculiar layout, there are three further important aspects of Group I to consider. First, as was noted above, according to the later rabbinic regulations the scriptural passages copied in this reconstructed slip alone could constitute an "arm tefillin." Another example of a single tefillin slip from Qumran, an opisthograph, containing these four passages is 4QPhyl C. Second, the wording of the four biblical pericopae copied in Group I reveals a rather "conservative" or "exact" scribal approach to the biblical texts (Chapter 2). There are only two instances where it deviates from the MT: a plene spelling (הזאות) in Exod 13:5 and an omission of several words in Exod 13:12 (suggested by the extant text and the size of the lacunae).[381] This "conservative" approach is especially remarkable, since the other three putative slips of this tefillin, Groups II–IV, exhibit a "revisionist" or "facilitative" approach. The third notable aspect of Group I is closely related to the second – it is the only group that Baillet was able to decipher in its entirety. It is quite clear that his difficulty to restore the lacunae in Group III or to identify some of the text in Groups II and IV had much to do with the fact that Groups II–IV often deviate from other ancient witnesses of Exodus and Deuteronomy.

---

379 See Cohn, "Material Features," 89–99.

380 Adler, "Content and Order," 223, suggests that Deut 6:4–9 was copied first. That Deut 11:13–21 was fitted in later is indicated by this scribe's attempts to squeeze in the words in the end of the lines.

381 The restored text of Exod 13:12 in Group I reads: ‏[והעבר]ת כל פטר רחם [בבהמת]‏ך אשר יהיה לך הזכרים ל[‏יהוה, whereas the MT has: ‏והעברת כל פטר רחם ליהוה וכל פטר שגר בהמה יהיה לך הזכרים ליהוה אשר (4QPhyl C and G read ‏בבהמה).

Group III. Baillet's Group III consists of frags. 17–25. The incipit and the top margin of this putative tefillin slip are still intact.[382] It contains Deut 10:12–19; Exod 12:43–51; and Deut 5:1–14. Group III has several notable features. First, the order of the biblical passages in Group III appears to be unique as far as other tefillin and mezuzot from the Judean Desert are concerned.[383] Of particular interest is its presentation of Deut 10:12–19 and Exod 12:43–51 as one textual unit. These two passages are linked thematically. Deut 10:18–19 calls for love for an alien resident, whereas Exod 12:48–49 legislates on the alien resident with reference to the Passover.[384] The scribal technique of aggregating verses dealing with the same topic (in this case, of a legal kind) is otherwise unknown in tefillin from the Judean Desert but is well established in other Second Temple texts, including such biblical manuscript as 4QRP[d] (4Q366) 4 i juxtaposing Sukkoth regulations from Numbers 29 and Deuteronomy 16 (as discussed in Chapter 2). Second, Group III features a wealth of textual variants, which include scribal lapses,[385] Aramaisms,[386] changes in word-order,[387] paraphrase,[388] omissions,[389] and additions.[390] There is also a noteworthy harmonizing reading: for the Sabbath com-

---

382 The right and left edges are present as well. The bottom margin is not preserved.

383 See Adler, "Content and Order," 222.

384 As expected in Type 2 tefillin, the scribe began transcribing Deuteronomy 10 with v. 12. Upon reaching the laws pertaining to an alien resident (10:18–19), he switched (without leaving a separating space) to another Type 2 pericope, Exod 12:43–51. Interestingly, he copied here the entire pericope, and not only verses 48–49 dealing with the alien resident. Having inscribed Exod 12:43–51, he, however, did not continue, as one might have expected, with Deut 10:20 (Deut 10:20–22 appears in Group II). Rather, he left the line containing v. 51 incomplete and moved on to yet another Type 2 passage beginning with Deut 5:1. Adler, "Content and Order," 222, observes that tefillin from Qumran routinely exhibit the same delineation of the biblical texts into textual units as the MT. The aforementioned juxtaposition of Deut 10:12–19 and Exod 12:43–51 without any formal separation is an exception from this rule. It lends further support to the proposal that Exod 12:43–51 was introduced here next to Deut 10:19 due to a similarity in the topic.

385 In Deut 5:2, where the MT reads כרת עמנו, 8QPhyl III has כרת עכרת. It appears as if the scribe began inscribing the word עמנו, but then, mistakenly (thus Baillet, DJD 3:153), wrote כרת once again.

386 Baillet lists the following Aramaisms: על כן בֹּעִיאֹת / אבתֹיכֹם (Deut 10:13), מֹצות דֹיהוה (vs. MT's רק באבתיך חשק; Deut 10:15).

387 E.g., והנורא והגבר vs. הגבר והנורא (MT Deut 10:17).

388 See וי[ד]בר vs. ויאמר (MT Exod 12:43), ומלתה את ערלתו vs. ומלת אתו (MT Exod 12:44). The curious reading לנֹוֹכֹרֹי in Exod 12:49, where other textual witnesses have לאזרח, may also belong here.

389 Among these are ואדני האדנים (Deut 10:17), וכל עבד איש מקנת כסף (Exod 12:44), ועצם כי לא ינקה (Deut 5:8), ואשר בארץ מתחת (Deut 5:5), כי יראתם (Exod 12:46), אחד לא תשברו בו (Deut 5:11). יהוה את אשר ישא ישא את שמו לשוא

390 See היום הֹזֹה vs. היום (MT Deut 5:1). In addition to the obvious longer and shorter readings, in several cases the lengths of the lacunae suggest that Group III may have had a shorter/

mandment (Deut 5:14) Group III provides a justification borrowed from Exod 20:11, as do also 4QPhyl G, 4QMez A, and Papyrus Nash.[391]

Group II

While the biblical texts copied in Groups I and III are relatively easy to identify, the case of Group II is different. This group is comprised of frags. 12–16. The left and right margins of this putative tefillin slip are preserved intact (frags. 12 and 15). The new images of frag. 14 feature an uninscribed space above Baillet's line 1, but it may not be large enough to warrant a top margin. Group II begins with some eight lines of text that Baillet was unable to match with the Types 1 or 2 passages. This section is immediately followed by Deut 6:1–3. After a full blank line comes Deut 10:20–22, possibly "complementing" Deut 10:12–19 inscribed at the top of Group III. Both Deut 6:1–3 and 10:20–22 feature a familiar array of scribal interventions: lapses,[392] omissions,[393] additions,[394] and alternative formulations.[395]

Next to Deut 10:20–22, at the bottom of this reconstructed slip, there are three lines of an unidentified text (lines 19–21). These three lines deserve further attention. They contain only a few letters. Most of these letters are found on a small scrap positioned near frag. 16 (encircled on Fig. 33). The PAM image reproduced here is not sharp enough to ascertain whether the shapes of the edges of the two fragments match.[396] Hence, it is unclear whether the small scrap belongs here at all.

---

longer text than the one found in the MT and other textual witnesses. For instance, line 9 could hardly accommodate Deut 10:18.

391 The excerpted scroll 4QDeut[n] provides both Deuteronomic and Exodus justifications for the Sabbath observance, and so does also Codex Vaticanus. See further Eshel, "4QDeut[n]," 145–47; Himbaza, "Le décalogue"; Brooke, "Deuteronomy 5–6," 68; Tov, "The Papyrus Nash and the Septuagint," 46.

392 One example of a scribal lapse might be found in Deut 10:22, where Group II reads ב[שבע נפש instead of the בשבעים נפש of the MT and the versions. Group IV, 7 (citing Deut 10:22) also reads בשבעים נפש.

393 These range from a definite article (וחקים in Deut 6:1), to a single word (והמשפטים, v. 1), to longer stretches of text (אשר ייטב לך ואשר תרבון מאד [v. 2], כל ימי חייך ולמען יארכן ימיך [v. 3]) which cannot fit the available lacunae.

394 See היום ה[זה] (Deut 6:2).

395 See בֹּאׄים vs. עברים (MT Deut 6:1), צוׄהׄ vs. דבר (MT Deut 6:3), ובו תקרב vs. ובו תדבק (MT Deut 10:20; Baillet, DJD 3:152, suggests an Aramaic influence here [cf. Tg. Ps.-J. ad loc.]).

396 On the recent images the tiny gap between the fragments visible on PAM 42.494 is no more apparent as they have been fully joined and are now supported by a rice paper on the verso.

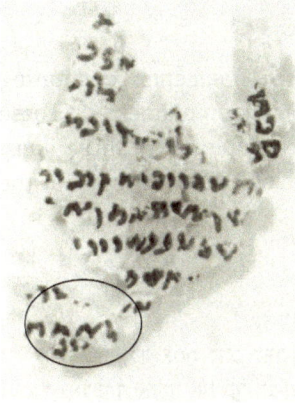

Fig. 33: Frag. 16 (PAM 42.494).[397]

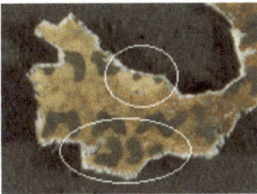

Fig. 34: Group II, lines 19–21 (Frag. 16; digitally brightened new full-color image).

Two further physical aspects of this small piece need to be noted. First, the shade of a tiny segment embedded in its first line (=line 19) differs from the rest of this scrap (encircled on Fig. 34). One wonders whether it might have been placed here by Baillet. Second, the images do not allow to ascertain whether another small misaligned segment of text read by Baillet as line 21 (encircled on Fig. 34) originates here or elsewhere.

---

397 https://www.deadseascrolls.org.il/explore-the-archive/image/B-283984. All the images included in this chapter are courtesy of the Leon Levy Dead Sea Scrolls Digital Library; Israel Antiquities Authority. The new infrared and full-color images are by Shai Halevi. The earlier PAM images are by Najib Anton Albina. As this monograph is submitted to the publisher, the new images have not yet been uploaded to the LLDSSDL website.

Group II: Revised Text

A close scrutiny of the old and new images of the fragments constituting
Group II suggests multiple revisions to Baillet's transcription of lines 1–8. These
allow the reader to partially identify scriptural texts employed in these lines.
Moreover, the revised text proposed below offers several new readings for the
remaining lines 9–21.[398]

Deut	Revised Text	
5:29	[מִי י]תֵּ֯ן והיֹֽה֯] לבבם זה להם [	1
5:30	[לך אמר להם שוב]֯וֹ לכם לֹא]הליכם ואתה פה]	2
5:31	[עמדי ואדברה אליך את כל המ[צ֯וֹ]א]והחֻק֯]ים והמשפטים אשר]	3
5:31	[תלמדם או]תם ועשֹו֯] בארץ אשר אנכי נתן]	4
5:31–32	להֹם לֹֹ֯]שתה לא תסרו י]מין [ושמאל [כא]שר צוה יהוה]	5
32+?	אלהיכם לֹ] [ ]אֹתכמֹ] [°א°[ ]°°°[	6
5:33	צ֯וֹה יהוֹ֯לֹ֯] בארץ]אשר תיר֯]שון [°°°[ ]ו֯]טוב֯[לכם [	7
6:1	[י]ומֹ°°[ ]אתכם לֹעֹ֯]שות וזא֯]ת ה]מ֯]צוא וחֻק֯]י֯]ֹם [א]שֹׁר]	8
	[צוה י]יהוה] אלהיכם]ללמד לֹמֹ] ב]ארץ אשר את]מ]	9
6:2	בֹא֯ים שמֹה֯] למען ת]ירא אֹ]ת א]ֹת יֹה]ו֯]הֹ אלֹֹהֹיך	10
	לשמור את] כל חקתיו] ומֹ֯]צֹותי ואשר] אנכי מ֯]צוֹ֯ך היום ה]זֹה]	11
6:3	אתה בנך ֹוֹבֹֹ֯ן] בנך ושמעת] י֯]שר]אל ושמרת לעשות	12
	כֹאשר צוֹֹ֯ה] יהוה אלהי אבתיכֹ]ם֯ לֹך֯ ארץ זבת חֹלב ודבש	13
	vacat	14
10:20	אֹ֯ת יֹ֯הוה אלהיך] תירא אֹת]ֹו֯ תעבד ובו תקרב ובשמו תשבֹֹע֯ו֯	15
10:21	[הוא ת]הֹלתך והו]א אלהיך א]שר עשה אתך אֹת֯] הגדלת וא]ֹת֯	16
10:22	[הנו]ֹרֹאות ואשׁ]ר ראו עיניך ב]שבע נפש ירדֹו֯] אבתיך מצרי]מה	17
11:1	[ועת]ֹה שֹ֯מֹך֯ יֹהֹ]וה כככֹ]בֹ֯י השמֹי֯]ם לרב ואהב]תם	18
11:1a+?	[יהוה א]לֹֹהֹיך ו֯]שמרת משמרתו [אשֹׁ] [שֹׁרֹ°[[	19
?	[ ]ל אֹת ה]ֹ [	20
?	[ ]°°יבֹ[[	21

398 Since this scribe rarely left spaces between the words, in the following transcription they have been added to assist the reader.

Notes to Readings[399]

Line 1]יהיה וֹתָ[יֹ (frag. 14). Baillet reads]תָייהוה[. Given several occurrences of a very short final *nun* in this column, a reading וֹתָ[יֹ appears to be possible.

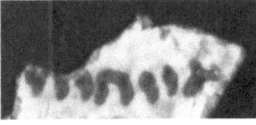

יֹ[מִין (line 5)   וֹבֹֻן[(Line 12)

Line 2 הליכם[לא לכם וֹ[שוב (frag. 14). Baillet reads here]לכמלשׁ○[. A top of a letter visible before a *lamed* may belong to a *vav/yod*. The last letter is clearly an *aleph* – not a *shin*.

Line 3 ים[והחקֹ]א[צֹוֹ]המֹ (frag. 14). Baillet reads the second letter as a *tav*. The images, especially the new one, suggest that this is a *he*. On an early image (PAM 42.494 reproduced below [right]), to the right of the *vav* additional traces are visible. Here they are read as a medial *tsade* and a *vav* (following the presumed scriptural context of this line).

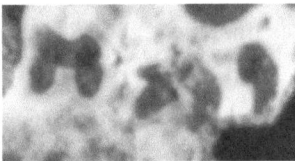

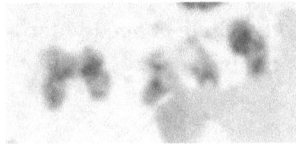

Line 4]וֹעשֹו (frag. 14). Baillet offers no reading for the last two letters. On the new image, there is a trace of a diagonal right stroke as in the right arm of a *shin*. This *shin* merges with a letter that might be read as a *vav/yod*, a *resh*, or a *dalet*.

---

399 Unless noted otherwise, the photographs utilized here are the recent infrared and full-color images. To assist the viewer, the images have been digitally brightened.

Line 5 שתה‎]לֹֿ לֹהֹם (frag. 12). Baillet reads ‎]°ליומסל[. The new images show a blank space prior to the *lamed*, indicating that this is the beginning of the line, as Baillet had assumed. What appeared to him to be a *yod* and a *vav* may well be, according to the new full-color image, a *he* (with a missing roof). The trace of a letter next to the second *lamed* visible on PAM 42.494 is tentatively read here as a *resh*.

מין‎]י. Baillet reads ‎]מיך[(frag. 13). The images may not preserve the top of the third letter in full. However, the extant vertical stroke better suits a final *nun*, rather than a final *kaph*. On a short final *nun* in this column, see Notes to Readings to line 1.

Line 6 אֿתכֹם‎[(frag. 13). Baillet reads the second letter as a *he*, but its left vertical stroke, slanted to the left at the top, is rather common in *tav* letters in this text. What the editor reads as a medial *pe* can be also be read as a medial *kaph*. Finally, the circle-shaped letter is most likely as final *mem*, though a *samekh* is also possible.

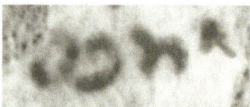

Line 7 ‎]לֹ°ל יהוה (frag. 12). There appears to be an interlinear correction between the lines above the letters *vav* and *he* in the word יהוה. Perhaps, this is a *lamed* followed by another letter.

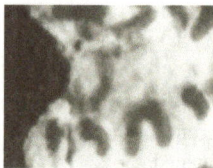

אשר תיר]שון[. Baillet reads]°תי שא[(frag. 13). The *resh* written next to a *shin* is visible on the new image. For the spelling with a *yod* cf. תירשון (Deut 6:1) in XQPhyl 2.

טוב]ו[. Baillet reads]°טי[(frag. 14). The tiny trace of the third letter visible on PAM 42.494 (encircled) can be variously construed. Here a *bet* is proposed.

Line 8 לע]שות (frag. 13). Baillet reads לעש]ות. No trace of a *shin* is visible on the images, old and new. **[א]שר** (frag. 15). Baillet reads an *aleph*, but the early images do not support this reading. The relevant piece of leather is lost on the new images.
　　Line 9]ללמד למ[(frag. 13). Baillet reads ללמד] אתכ[ם. On the new image, the *dalet* is followed by a *lamed* and a medial *mem*.

Line 10 ת]ירא א]ת (frag. 13). Baillet reads ת[יר]א°°°[. On the new image there are traces suggesting another *aleph*. **יה]ו[ה** (frag. 14). Baillet reads יה]ו[ה. The new image indicates that the second *he* is present.

Line 11 ה]זה[(frag. 15). Baillet reads ה°. According to the images, there is no additional letter next to the *he* (which has an elongated roof).

Line 12 וּבֹן] (frag. 12). Baillet reads וֹבֹ[ן]. The tiny final *nun* is visible on the new image.

Line 13 אבתיכ]ם (frag. 16) Baillet read אב[תיכֿם. However, only a trace of what might be a final *mem* is visible on PAM 42.494. Perhaps, he assumed that a small scrap appearing on the same image near frag. 15 (frag. 46) contains the missing letters. Yet, this seems unlikely, as his transcription of frag. 46 includes those letters. In any case, the shapes of the edges of the two fragments do not match.

Line 15 ובשמו (frags. 16 + 15). Baillet reads ובעֿמֿו and suggests a scribal error. On the new image of frag. 15 the little scrap bearing what Baillet read as an *ayin* and a medial *mem* appears upside down. One wonders whether on the earlier image (PAM 42.494; reproduced below on the left) this scrap should have been moved a little to the left. Then what Baillet read as an *ayin* could be read as a *shin* (its rudimentary middle arm is present in the curve of the left arm) and a medial *mem*.

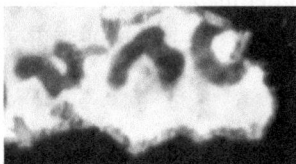

Line 17 הנו]ראות ואש]ר (frag. 12). Baillet reads הנו]ראוֹ יאש]ר taking the zig-zag-shaped *tav* as a *vav* added above the line. This *vav* is, however, present, though it is written closely to a small *aleph*.

Line 18 ‏וה|יֹה שֵׁמֹךֹ ה[ועת]‏ (frag. 12). Baillet suggests ‏[°אמור°]‏. What he reads as an *aleph* may as well be a *shin*, as can be seen on PAM 42.494 (reproduced below, on the left; the new images lack the detached scrap containing these traces). It is preceded by a tiny trace of an upper horizontal stroke. Perhaps this is a roof of a *he*. Next to the *shin*, there is a medial *mem*. Given the context, what the editor read as a *vav* could also be a final *kaph* – a short final *kaph* without a roof is attested to elsewhere in this this column, in ‏אתך‏ in line 16.

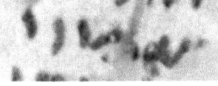

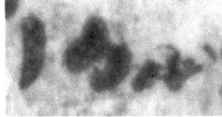

‏אתך‏ (line 16)

‏תם[‏ (frag. 15). Baillet reads only a *tav*.

Line 19 ‏שמרת ו|ל'הֹיך א[יהוה[‏ (frag. 12). Baillet reads here only a final *kaph*. On PAM 42.494 there appears to be a top of a *lamed*. The tops of the two vertical strokes that follow (separated by a gap) could belong to a *he*. The *yod* before *kaph* is certain. The vertical stroke next to the final *kaph* may be read as a *vav*.

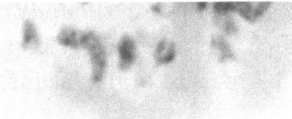

Line 21 ‏[°יב°]‏ (frag. 16). Baillet reads only a *bet*. The new image suggests that there is a *vav/yod* prior to it.

Group II: Discussion

The revised reading of lines 1–8 securely places them within the concluding verses of Deuteronomy 5.[400] The scribe proceeded from chapter 5 to chapter 6 without leaving a blank line. Clearly, he considered them to be a single textual unit, unlike Deut 10:20–22 separated here from Deut 6:3 by a full blank line.

What is also clear is that in lines 1–8 the scribe did not follow the text of Deut 5:29–33 as known from other ancient textual witnesses of Deuteronomy. Verse 29 does not appear to fit the lacunae in its entirety, whereas v. 31b seems to be too short for the available space (line 4). The order of the clauses in v. 32 is reversed. Of v. 33 only two phrases are recognizable (lines 6–8a). As discussed in Chapter 2, several tefillin and mezuzot from Qumran (4QPhyl A; B; J; 4QMez C) feature shorter texts of Deut 5:32–6:2. In comparison to those slips, Group II seems to offer for those verses a wider array of scribal techniques which encompass not only Deut 5:32–6:2 but also the preceding Deut 5:29, 31 and the following Deut 6:1–3.[401]

If the proposed reading is correct, line 18 containing Deut 10:22b continued with Deut 11:1, probably leaving a short blank space between the two.[402] The beginning of line 19 appears to contain Deut 11:1, while the rest of it does not match the wording of this verse. Similarly, lines 20–21 have no parallel in the following verses of Deuteronomy 11. However, as was suggested above, it is possible that the small scrap containing the non-matching text of lines 19–21 does not belong here.

Finally, the wording of lines 18–19, [יהוה] / ואהב[תם, differs from that of the MT Deut 11:1: ואהבת את יהוה (thus also reads a parallel text in Group IV). While the pl. masc. ואהב[תם has parallels elsewhere (cf. Tg. Ps.-J. and Tg. Neof. ad. loc.), the presumed omission of את (suggested by the size of the lacuna) appears to be unique to 8QPhyl II.

Group IV

Group IV is comprised of frags. 26–29 preserving the right, left, and bottom margins. This reconstructed tefillin slip yields a peculiar (as far as other tefillin

---

400 Upon the completion of this chapter, I found out that Yadin, *Tefillin from Qumran*, 33n45, has already suggested (without elaborating) that lines 1–8 may contain Deut 5:22–33.

401 For the scribal phenomena attested to in these verses see notes 392–395. To those one could add that the wording and lacuna in line 10 may suggest a slightly longer text of Deut 6:2a.

402 For a continuous text of Deuteronomy 10–11 without a separating space cf. 4QPhyl K.

and mezuzot from Qumran are concerned) arrangement of biblical verses. According to Baillet, its first nine lines contain the following sequence: Deut 10:13?, 11:2+10:13?, 11:2, 11:5, 11:3?, 10:21–22. The next thirteen lines feature Deut 11:1, 6–12.

It appears that the puzzling order of biblical texts in the first nine lines is partially a result of an imprecise placement of frag. 26. Baillet correctly identified it as containing the top right corner of the reconstructed Group IV. He read and restored it as follows:

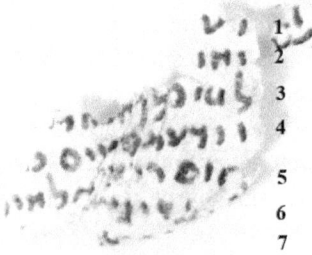

1 ‏וֹל‏[ו°‏
2 ‏יהו‏]ה‏
3 ‏לטֹוב לך הֹנֹה °י‏[°‏
4 ‏וידעתם היום כי‏[‏
5 ‏מוסר יהוה אלהיכ‏]ם‏
6 ‏[במד‏]בר ובא‏]רץ‏
7 ‏הכ‏] ‏]בֹ[‏
8 ‏וֹאֵת הֹנֹ‏]וראות‏
9 ‏מֹצֹרֹיֹם‏]°‏
10 ‏[לר‏]בֹ וֹ‏]אהבת‏

Fig. 35: Frag. 26 (PAM 42.494).

Baillet's lines 8–10 are not visible on the PAM images. It seems that this section of the fragment is still folded on the PAM photographs. On the new images it has been unfolded, as can be seen on Fig. 36 (right):

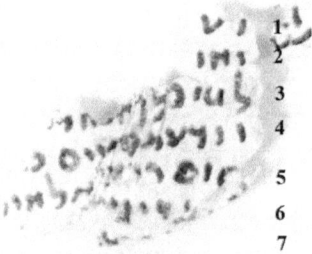

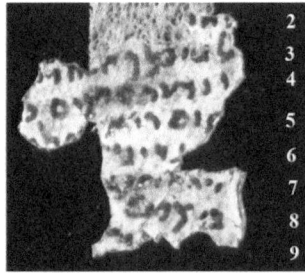

Fig. 36: PAM 42.494 (left) and a new infrared image (right; digitally brightened).

The new photograph indicates that the first line of this fragment was lost since the PAM images were taken. More importantly, it suggests that overall frag. 26 contains nine lines of text, and not ten as Baillet assumed. It seems that the traces which he read as line 7 (‏בֹ[ ]הֹכֹ‏) belong to to his line 8. What this means is that frag. 26 needs to be slightly repositioned within Group IV. Following the sequence of biblical passages cited here, particularly Deut 11:2, it seems that it should be placed one line "lower" vis-à-vis frag. 27. In the revised text proposed below frags. 26 and 27 are also placed slightly closer to one another than in Baillet's reconstruction. Overall, this re-arrangement yields a more coherent reading of lines 4–9.[403]

Group IV: Revised Text

Several tefillin from Qumran attest to a scribal technique of splitting a word between the lines when the space at the end of a line is too short to accommodate it in full. The scribe of 8QPhyl refrained from splitting the words in the end of lines 6, 7, 9, 11–14, 16, and 18. Instead, he used several strategies to fit them in. These can be seen on the images, as well as on Baillet's drawing in DJD 3:155.[404] In the transcription that follows the letters that the scribe adjusted are presented in a smaller font.[405]

Deut	Revised Text	
10:12?	וֹעַ]תה ישראל מה[	1
10:13	יהו]ה אלהיך שאל מעמך ל[שֹׁמֹ]ר את מצות יהוה ואת חקתיו[	2
10:13–14a	לטוב לך הֹנֹה לֹי[הוה א]נֹכי מצוך היוֹ]ם [	3
11:2	וידעתם היום כֹיֹ] לא [את בניכם אשר ל[א ידעו ואשר לא ראו את[	4
	מוסר יהוֹ]ה [אלוֹהֹיכם ואת מֹכֹת יהֹוֹהֹ הגֹדוֹל]ה ואת ידו החזקה[	5
11:5?; 11:3	[במד]בֹר ובאֹ]רֹץ וא[ת מעשה אשר עשהֹ] בתוך מצרים לֹפֹרֹ[עֹ]ה	6
10:21–22	וֹאֹת הֹנֹוֹ]אֹות האֹ]לֹה אֹשׁר ביעיֹנֹיכם כי בֹשֹׁבֹעֹים נפש ירד אֹבֹתיך	7
10:22	מצרֹי]ם [ ] וֹעתֹ]ה שֹׁמֹית יהוה אלהיך ככבי השמים	8
10:22; 11:1	[לרב]וֹאֹ]הבת את]יֹ]הֹ]וֹהֹ] א]להיך ושמרת משמרת חקיו ומשפֹטיו	9
11:6	ומצוֹ]תיו כֹל] הימים[ ]ף לדתֹ]ן[ ]ולאבֹהֹן בני אליב בן	10
	רבֹנֹ אֹ]שר פצתה הארץ את]פיה ותבֹלֹעו את בתיהכם ואת	11
11:7	כל הֹ]יקום אשר ב]רֹ]גֹ]ליהֹם ק בקֹ]רֹ]בֹ [כֹ]ל ישראֹל כי עיניכם הרו אנן	12
	את כֹ]ל מעשה יֹ]הוה הגֹדול אשר אתא אֹתה גדול אתה	13

---

403 Also, Baillet suggests that frag. 29 can be placed in between the large frags. 26–28 adding a few words that fit the context. However, neither his reconstruction nor the one proposed below warrants this placement.

404 A similar set of techniques is attested to in XQPhyl 1–3. On these see further Cohn, *Tangled Up*, 71.

405 The decision as to which letters were adjusted by the scribe is sometimes a difficult one. My interpretation differs slightly from that of Baillet (lines 11–13). Moreover, since this scribe rarely left spaces between the words, they have been added here to assist the reader.

11:8	14 הניך לֹמֹעֹן תֹחיו ויטבוֹ יֹמֹים בארץ אשׁר אתם באים שם
11:9	15 לרשתה ולמען ירבו ימיכה על האדמה אשר נשבע יהוֹה
	16 לאבתיכם לתת להם ולזרעם אֹחריהם אֹ[ר]ץ [ז]בת חלב[ודב]שׁ
11:10	17 כי הארץ אשר אתם באים שמ[ה] לרשתה ו[°°תם לֹא אֹ⁙
11:11	18 מצרים [ה]ֹיֹא לא מיצצרֹים היא אֹרֹץ ארץ הרים ובקעותם
11:12	19 מֹמטר השמים תשת[ה] מים אֹשׁר יה[וה] אֹלֹהֹיך בֹה
	20 רובֹץ אותה תמֹד עיני יהוה אלֹהֹיֹךֹ] בה מרשית השנה ועד אחרית]
	21 שנה

Notes to Readings[406]

Line 1 וֹעֹ]תה (frag. 26). Baillet reads וֹלֹ[°]. The traces next to the *vav* appear to be consistent with the *ayin* letters in this text (cf. *ayin* in וידעתם in line 4 reproduced here on the left [PAM 42.494]).

Line 3 הֹנֹה לֹי]הוה (frag. 26). Baillet reads a *yod* next to הֹנֹה. However, the letter appears to be too wide for a *yod*. Perhaps, this is the lower part of a *lamed*. A vertical stroke, read here as a *yod*, follows.

Line 5 יהֹוֹ]ה (frag. 26). Baillet suggests יֹהוה. The images, both old (PAM 42.494, left) and new (right), support only the first three letters.

---

406 Unless noted otherwise, the images utilized here are the recent infrared images. To assist the reader, they have been digitally brightened.

מכת יהוה (frag. 27). Baillet reads מ̇כּתי̇ו̇.. On the new image, traces of four letters are visible next to *tav*. They appear to be consistent with י̇ה̇ו̇ה̇.

Line 6 ו̇]א[ת (frag. 27). Baillet does not read the trace visible on PAM 42.494 prior to the *tav*. It appears to be consistent with a *vav/yod*.

לפֹר̇]ע[ה (frag. 27). Baillet offers no reading for the traces visible on the images. I tentatively suggest that a bottom tip of a letter on PAM 42.494 (left) belongs to a bottom hook of a *lamed*. The following semi-circular letter could be a medial *pe*, while the third letter is probably a *vav/yod* or a *dalet* or a *resh*. The earlier PAM images leave it somewhat unclear whether there is a hole in the leather before *he*, as the new infrared image (right) indicates. Finally, there might be a trace of an ink above the *he* (PAM images), possibly belonging to the now-lost letter that was inscribed above it.

Line 7 הנּוֹר̇]אות (frag. 26). Baillet reads הנּ]וראת. Traces of three letters are visible on the new image after a large *he*. These seem to be consistent with a medial *nun*, a *vav*, and a *resh*, represented by a slanted vertical stroke.

בּשׁבּעׁים (frag. 27). Baillet reads בש]בעי[ם. On the new image traces of the missing letters are visible.

ירד (frag. 27). Baillet reads רֹרֹ. The *yod* is visible on the new image.

Line 9 |לרב [וֹאֹ]הבת (frag. 26). Baillet reads לֹ[רב וֹא]הבת. There are no traces of ink in the beginning of the line in frag. 26. The traces that are visible at the end of the line may suit a *vav* closely followed by an *aleph*.

ומשפטיו (frag. 27). Baillet reads a final *mem*, ומשפטים. The image seems to indicate a large hook-shaped *vav*.

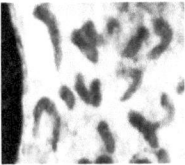

Line 10 ולאבהו [לדת]ן (frag. 27). Baillet reads לדתולאבהו. As the new image indicates, there is a gap in the leather which might have destroyed the final *nun* in דת[ן]. This gap is not apparent on PAM 42.494 (right).

Line 11 ותבֹלֹעוֹ. Baillet reads ות[בל]עֹמֹ (frag. 27). The reading is difficult. The new image (right) contains a gap and fewer traces than the early ones. PAM 42.494 (left), however, seems to preserve traces of a *bet* and a *lamed*. The final letter is not consistent with a final *mem*, but rather appears to be a *vav* or a *yod*.

Line 12 ב[ר]ג[לייהם ק בק[ר]ב [כ]ל ב[ר]גליהם בקרב (frags. 27–28). Baillet offers בקרב ב[ר]גליהם
כל. The images, both old and new, do not seem to contain the *gimel* and the
resh. A trace that might be the left tip of a base stroke of a *bet* is visible on PAM
42.494. There appears to be a *qoph* prior to the *bet*. It is visible on the old and
new photographs.

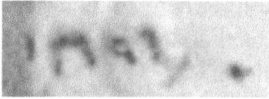

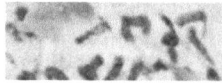

הרו / אנן (frag. 27). This is Baillet's reading. The penultimate letter closely
resembles a medial *nun* (PAM 42.494). One wonders, however, whether a *yod*
might have been intended, הרואין.

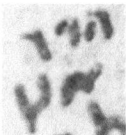

Line 13 אתא אתה (frags. 27). Baillet אתאלֹהֹ. The trace he reads as a *lamed*
can also be a left diagonal stroke of an *aleph*. As to the next letter, as seen on
PAM 42.494, the left vertical stroke projecting above the roof is more consistent
with a *tav*, rather than with a *he*.

Line 14 הניך לֹמֹעֹן (frag. 28). Baillet reads הֹנוֹך. The third letter can be either a
vav or a *yod*. יֹמֹים (frag. 27). The fist *mem* appears to be a final *mem* in a medial
position (PAM 42.494, below). Compare the use of an almost a round *mem* in a
medial position in תמד in line 20.

Line 15 ימיכה (frag. 28). Baillet suggests ימיכם. The image (PAM 42.494) indicates that the last letter is a *he*.

Line 16 אֹ[ר]ץ [ז]בֿת (frag. 27). Baillet reads אר̇ץ זבת. *Resh* and *zayin* are not visible on the images. The latter is probably concealed by a wrinkle in the leather.

ו[דב]ש̇. Baillet reconstructs the *shin*. It is visible on the new image.

Line 17 שמ[ה] (frag. 28). Baillet sees a *he*, but there are no traces of it on the images, either old (PAM 42.494) or new.

ו[ ]∘∘תם (frag. 27). Baillet reads ו[ ]עֿכֿתֿם. The reading is difficult here due to the shrinking of the leather on the early images and the apparent absence of some scraps on the new ones. The traces prior to the *tav* can be variously construed.

לֹא אֹר̇ץ̇ (frag. 27). Baillet reads לאא[. Traces of Baillet's second *aleph* seem to be visible on PAM 42.494. He sees a trace of another letter prior to the *resh* written slightly below the line. It is absent from the images.

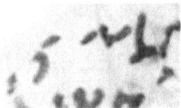

Line 18 [ה]יֹא מיצצרים (frag. 28). Baillet reads הוא לאכֿמֿצרים. It is unclear whether a vertical stroke before the *yod* in [ה]י̇א is an ink (PAM 42.494, below, left) or a hole in the leather, as might be suggested by a large gap on the new image (below, right). The photographs indicate rather clearly that there is no

medial *kaph* before מיצצרם, and that there is a *yod* next to the medial *mem*. Whether there is a *yod* between the *resh* and the final *mem* is somewhat uncertain.

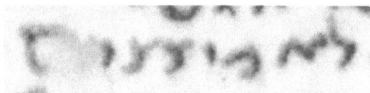

Group IV: Discussion

The newly-proposed reading and reconstruction of the top lines in Group IV seem to clarify some of the difficulties Baillet could not resolve. The new reading of line 1, וֹעֵ]תה, links it to Deut 10:12. This verse is rather long and cannot be fully accommodated in line 1. Since line 3 utilizes the wording of Deut 10:14 and line 2 contains two letters that can be reconstructed as ר]שֹׁמ[ל of Deut 10:13, I suggest that the scribe omitted much of v. 12 and skipped to v. 13. My tentative reconstruction takes line 1 as the first short line of Group IV (cf. the first line in Group III). Other reconstructions assuming a longer line 1, as the one proposed below, are equally possible:

Deut	Revised Text	
10:12?	[את לעבד אם כי מעמך שאל אלהיך יהוה מה ישראל וֹעֵ]תה	1
10:13	[חקתיו ואת יהוה מצות את ר]שֹׁמ[ל לבבך בכל אלהיך יהֹו]ה	2
10:13–14a	[היֹו]ם מצוד אٰ[נٰכי א]לֹהֹו[ה לٰיٰ הٰנֹה לך לטוב	3

I was unable, however, to offer a plausible reconstruction for line 3. It appears to juxtapose wording from Deut 11:13 (לטוב לך), Deut 11:14 (הٰנٰה לٰיٰ]הٰוה; cf. the MT's הן ליהוה), and Deut 11:13 again (א]נٰכי מצוד היٰו]ם). The latter phrase could not have been accommodated into the reconstructed line 2 due to the space limits suggested by lines 4 ff. It would appear as if the scribe began copying v. 14 and then recalled that he omitted a phrase from v. 13. Whether he resumed his work on v. 14 is unknown.

If correct, the revised text of Group IV employs Deut 10:12–14; 11:2, 3, 5(?); 10:21–22; 11:1, 6–12. As with Groups II and III, this tefillin slip features the familiar scribal phenomena. In addition to the scribal interventions suggested by my reading and reconstruction of lines 1–3, there are further instances of lapses,[407]

---

407 E.g., ירד vs. ירדו, שֹׁמֵית vs. שמך (MT Deut 10:22), הרו / אנן (yet see also Notes to Readings]) vs. הראת (MT Deut 11:7). Note also the doublet אתא אתה (MT Deut 11:7) and several

omissions (some of which are rather extensive),[408] and paraphrase.[409] Two other aspects of Group IV deserve further attention: the order in which it presents scriptural texts and several longer readings it attests to.

Group IV features a unique, as far as the published tefillin from Qumran are concerned, sequence of biblical texts. At the first sight, it appears to contain the running text of Deut 10:12–11:12. We have already seen that Deut 10:12–19 and Deut 10:20–11:1 are copied in Groups III and II (respectively). Yet while in Groups II and III these verses appear in a familiar order, here the entire section found in Deut 10:15–20 is missing. Instead, the scribe copied (or, better, paraphrased) some of the wording found in Deut 11:2–3 and possibly 5. These very verses are absent from the following text of Deuteronomy 11. The motivation behind these omission and re-ordering is not entirely clear. One could tentatively suggest that the scribe might have associated the wording of Deut 10:13 cited in line 3 – א[נֹ]כִי מצוך **היו[ם** – with Deut 11:2 copied in line 4 which opens with **וידעתם היום**. The link between Deut 11:3 (line 6) and the following Deut 10:21–22 (lines 7–9a) is somewhat easier to explain. Both texts deal with God's mighty deeds during Exodus, featuring the phrase ואשר עשה (10:21; 11:3–5). If correct, this is yet another example of a technique I observed in Group II where the scribe juxtaposes passages dealing with the same topic.

Group IV also yields two intriguing expansions. Both appear to employ phraseology found elsewhere in the Hebrew Bible. Thus in Deut 11:2, instead of the MT's את גדלו, Group IV employs the phrase ואת מכת יהֹוה הגדֹול[ה ("YHWH's

---

.לֹא אֶרֶץ / מצרים [ה]יֹא לֹא מיצצרים היא אֶרֶץ הרים ובקעותם :doublets in Deut 11:10. The reading ובקעותם vs. ובקעת (MT Deut 11:11) also appears to be a scribal oversight.

408 In Deut 11:2–3 the list of the manifestations of the divine power is shorter (excluding וזרעו הנטויה ואת אתתיו). Deut 11:4 appears to be completely omitted, and so does most of verse 5. In fact, the only possible allusion to v. 5 (ואשר עשה לכם במדבר) is a reconstructed reference to the wilderness in line 6, [במד]בר]. The preceding lacuna can be restored either with the wording of this verse or with v. 2 (continuing with the reference to ואת ידו החזקה / [במד]בר ובא[רץ) :מכה גדולה. Further omissions are found in verse 8 אשר יצאתם משם אשר תזרע) and in vv. 10–11 (ושמרתם את כל המצוה אשר אנכי מצוך היום) את זרעך והשקית ברגלך כגן הירק והארץ אשר אתם עברים שמה לרשתה). The latter might be a result of a homoioteleuton (לרשתה ... לרשתה).

409 Group IV omits Deut 11:8a picking up the biblical language beginning with the conjunction ולמען. However, instead of תחזקו, Group IV introduces a phrase לְמַעַן תֵחיו ויטבֹו יֹמֹים בארץ echoing the beginning of 11:9 copied next. Moreover, the MT's עברים is replaced here with באים (as in v. 10). In 11:9, instead of the MT's תאריכו ימים, one finds ירבו ימיכה. In Deut 11:12, where the MT has אֶרֶץ אשר יהוה אלהיך דרש אתה, Group IV reads אֲשֶׁר יה[ו]ה אֱלֹהֶיךָ בֹה / רובֹץ אותה. It appears as if the scribe replaced the verb דרש with a peculiar construction רבֹ(ץ) / בֹה / רובֹץ) never appears in the Hebrew Bible with reference to God) almost mechanically, retaining the superfluous אותה.

gre[at] blow"). The phrase מכה גדולה ("great blow"), echoing several biblical accounts of divine victories (e.g., Josh 10:10, 20; 1 Sam 4:10; 6:19; 19:8; 23:5), fits well in a context dealing with the events of Exodus. In Deut 11:7 Group IV expands the Deuteronomic את כל מעשה יהוה הגדל אשר עשה ("all YHWH's great deeds that he performed") referring to God in the third person with what appears to be a direct address to the deity: את כֹּ[ל מעשה י[הוה הגדֹול אשר אתא אתה / גדול אתה הניך ("al[l Y]HWH's great [deeds] that you (?) you great are you you are," reading אתא and הניך as a phonetic spelling of אתה and הנך). The formula גדול אתה occurs in several biblical passages (גדול אתה וגדול שמך [Jer 10:6]; כי גדול אתה [Ps 86:10]; cf. also גדול אתה מֹושיא in Miriam's Song in 4QRPᶜ [4Q365] 6a ii, 6c 3). Of all the published tefillin and mezuzot, only 8QPhyl IV introduces a language of praise (or prayer) into its text of Deuteronomy.

Identifying 8QPhyl's "Unidentified Fragments"

Out of 77 fragments assigned to 8QPhyl, Baillet identified and placed 29. The remaining 48 fragments are included in the *editio princeps* as "unidentified." For some of them he proposed a tentative reading, while many others, mostly the minute ones, are not transcribed. The latter are found on the plates accompanying the DJD edition.[410]

Already in the DJD edition, Baillet noted that frag. 30 2 may point to Deut 5:5. The discussion below confirms this proposal. In a subsequent study he made several further suggestions as to what some of his "unidentified fragments" may contain.[411]

Frag. 32. Baillet suggested that this fragment belongs at the bottom of Group III. He assumed that frag. 32 1–4 run parallel to Deut 5:11, 13 (cf. Exod 20:10–11). See further below.

Frag. 33. Baillet proposed that frag. 33 4 quotes Deut 5:21 (cf. Exod 20:17). However, what Baillet read as א]שת רֹעֶ֯ך[(line 4; DJD 3:157) appears to be]שׁולא[on the new image (reproduced here). Grouped as]שׁו לא[, these letters could be construed as Deut 5:20–21: ולא תענה ברעך עד שוא ולא תחמד אשת רעך. Such a reading would only be possible, if one is willing to assume that שׁוא is spelled here phonetically, שׁו (as in 4QPhyl B and J; cf., however, לשוא in Deut 5:11 in Group III, 23) and that a *vav* of ולא is absent, as is the case in

---

410 Most of the recent images reproduced in this section have been digitally brightened.
411 Baillet, "Nouveaux phylactères de Qumran," 414.

multiple textual witnesses of Deuteronomy (4QDeut[n]; XQPhyl 3; Papyrus Nash; SamP; LXX and more).[412]

Frag. 36. Baillet suggested that frag. 36 3 reading ‏[בֹתֹ֯ך ובֿ֯]‏ may contain Deut 6:9 or 11:20: ‏וכתבתך על מזזת ביתך ובשעריך‏. This fragment appears to be missing from the new images of 8QPhyl. The early PAM 42.494 is of poor quality as far as this fragment is concerned (reproduced here; digitally brightened). Still, it appears legible enough to allow for a reading ‏[בֿ]ֿי[תֿ]ך ובֿ[שעריך‏. Both Deut 6:9 (cf. also v. 7) and 11:20 (cf. also v. 19) are included in Group I.

Frag. 40. Line 2 in frag. 40 reads ‏[ריכֿוֿ]‏. Baillet proposed that this fragment may belong at the bottom of Group III. He pointed to Exod 20:11–13, yet did not elaborate as to how this fragment fits this passage. Baillet's reading of line 2 needs to be slightly corrected. The third letter appears to be a *bet*. This, however, does not resolve the problem of its identification.

A close scrutiny of the remaining "unidentified fragments" suggests that most of them yield too little text to allow for a positive identification. With this category belong frags. 34, 38–39, 41, 43–45, 47–57, 59–77. Several others contain some legible text of a highly general nature (frag. 42: ‏אלהי[ך אשׁ]ר‏, frag. 58: ‏[היֿ/וה]‏). A few relatively large fragments, frags. 31, 32, 35, and 37 feature phrases found in the scriptural passages used in tefillin. However, the rest of their poorly preserved text does not match the wording of those passages. Finally, there are fragments that can be linked to the biblical verses copied in tefillin (frags. 30 and possibly 46). The following discussion focuses on the two latter categories.

---

412 As discussed below, frag. 37 may contain Deut 5:20–21. My attempts to place these two fragments together were unsuccessful.

"Unidentified Fragments" Matching Type 2 Texts

Frag. 30

On both old and new images frag. 30 is not fully disentangled (Fig. 37). Several unplaced scraps of leather with traces of letters are piled on its left side.[413]

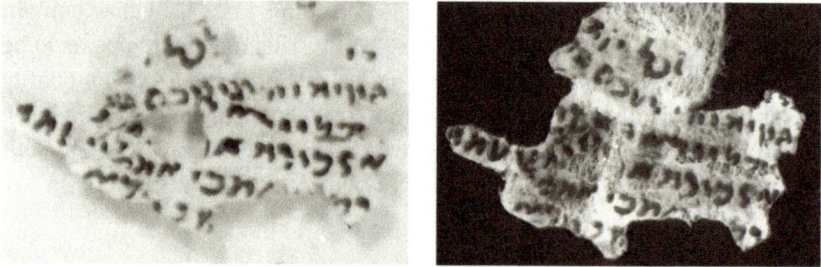

Fig. 37: Frag. 30 on PAM 42.494 (left) and a new infrared image (right; digitally brightened).

DJD Edition		Revised Text
]לֹ[וֹ] [לכל[לֹ	1	ד[בֹּרֹ] יהוה]לכל קה[לכם
]בין יהוה וביניכם ביו[	2	]בין יהוה וביניכם בעֹ]ת ההיא
]מֹ°[[ ] .. אֹוֹרֹיֹרֹ°°[	3	יה]וֹה כי יראתֹ]ם [°°[
]...[ ]אֹנכי והֹאֹרֹ[	4	]אנכי יה אל]היך
]וֹתֹ°[ ]את כי אתם וֹ°[	5	הבר]יֹתֹ הֹזֹאֹת כי אתם]
]הבֹיֹדֹ א[	6	השב]תֹ כבֹדֹ א]ת

Notes to Readings

Line 1]בֹּרֹ[ד. Baillet reads]לֹוֹ[. On the new full-color image traces of a roof, a base, and a vertical stroke are visible. These might suit a small *bet* slightly tilted to the left. The bottom tip of the second letter might belong to a *resh*.

---

413 In the following transcriptions intervals between words have been added to assist the reader.

קה]לכם. Baillet offers no reading here. The new infrared image reveals a *qoph* and a *he*.

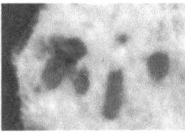

Line 2 בע̇]ת. Baillet sees traces of two letters after the *bet*. On an early image (PAM 42.494, right) these are consistent with an *ayin* – both of its arms are clearly visible. On the new image (left) its right arm alone is extant.

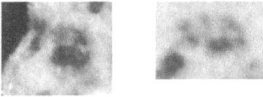

Line 3]∘∘[ם] יראת̇ כי יה]ו̇ה. Baillet was unable to suggest a plausible reading in this line. A *vav* and a *he* are well preserved on the new image.

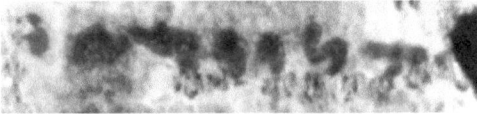

What may appear as a small *lamed* is most likely a medial *kaph* with a serif (cf. medial *kaph* in אנכי[, line 4). Two *vav/yod* letters follow. Next there are a *resh* – its roof is well visible on the images – and a small *aleph*. The following trace shaped as an inverted chevron suits a *tav* (see below discussion of scrap #1 which may yield the missing final *mem*). The interlinear space between lines 2 and 3 preserves traces of two letters:

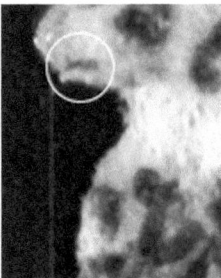

Below I read them as a *yod* and a *he* in light of the presumed context.

Line 4 היך]אלֹ יה. Baillet suggests]וֹהֹאֹר. The fourth letter, which he reads as a *resh*, might also be a lower part of a *lamed* (cf. the second *lamed* in לכל[in line 1 as seen on PAM 42.494 reproduced below). On PAM 42.494 there might be a trace of this *lamed*'s mast:

לכל[(line 1)   A trace of *lamed*'s mast

Line 5 בר]יֹת הֹזֹאֹת. Baillet reads the first letter as a *tav*. According to the recent full-color image (below, left), the vertical stroke with a widened top may rather be a *vav/yod*. On PAM 42.494 (below, right) the gap between the following *tav* and the *aleph* seem to contain traces of two letters. In agreement with the presumed context of this line, these might a *he* and a *zayin*.

אתם. Baillet suggests]ֹתֹיֹ אתם. His last four letters are written on the separate scrap # 4 discussed below.

Line 6 השב]תֹ כבֹד א]ת. Baillet has]א ך[הב]ֹ. The first letter may as well be a *tav* – a little horn at its left upper corner supports this reading. The second letter matches a medial *kaph*, as there is no typical base stroke of the *bet*. The third letter has a roof and a vertical stroke which could suit a *bet*. A letter that might match a *dalet* or a *resh* follows.

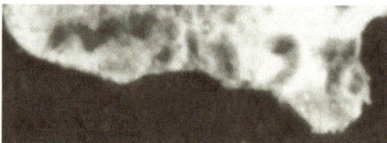

Scraps 1–4

There are several scraps of leather on the left side of frag. 30. On the following image they are tentatively numbered 1–4, though there appear to be more of them (the images do not allow for more precision; Fig. 38):

Fig. 38: Small scraps of Frag. 30 (digitally brightened new full-color image).

#1 This scrap contains a final *mem* and another letter. It could be placed at the end of line 3 where a final *mem* is missing: יה[וֹה כי יראתֹם]ᵒ.

    #2 Once rotated, this scrap yields four letters, [ᵒתֹרᵒ].

#3 It is unclear whether this is a large *shin*, a reversed *gimel*, or something else.

    #4 Baillet reads here [ᵒתוֹ̇ᵒ]. The new images make it clear that the first letter is an *ayin*. This scrap appears to the left of line 5 already on the earlier PAM photographs. However, as Fig. 38 indicates, such a placement is quite uncertain as the edges of the fragments do not match.

Frag. 30: Discussion

If the proposed reading of frag. 30 is correct, its wording can be traced back to Deuteronomy 5:

Deuteronomy	Frag. 30
5:22	1 [האלה ד[בֹ̇רֹ] יהוה]לכל קה]לכם
5:5	2 [אנכי עמד]בין יהוה וביניכם בעֹ̇]ת ההיא להגיד לכם]
5:5	3 [את דבר יה[וֹה כי יראתֹ]ם מפנ[יֹ הֹ]אש ולא עליתם]
5:6	4 [בהר לאמר]אנכי יה אל]היך
5:3?	5 [הבר]יֹ̇ת הֹזֹאת כי אתם]
5:15–16	6 [את יום השב]ת כבֹד א]ת

Frag. 30   **Deuteronomy**

1. [those (words) YHWH s]poke to [your] whole congregat[ion   5:22
2. [I stood]between YHWH and you at [that] t[ime to tell you]   5:5
3. [the words of YH]WH, for [you] were afrai[d of the fire and   5:5
   did not go up]
4. [the mountain saying,] "I am Yah [your]Go[d   5:6
5. [   ]this [cove]nant, for you (or for with them)[5:3?
6. [the sabba]th[day.] Honor [5:15–16

This fragment does not contain a running text of Deuteronomy 5. Rather it deviates from other ancient versions of this chapter in several ways. First, the order
of the verses here is strikingly different. In the MT, verse 22 comes next to the
last of the Ten Commandments. In frag. 30 it precedes the Decalogue. At the
same time, a phrase reminiscent of verse 3 interjects between the reference to
the first commandment and the Sabbath commandment. Second, the presumed
length of lines, suggested by the reconstructed lines 2–3, indicates that frag. 30
could not have accommodated some of the verses listed in the chart above in
their entirety. Such is clearly the case with the lengthy verse 22. The use of the
shortened form of the Tetragrammaton in line 4 may also reflect an attempt to
offer a succinct version of verse 6. Moreover, the fragment apparently omits a
significant amount of text found between the references to what was perceived
by some ancient sources as the first of the Ten Commandments (אנכי יה אל̇[היך,
verse 6)[414] and the Sabbath commandment (verse 15). Third, line 5, הבר[י̊ת̊
הז̊את כי אתם], alluding to Deut 5:3, "it was not with our fathers that the Lord
made this covenant, but with us (הברית הזאת כי אתנו)," suggests a paraphrase
of some kind. The last two words can be vocalized as either כִּי אִתָּם, "for with
them," or as כִּי אַתֶּם, "for you." The former reading would differ rather sharply
from the other versions' emphatic use of the first-person speech here, as in MT's
כי אתנו אנחנו אלה פה כלנו חיים ("but with us, the living, every one of us who
is here today").[415] The latter reading assumes, more plausibly, a second-person
plural address shared by Deut 5:1 and 4–5 (for the language, compare Deut 7:7;

---

414 Thus Philo, *Decal.* 52 ff and Josephus, *Ant.* 3:91. On the divisions of the Decalogue see
Mordechai Breuer, "Dividing the Decalogue into Verses and Commandments," in *The Ten Commandments in History and Tradition*, ed. Ben-Zion Segal and Gerson Levi (Jerusalem: Magnes
Press, 1985), 314–26; Kugel, *Traditions of the Bible*, 641–43.
415 LXX Deut reads here πρὸς ὑμᾶς ὑμεῖς. Carmel McCarthy, *Deuteronomy*, Biblia Hebraica
Quinta 5 (Stuttgart: Deutsche Bibelgesellschaft, 2005), 18, suggests that this is a contextual
harmonization (for 2nd pl. see vv. 1, 4, 5).

11:31; 29:15; see also Deut 4:12: שמעים **אתם** דברים קול and Exod 20:22: **אתם**
(ראיתם כי מן השמים דברתי עמכם).

What is this text? Two suggestions can be made. First, it seems likely that
lines 2–6 contain some kind of abbreviated text of the Decalogue. One may only
speculate whether the wording of line 4 stood for both the first and the second
("do not worship") commandments. It is equally unknown whether lines 4 or 5
made a reference to the third commandment, prohibiting taking up God's name
in vain. Second, the peculiar order of the verses may serve an exegetical purpose. As is well known, the Decalogue lends itself easily to a division into two
broad units according to the voice of the speaker. The first two commandments
are phrased in the first person, whereas the remaining eight refers to God in the
third person. Attentive to this feature, later rabbinic midrash asserts that the
first two commandments were delivered to Israel directly by God, while the rest
were given through the mediation of Moses.[416] As was discussed in Chapter 2,
this exegetical tradition may underlie the arrangement of the Decalogue in
4QRPᵃ (4Q158) 6, 7–8 (cf. also the longer text of Deut 5:1–2 in 4QPhyl G as discussed also in Chapter 2). One wonders whether the placement of verses 22 and
3 in frag. 30 reflects a similar understanding of how the Ten Commandments
were communicated. Indeed, the reference to verse 22 prior to verse 5 in lines
1–3 may establish a "proper" sequence of events: God speaks directly to Israel
and then Moses comes in as a messenger. This order might be re-affirmed by a
reference to Deut 5:3 containing Moses's words in line 5. After the first commandment was delivered by God himself (line 4), Moses began to address Israel.
Naturally, given the broken state of the fragment, this proposal must remain
tentative. At the very least, one can observe that the placement of v. 22 before
v. 5 highlights the divine origin of Moses's pronouncements, while the insertion
of v. 3 after v. 6 seems to identify the Decalogue with the covenant between God
and Israel.

Finally, two further aspects of frag. 30 must be noted. Group III contains a
full running text of Deut 5:1–14 (+Exod 20:11). Thus, some of the Decalogue appears to be represented twice in 8QPhyl. Also, the new reading of frag. 30 adds
two items to the extensive list of variants compiled by Baillet. First, there is the
use of יי instead of יהוה in Deut 5:6, a reading that is otherwise unattested to
in ancient versions of Deuteronomy. Second, while multiple witnesses of Deut
5:22 (MT, as well as 4QDeutⁿ; 4QPhyl B; H; and SamP) read אל כל קהלכם,
frag. 30 has [לכל קה]לכם ([XQPhyl 2 1 reads עם כל קהלכם).

---

416 See note 221.

Frag. 46

The photograph PAM 42.494 indicates that this fragment has two lines. On the new image the second line is absent. It is not impossible that PAM image displays two small fragments placed one above the other. This might explain the small distance between the first letters in these two lines. The transcription below follows Baillet's reading of the first line (including a *yod* shaped as an inverse chevron) and offers a tentative reading of the second line – a *he* or a *tav*.

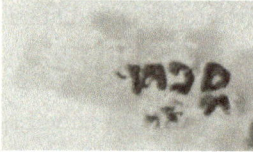

PAM 42.494	New Image (digitally brightened)	Revised Text	
		]ם בֹּיֹדֹ[	1
		]ooהֹ[	2

The sequence of letters found here matches Deut 5:15: ויצאך יהוה אלהיך משם בְּיָד חזקה. This verse is not extant in Group III copying Deuteronomy 5. In fact, as was mentioned earlier, Group III utilizes the wording borrowed from Exod 20:11 as the reason for observing the Sabbath. If the proposed reading is correct, one could tentatively suggest that this fragment belongs with Group III. This would imply that it provided two reasons for keeping the Sabbath found in the two versions of the Decalogue, in Exodus 20 and Deuteronomy 5. The scroll 4QDeut[n] does precisely that, citing first the Deuteronomic justification of the Sabbath observance and then the one found in Exodus.[417]

"Unidentified Fragments" Partially Matching Type 2 Texts

Several of Baillet's large "unidentified fragments" feature some wording that can be matched to scriptural verses included in tefillin and some that has no parallel in these biblical texts.

Frag. 31

On PAM 42.494 frag. 31 appears to be comprised of two long narrow scraps placed near each other. These are numbered on the full-color image below as #1 and #3. The latter image displays the small piece containing the letters הֹם

---

417 See further note 391.

of line 5 as a self-standing scrap of leather, #2. There seems to be little physical justification for placing #1 and #3 together. The shapes of their edges do not match. The same is true for #1 and #2. These observations suggest that line 5 is likely to be an artificial construction and that lines 1–4 and 6–10 may come from different contexts. Still, for an easy comparison the revised transcription below retains Baillet's arrangement of the scraps.

PAM 42.494	New Image (digitally brightened)	DJD Edition		Revised Text	
		]בֹּ֯רׄ יהוהלֹ[	1	]ׄ°°°°°°°°°בׄ[	1
		]ׄ° םׄיׄ°[	2	]° שׄם[	2
		]בֹרֹכֹ[	3	]°רׄ°[	3
		]ׄם כׄיׄ[	4	]°ׄםׄ°[	4
		]חֹלֹתֹֿםֿ[	5	]הלהֹֿםֿ[	5
		]את חקׄ֯יׄוׄ[	6	]את חקׄ֯יׄוׄ[	6
		]כוֹחֹ °° םׄ° [7		]°יׄכׄתׄ°°םׄ°° [7	
		]ׄכׄׄׄ°[	8	]°ׄכׄיׄ°[	8
		]ׄבֹּׄאׄ°[	9	]ׄאׄשֹׁ°[	9
		]ׄוֹׄכֹׄׄ°[	10	]°ׄהׄיׄ°[	10

Notes to Readings

Line 1. Baillet reads]בֹּ֯רׄ יהוהלֹ. While the first letter indeed resembles a *bet* or a medial *kaph*, the rest of the traces can be variously construed.

Line 2. The traces preceding the final *mem* are consistent with a *shin*, not a *yod* (Baillet).

Line 3. Baillet reads]בֹרֹכֹ[. It is however somewhat unclear whether a trace of a roof on PAM 42.494 is actually an ink or a damage to the parchment, as appears to be the case on the full-color image reproduced above.

Line 4. Only a final *mem* appears to be certain here.

Line 5. As suggested above, this line might be an artificial construction by the editor. In any case, the first letter, which Baillet reads as a *khet*, is more consistent with a *he* – its long roof projects to the left. The fourth letter is also probably a *he*, as its left vertical stroke does not extend above the roof as is the case with several *tav* letters in this fragment.

Line 7. On the new images, there is a certain *tav* before the medial *kaph*. As to Baillet's כוח, what he reads as a *khet* is quite different from the *khet* in line 6. Perhaps these are two letters, with the second being a medial *nun*.

Line 9. There are traces of a *shin*, and not a *bet*, in the beginning of the line visible on both old and new images.

Line 10. A *he*, and not a medial *kaph* and a *vav*, is clear on all the images.

Frag. 31: Discussion

While frag. 31 is quite large, the legible text it preserves is rather meager. Moreover, it may well be an assemblage of unrelated scraps. Hence, little can be said about the contents of this fragment. Some of Baillet's readings, such as a form of בר״ך and nouns מ[חֹלֹתֹם (my reconstruction) and כוֹח have no parallel in Types 1 or 2 texts. However, those readings are highly uncertain. The only certain reading in this fragment is]וֹۣוۣקח את[. This construction does not occur in the Types 1 or 2 texts as found in the MT. However, in Group III Deut 10:13 reads חקיו את׳, instead of the MT's ואת חקתיו.[418] While this is a possible match, the rest of the fragment (lines 7–10) does not lend itself easily to a reconstruction with Deuteronomy 10.

Frag. 32

PAM 42.494	New Image (digitally brightened)	DJD Edition		Revised Text	
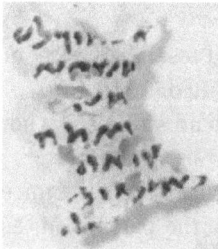	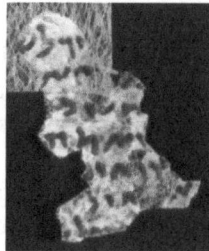	[שׁל אלֹהיך [	1	[שׁל אלֹהיך [	1
		]ׂאׁשׁהֹאׂ[	2	]אׁהׂשׁ°[	2
		]תׁאׂ[	3	]תׂיׂוׂב[	3
		]°°אתׁ°[	4	]אתהׂ°[	4
		]רׁוׂאׁבֹ[	5	]°ۣאۣיۣ°[	5
		]לׂאׁרׁלׁאׁוׂלׂ[	6	]לׁאׁתׂ°°וׂלׂ[	6
		]°לׂ°°[	7	]°לׂ°°[	7

Notes to Readings

Line 2. Baillet's *aleph* is quite uncertain. There is no trace of another letter after the *aleph* in the end of the line.

---

418 In fact, our fragment could also allow for a reading את[חקۣוۣתۣ]יۣ.

Line 3. What Baillet reads as an *aleph* may be a *shin* followed by a *vav*. On the new image a *bet* is visible at the end of the line.

Line 4. The *he* at the end of the line is clear on both old and new images.

Line 5. The proposed transcription is somewhat more cautious than that of Baillet. The second vertical trace in this line appears to be a final letter, perhaps a final *nun*.

Line 6. Baillet's *resh* resembles some of the *tav* letters in 8QPhyl. The following traces are difficult to read.

Frag 32: Discussion

The only legible phrase in line 2 matches several passages included in Type 2 tefillin, such as Deut 5:11 (אלהיך לשוא; cited in Group III) and 6:2 (אלהיך לשמר; cited in Group II). The rest of the text is fragmentary and difficult to match with Deuteronomy 5 or 6.

Frag. 35

I was unable to locate frag. 35 on the new images of 8QPhyl. The few revisions to Baillet's readings suggested below rely on the PAM images. At the end of line 2 a small *yod* and a vertical stroke as in *he* suggest a reading and reconstruction יֿה[וה]. It is not impossible that the third letter in this line is a *dalet*, עבדו את יֿה[וה]. In line 3 the very last letter is consistent with the medial *nun*, another instance of which appears earlier on in this line.

PAM 42.494	Baillet	Revised Text
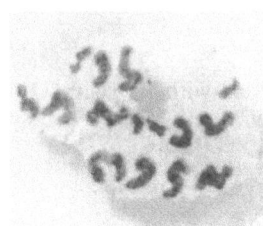	1]° [°לר°[	1]°לר°[ ]°
	2 עבۥואתۥ[	2 עבۥו את יֿהۥ[וה]
	3 אנכיۥ °[	3 אנכי נۥ[ותן]

The wording preserved in line 3 is attested to in Deut 5:31. This verse is partially preserved in Group III, though this particular phrase is not extant there. The phrase עבדו את יֿה[וה] occurs in Exod 12:31. This verse is not included in other tefillin from Qumran.

Frag. 37

New Image (digitally brightened)	DJD Edition	Revised Text
		]° וֹאת[1
	ע]יִֹנִיֹכֹם הרֹ[1	א]להיכם הי[וֹם 2
	שֹֹהרֹיֹעֹ] [° 2	א]שֹׁת רעֹךֹ] 3
	והאלֹכֹ[3	יה]וֹה אל כ]ל קהלכם 4

Notes to Readings

Line 1]° וֹאת[. Baillet offers no transcription for this line. A *vav*, an *aleph*, and a *tav* are clearly visible on the recent images.

Line 2 א]להיכם הי[וֹם. Baillet reads ע]יִֹנִיֹכֹם הרֹ[. A *lamed* and a *he* are certain on the new image. The last letter in this line can be also read as a *vav/ yod*.

Line 3 וֹא]שֹׁת. The second letter appears to have a feature that often distinguishes a *he* from a *tav* in 8QPhyl – its left leg protrudes above the roof. רעֹךֹ]. The shape of the letter next to the *ayin* resembles the top of a final *kaph* (cf. final *kaph* in הניך in Group IV, 14, reproduced here [below, left]).

Tentative Reconstruction with the MT Deut 5:21–22

Lines 3 and 4 in frag. 37 lend themselves to a reconstruction with MT Deut 5:21–22:

]° וֹאת[1

א]להיכם הי[וֹם 2

ולא תחמד א]שֹׁת רעֹ[ך ולא תתאוה בית רעך שדהו ועבדו ואמתו שורו וחמרו וכל אשר לרעך[3

[את הדברים האלה דבר יה]וֹה אל כ]ל קהלכם 4

The reconstructed lines 3–4 suggest a line that is some 65 letters long. Such a line might fit rather well at the bottom of Group III. For instance, the almost complete line 23 there has 62 letters. Group III includes Deut 5:1–14. Hence, one might assume that frag. 37 belongs with its now-lost section containing the rest of Deuteronomy 5. The difficulty with this proposal, however, is that the wording of line 2 in frag. 37 does not match that of the preceding verses of Deuteronomy 5.[419]

8QPhyl: Discussion

The foregoing study of the unidentified segments of text in 8QPhyl contributes to a better understanding of this tefillin in four ways.

First, a close scrutiny of the fragments suggests that, in addition to the biblical passages identified by Baillet, 8QPhyl includes also the following verses:

Deut 5:15 (frag. 46?)
Deut 5:29–33 (Group II, 1–8)
Deut 5:22, 5–6, 3, 15–16 (frag. 30)
Deut 6:9 or 11:20 (frag. 36?)
Deut 10:12 (Group IV, 1?)
Deut 11:1 (Group II, 18–19)

Second, this analysis does not fully eliminate a possibility noted by Cohn that 8QPhyl incorporates text that does not match Types 1 and 2 tefillin from Qumran.[420] The wording of several fragments can be only partially matched with the biblical pericopae copied in Type 2 tefillin (frags. 31, 32, 35, 37). Still, it is not unlikely that the difficulty to read and reconstruct these fragments with Types 1 and 2 passages is a result of their highly fragmentary (and potentially composite) nature and the fact that Exodus and Deuteronomy texts in Groups II–IV often deviate significantly from other textual witnesses.

Third, this study suggests that the fragments assigned to 8QPhyl contain duplicate versions of several biblical passages. Two such duplications are found already in the text identified by Baillet:

a. Deut 10:12–13 (Groups III and IV; on the proposed identification of v. 13 in Group IV see above)
b. Deut 10:21–22 (Groups II and IV)

---

419 As discussed above, frag. 33 may contain Deut 5:20–21. My attempts to place these two fragments together were unsuccessful.
420 Cohn, *Tangled Up*, 72.

The newly-identified text yields further cases of duplication:

c. Deut 5:3, 5–6, copied in full in Group III, appears to be cited in a truncated and rearranged form in frag. 30
d. Deut 6:9 (=11:20) might be cited in both Group I and frag. 36
e. Deut 11:1 appears to be partially copied in Group II, 18–19 (as a direct continuation of Deut 10:20–22) and in Group IV containing much of Deut 11:1–12

Further possible instances of duplication are found in frags. 31, 32, 35, and 37. These are fragments which cannot be fully matched with the Types 1 and 2 pericopae:

f. Deut 5:11 or 6:2 copied in Groups III and II respectively may occur once again in frag. 32
g. Deut 5:21–22 might be cited in frag. 37, while v. 22 (the same phrase) occurs also in frag. 30 (cf. also frag. 33)
h. Deut 5:31 may appear in both Group III and frag. 35
i. Deut 10:13 may be attested for the third time (in addition to Groups II and IV) in frag. 31

A comparison of the better-preserved duplicate texts a, b, and c is instructive.

a. Deut 10:12–13 (MT):

ועתה ישראל מה יהוה אלהיך שאל מעמך כי אם ליראה את יהוה אלהיך ללכת בכל דרכיו
ולאהבה אתו ולעבד את יהוה אלהיך בכל לבבך ובכל נפשך לשמר את מצות יהוה ואת חקתיו
אשר אנכי מצוך היום לטוב לך

Group IV	Group III
1 וֹעַ֯]תה ישראל מה[	1 ועתה ישראל מה
2 יֹהו֯]ה אלהיך שאל מעמך ל[שֹׁמֹ]ר את מצות יהוה ואת חקתיו[	2 יהוה אלהיך שואל מעמך
3 לטוב לך הֹנֹה לֹי֯[הוה א]ֹנֹכי מצוך היֹו֯[ם	3 כי אם ליראה את יהוה אלהֹי֯ך֯
	4 ללכת בדרכ]יו ו[לאהבה אתו ולעבד את יהוה אלהיך
	5 בכל לבבך ובכ]ֹל נפ[שך לשמור אֹת מֹצות דֹיהוה
	אלהיך יאֿת חקיו אשר אנכי מצוך
	6 היום לטוב] לך

b. Deut 10:21–22 (MT):

הוא תהילתך והוא אלהיך אשר עשה אתך את הגדלת ואת הנוראת האלה אשר ראו עיניך
בשבעים נפש ירדו אבתיך מצרימה ועתה שמך יהוה אלהיך ככוכבי השמים לרב

Group IV	**Group II**
7 וֹאֹת הֹנוֹרֹ[אות הא]לֹהֹ אשר ביעינֹיֹכם	[הוא ת]הלתך והו[א אלהיך א]שר עשה אתך את] 16
כי בֹשֹבֹעֹיֹם נפש ירד אבתיך	הגדלת וא[ת
8 מצרי̇ם] ועת[ה שֹמֹית יהוה	[הנו] רֹאות ואש[ר ראו עיניך ב]שבע נפש ירד[וֹ] 17
אליהך ככבי השמים	אבתיך מצרי[מה
9 [לרב]	כככֹבֹי̇ השמֹי[ם לרב [ועת]ה̇ שֹמֹך יה̇]וה 18

In both instances, Group IV appears to modify the texts to a greater extent than Groups II and III. In the case of "c," while Group III presents a running text of Deuteronomy 5, frag. 30 abridges and rearranges it. Thus, not only there are duplicate texts in 8QPhyl, but they also seem to reflect varying degrees of scribal intervention.

Such duplications are unknown in other tefillin and mezuzot from the Judean Desert. How might one account for them? It is possible that 8QPhyl contains remains of more than one tefillin. Such a proposal is not entirely new. As was noted in the introduction to this chapter, Yadin suggested that Group I, featuring four biblical passages prescribed for tefillin by the later rabbinic halakhah, is a distinct tefillin unit, an "arm tefillin," while the rest of 8QPhyl belongs to a "head tefillin." Against Yadin, Baillet argued that Groups I and II–IV, written by the same scribe, complement each other, while Adler supported Yadin by adducing the MT-like textual profile of Group I vis-à-vis Groups II–IV which often deviate from the MT. The presence of a small frag. 36 citing Deut 6:9 (or 11:20) – duplicating a passage found in 8QPhyl I – lends some support to Yadin's suggestion. At the same time, the rest of the duplications listed above involve Type 2 passages from Deuteronomy 5, 10, and 11. In light of these, if Yadin's proposal were to be maintained, one would have to assume that, in addition to his Type 1 "arm tefillin" (Group I), 8QPhyl contains also remains of two Type 2 tefillin. Alternatively, accepting Baillet's argument that (some of) Type 2 texts were intended to complement 8QPhyl I, two Type 2 tefillin can be posited.[421] In either of these two scenarios, one might speculate that Group IV and frag. 30, with their distinctly "revisionist" approach to the biblical text, belong to the same tefillin. It is not unlikely that the aforementioned frags. 31,

---

421 One could probably harmonize Yadin and Adler's observations with those of Baillet by speculating that Group I's distinct textual profile reflects a special "status" accorded by its scribe to the Type 1 texts. Or, perhaps, it was a "generic" tefillin slip, one that had been prepared separately and was later expanded by the same scribe (perhaps upon customer's request) with additional slips including Type 2 passages. The striking difference in their textual profiles may have to do with the *Vorlagen* utilized for these two tasks or this scribe's more facilitative approach to Type 2 texts.

32, 33, 35, and 37, featuring some unidentified text, are to be grouped with them as well.

This leads me to the fourth contribution of this study to a better understanding of 8QPhyl: it highlights the wide array of scribal strategies in Groups II–IV and frag. 30. These include: (a) stringing together of thematically linked biblical passages, involving both law and narrative (Groups II and IV), (b) extensive paraphrase (Group IV), (c) additions, including a brief doxology in Group IV, and (d) omission and reordering in frag. 30. As was discussed in Chapter 2, all these scribal techniques are attested to in other copies of Exodus and Deuteronomy from Qumran, especially in such "revisionist" or "facilitative" texts as the 4QRewritten Pentateuch scrolls. In particular, one could mention the rearrangement of the Decalogue in 4QRP[a] (4Q158), the extended "Song of Miriam" in 4QRP[c] (4Q365), and the juxtaposition of the thematically related passages dealing with Sukkoth in 4QRP[d] (4Q366). As is well known, 4QRewritten Pentateuch texts were initially classified as Rewritten Bible works. The affinities between tefillin/mezuzot and Rewritten Bible have been highlighted by Brooke (see Chapter 2).[422] In his detailed study of variant readings found in tefillin from Cave 4, he refers to 8QPhyl only occasionally. However, it seems that of all the published tefillin and mezuzot from the Judean Desert, it is 8QPhyl (especially, Group IV and frag. 30), with its juxtaposition of related texts, extensive paraphrase, abridgement, and rearrangement, that comes closest to the realm of the Rewritten Bible texts, standing between what Molly Zahn recently described as a "revision" of a text and a "reuse" thereof.[423] I do not wish to argue here that 8QPhyl is to be classified as a Rewritten Bible. Rather, to my mind, all this underscores Tov's observation (see Chapter 2) that, as biblical texts, Qumran tefillin mirror the variety of texts reflected in biblical manuscripts found among the Dead Sea Scrolls, including such "border-line" texts as 4QReworked Pentateuch.

---

422 Brooke, "Deuteronomy 5–6."
423 Molly Zahn, *Genres of Rewriting in Second Temple Judaism: Scribal Composition and Transmission* (Cambridge: Cambridge University Press, 2020), 28–55. I am grateful to Prof. Zahn for sharing with me a copy of her book prior to its publication.

Conclusion

Growing out of an earlier research on several fully and partially undeciphered tefillin and mezuzot from the Judean Desert, this study sought to answer three questions.[424] First, I wanted to find out whether other published tefillin and mezuzot contain substantial segments of text where further work could shed new light on their contents. As this monograph indicates, they certainly do! Of the six texts studied here, three in particular fall into this category. Thus, in 1QPhyl a fresh analysis assisted by full-color images allowed me to read and identify some ten fragments. Also, a scrutiny of the imprints of letters in 4QPhyl L revealed a stretch of text that is no more extant on the parchment. Finally, a detailed study of 8QPhyl led to several new identifications, including a remarkable fragment containing what appears to be an abridged and rearranged text of the Deuteronomic Decalogue.

My earlier work on 4QPhyl T, 4QPhyl U, and Mur5 – two of which are revisited here with new proposals illuminating their reconstruction (4QPhyl T), method of folding (4QPhyl T), and reading (4QPhyl U) – suggested the second question that guided this study. These fragments, closely resembling slips of tefillin and mezuzot, feature texts that do not match (or, at least, do not fully match) the familiar verses from Exodus 12–13 and Deuteronomy 5–6, 10–11. While working on the neglected fragments of the published tefillin and mezuzot, I wondered whether any of them contains anything besides these biblical passages, be it a non-biblical text or another scriptural pericope, as is the case with 4QPhyl N yielding verses from Deuteronomy 32. Overall, my sifting of the published tefillin and mezuzot reveals no certain instances of a use of any texts outside of the aforementioned Type 2 range of scriptural verses.[425] There is,

---

424 See bibliography provided in notes 15–16.

425 This is possibly true also for the slip XQPhyl 4. Yadin, the editor of XQPhyl, was unable to decipher it. Still, he tentatively identified several phrases inscribed on its recto as belonging to Exodus 13 (Yadin, *Tefillin from Qumran*, 30–31). Baillet concurred and offered a few improvements to Yadin's readings (Baillet, "Nouveaux phylactères de Qumran," 413–14). Unlike most of the fragments studied in his volume, there are no recent images of this slip. Moreover, the images included in Yadin's edition are unavailable in an electronic form. An inspection of the printed photographs seems to support Yadin's readings in lines 6–8. In the beginning of line 6 he reads תכל מצת (Exod 13:6: תאכל מצת). Line 7 opens with חמץ לא יראה לך (Exod 13:7; Yadin read a final *kaph* in לך, but the photograph indicates a non-final letter). In both cases, the remaining traces on the image do not lend themselves easily to a reconstruction with Exod 13:6–7. Line 8 according to Yadin begins with ב]צאתי ממצרים (Exod 13:8). Baillet was able to match more letters visible in this line with v. 8. He proposed that the line ends with למען of the same verse. I am less certain about Yadin and Baillet's suggestions for lines 1–5, though רחם (Yadin) in line 1 appears to be likely. Neither Yadin nor Baillet offered a reading of the

https://doi.org/10.1515/9783110725377-010

however, a caveat to this observation. Several fragments of 8QPhyl only partially align with the Exodus and Deuteronomy passages included in Qumran tefillin. This (or, better, these) tefillin, however, often deviates from other known ancient versions of Exodus and Deuteronomy. Hence, it is possible that the aberrant wording of these fragments reflects this scribe's tampering with the familiar Type 2 biblical texts. Perhaps, this is true also in the case of the non-matching line in 4QMez C, frag. 2.

The third question I sought to explore as I searched for the undeciphered fragments of the published tefillin and mezuzot had to do with the kinds of texts of Exodus and Deuteronomy they attest to. Earlier studies have noted the diversity of the textual profiles in Qumran tefillin and mezuzot, mirroring the textual variety exhibited by the biblical scrolls from Qumran. This study affirms and, hopefully, deepens our appreciation for the wealth of scribal techniques reflected in these texts, particularly in 8QPhyl. Groups II–IV and frag. 30 of this/these tefillin feature paraphrase, abbreviation, rearrangement, and juxtaposition of thematically related passages – the kinds of scribal interventions abundantly attested to in the Exodus and Deuteronomy texts from the 4QReworked Pentateuch scrolls. In fact, just like the latter scrolls have significantly expanded our perceptions of the limits of variation in the authoritative scriptural texts in Second Temple times, so do the fragments of 8QPhyl push the boundaries of what could qualify as a tefillin text in this period.

As was suggested in the introduction, this monograph is by no means a comprehensive study of tefillin and mezuzot from Qumran. After all, some nine tefillin await to be unfolded, deciphered, and published. They may shed new light on each and every aspect of these remarkable objects: the craftmanship of the cases, the scribal practices, and the contents of the slips. However, these unfolded tefillin are not the only feature of the corpus that calls for further exploration. Though much work has already been done to integrate tefillin and mezuzot from the Judean Desert into the biblical scholarship, they still remain on its margins. One area where they hold a great promise is the study of the early reception of Exodus and Deuteronomy.[426] Indeed, these artifacts offer a rare window into the ways in which these books were read and understood in Second Temple times. It is my hope that this volume shedding new light on these precious texts contributes to the quest for the complex textual histories of Exodus and Deuteronomy in the Second Temple period.

---

verso. As this book is submitted for publication, my long negotiations to have the negatives of XQPhyl 4 scanned and made available for an examination remain unsuccessful.

426 For the relevant bibliography see Chapter 2.

Bibliography

Abegg, Martin. "Qumran Scribal Practice: Won Moor Thyme." In *Scribal Practice, Text and Canon in the Dead Sea Scrolls: Essays in Memory of Peter W. Flint*, edited by John J. Collins and Ananda Geyser-Fouché, 175–204. STDJ 130. Leiden: Brill, 2019.

Abegg, Martin. "Scribal Practice and the Pony in the Manure Pile." In *Reading the Bible in Ancient Traditions and Modern Editions: Studies in Memory of Peter W. Flint*, edited by Andrew B. Perrin, Kyung S. Baek, and Daniel K. Falk, 65–88. Atlanta: SBL Press, 2017.

Ableman, Oren. "Newly Identified Pentateuchal Fragments: 4QExod^G (4Q18, Exod 12:51–13:3), 4QDeut^{K3} (4Q38B, Deut 30:13–18)." *RevQ* 30 (2018): 91–100.

Adler, Yonatan. "A Tefillin Case from the Cave of the Scrolls (Cave 34) at Naḥal Ṣeʾelim." In *the Highland's Depth, Ephraim Range and Binyamin Research Studies* 7 (2017): 145–62 (Hebrew).

Adler, Yonatan. "A Typological Distinction between Two Types of Tefillin Cases from Qumran." *Judea and Samaria Research Studies* 28 (2019): 81–99.

Adler, Yonatan. "Identifying Sectarian Characteristics in the Phylacteries from Qumran." *RevQ* 23 (2007): 79–92.

Adler, Yonatan. "Remains of Tefillin from Naḥal Ṣeʾelim (Wadi Seiyal): A Leather Case and Two Inscribed Fragments (34Se 1 A–B): With Paleographic Analysis by Ada Yardeni." *DSD* 24 (2017): 112–37.

Adler, Yonatan. "The Content and Order of the Scriptural Passages in Tefillin: A Reexamination of the Early Rabbinic Sources in Light of the Evidence from the Judean Desert." In *Halakhah in Light of Epigraphy*, edited by Albert Baumgarten et al., 205–30. Göttingen: Vandenhoeck & Ruprecht, 2010.

Adler, Yonatan. "The Distribution of Tefillin Finds among the Judean Desert Caves." In *The Caves of Qumran: Proceedings of the International Conference, Lugano 2014*, edited by Marcello Fidanzio, 161–73. STDJ 118. Leiden: Brill, 2016.

Baillet, Maurice. "Nouveaux phylactères de Qumran (XQ Phyl 1–4): à propos d'une édition récente." *RevQ* 7 (1970): 403–15.

Becker, Andrea. "Phylakterion." In *Brill's New Pauly Encyclopedia of the Ancient World*, edited by Helmuth Schneider et al., 11:206–207. Leiden: Brill, 2007.

Bernstein, Moshe. "What Has Happened to the Laws? The Treatment of Legal Material in 4QReworked Pentateuch." *DSD* 15 (2008): 24–49.

Blumell, Lincoln H. "A Proposal for a New LXX Text among the Cave 7 Fragments." *RevQ* 29 (2017): 105–17.

Bohak, Gideon. "Mezuzot with Magical Additions from the Cairo Genizah." *Dine Israel* 26–27 (2009): 387–403 (Hebrew).

Breuer, Mordechai. "Dividing the Decalogue into Verses and Commandments." In *The Ten Commandments in History and Tradition*, edited by Ben-Zion Segal and Gerson Levi, 314–26. Jerusalem: Magnes Press, 1985.

Brooke, George J. "Between Scroll and Codex? Reconsidering the Qumran Opisthographs." In *On Stone and Scroll: Essays in Honour of Graham Ivor Davies*, edited by James K. Aitken et al., 123–38. Berlin: De Gruyter, 2011.

Brooke, George J. "Deuteronomy 5–6 in the Phylacteries from Qumran Cave 4." In *Emanuel: Studies in the Hebrew Bible, Septuagint, and the Dead Sea Scrolls in Honour of Emanuel Tov*, edited by Shalom Paul et al., 57–70. SVT 94. Leiden: Brill, 2003.

https://doi.org/10.1515/9783110725377-011

Brooke, George J. "E Pluribus Unum: Textual Variety and Definitive Interpretation in the Qumran Scrolls." In *The Dead Sea Scrolls in Their Historical Context*, edited by Timothy H. Lim et al., 107–22. Edinburgh: T&T Clark, 2000.

Brooke, George J. "The Qumran Scrolls and the Demise of the Distinction between Lower and Higher Criticism." In *Reading the Dead Sea Scrolls: Essays in Method*, 1–17. Early Judaism and Its Literature 39. Atlanta: SBL, 2013.

Brooke, George J. "The Rewritten Law, Prophets and Psalms: Issues for Understanding the Text of the Bible." In *The Hebrew Bible and the Judaean Desert Discoveries*, edited by Edward D. Herbert and Emanuel Tov, 31–40. London: British Library, 2002.

Busa, Anna. *Die Phylakterien von Qumran (4Q128.129.135.137) aus der Heidelberger Papyrussammlung*. Heidelberg: Universitätsverlag Winter, 2015.

Cohen, Naomi G. "On the Special Laws 1–4." In *Outside the Bible: Ancient Jewish Writings Related to Scripture*, edited by Louis H. Feldman et al., 1:1033–1133. Philadelphia: JPS, 2013.

Cohen, Naomi G. "Philo's Tefillin." *Proceedings of the World Congress of Jewish Studies: Division A: The Period of the Bible*, 1985, 196–206.

Cohn, Yehudah. "Rabbenu Tam's Tefillin: An Ancient Tradition or the Product of Medieval Exegesis?" *Jewish Studies Quarterly* 14 (2007): 319–27.

Cohn, Yehudah. "Reading Material Features of Qumran Tefillin and Mezuzot." In *Material Aspects of Reading in Ancient and Medieval Cultures*, edited by Anna Krauß, Jonas Leipziger, and Friederike Schücking-Jungblut, 89–100. Materiale Textkulturen 26. Berlin: De Gruyter, 2020.

Cohn, Yehudah. *Tangled Up in Text: Tefillin and the Ancient World*. Providence: Brown University, 2008.

Cohn, Yehudah. "Were Tefillin Phylacteries?" *JJS* 59 (2008): 39–61.

Dahmen, Ulrich. "Das Deuteronomium in Qumran." In *Das Deuteronomium*, edited by Georg Braulik, 269–310. OBS 23. Frankfurt am Main: Peter Lang, 2003.

Dahmen, Ulrich. "Neu identifizierte Fragmente in den 'Deuteronomium'-Handschriften vom Toten Meer." *RevQ* 20 (2002): 571–81.

Davila, James R. "Exodus, Book of." In *The Encyclopedia of the Dead Sea Scrolls*, edited by Lawrence H. Schiffman and James C. VanderKam, 1:277–79. New York: Oxford University Press, 2000.

Davis, Kipp. "Caves of Dispute: Patterns of Correspondence and Suspicion in the Post-2002 'Dead Sea Scrolls' Fragments." *DSD* 24 (2017): 229–70.

Davis, Kipp, Ira Rabin, Ines Feldman, Myriam Krutzsch, Hasia Rimon, Årstein Justnes, Torleif Elgvin, and Michael Langlois. "Nine Dubious 'Dead Sea Scrolls' Fragments from the Twenty-First Century." *DSD* 24 (2017): 189–28.

Doering, Lutz. "Excerpted Tests in Second Temple Judaism: A Survey of the Evidence." In *Selecta Colligere, II: Beiträge zur Technik des sammelns und kompilierens griechischer Texte von der Antike bis zum Humanismus*, edited by Rosa M. Piccione and Matthias Perkams, 1–38. Hellenica 18. Alessandria: Ediziioni dell'Orso, 2005.

Duncan, Julie A. "Deuteronomy, Book of." In *Encyclopedia of the Dead Sea Scrolls*, edited by Lawrence H. Schiffman and James C. Vanderkam, 1:198–202. Oxford: Oxford University Press, 2000.

Duncan, Julie A. "Excerpted Texts of 'Deuteronomy' at Qumran." *RevQ* 18 (1997): 43–62.

Elgvin, Torleif, and Michael Langlois. "Looking Back: (More) Dead Sea Scrolls Forgeries in The Schøyen Collection." *RevQ* 31 (2019): 111–33.

Eshel, Esther. "4QDeut^n – A Text That Has Undergone Harmonistic Editing." *HUCA* 62 (1991): 117–54.

Eshel, Esther, and Hanan Eshel. "A Preliminary Report on Seven New Fragments from Qumran." *Meghillot* 5–6 (2007): 271–78 (Hebrew).

Eshel, Esther, Hanan Eshel, and Armin Lange. "'Hear, O Israel' in Gold: An Ancient Amulet from Halbturn in Austria." *JAJ* 1 (2010): 43–64.

Falk, Daniel. "Liturgical Texts." In *T&T Clark Companion to the Dead Sea Scrolls*, edited by George J. Brooke and Charlotte Hempel, 423–34. London: T&T Clark, 2019.

Falk, Daniel. "Material Aspects of Prayer Manuscripts at Qumran." In *Literature or Liturgy*, edited by Clemens Leonhard and Hermut Löhr, 33–87. Tübingen: Mohr Siebeck, 2014.

Feldman, Ariel. "Deuteronomy in the Texts from the Judean Desert." In *Oxford Handbook of Deuteronomy*, edited by Don C. Benjamin. Oxford University Press, 2020. https://www.oxfordhandbooks.com/view/10.1093/oxfordhb/9780190273552.001.0001/oxfordhb-9780190273552-e-22.

Feldman, Ariel. "On Amulets, Apotropaic Prayers, and Phylacteries: The Contribution of Three New Texts from the Judean Desert." In *Petitioners, Penitents, and Poets*, edited by Timothy J. Sandoval and Ariel Feldman, 169–98. De Gruyter, 2020.

Feldman, Ariel. "The Sinai Revelation According to 4Q377 (Apocryphal Pentateuch B)." *DSD* 18 (2011): 155–72.

Feldman, Ariel. "The Song of Miriam (4Q365 6a ii + 6c 1–7) Revisited." *JBL* 132 (2013): 905–11.

Feldman, Ariel, and Faina Feldman. "4Q147: An Amulet?" *DSD* 26 (2019): 1–29.

Feldman, Ariel, and Faina Feldman. "4Q148 (4QPhylactère U): Another Amulet from Qumran?" *JSJ* 50 (2019): 197–222.

Feldman, Ariel, and Faina Feldman. "Is Mur 5 a Mezuzah?" *RevQ* 32 (2019): 291–98.

Feldman, Ariel, and Tal Feldman. "4Q150 (4QMez B) and 8Q4 (8QMez) Revisited." *RevQ* 33 (2021): 121–38.

Fridman, Rachel. "Searching for Holiness: The Song of the Sea in the Bible and in the Liturgy." In *Sanctification*, edited by David Birnbaum and Benjamin Blech, 211–22. New York: New Paradigm Matrix, 2015.

Goren, Shelomo. "The Tefillin from the Judean Desert in Light of Halakhah." In *Torat Ha-Moadim*, 496–510. Tel-Aviv: Abraham Zioni, 1964 (Hebrew).

Gruen, Erich S. "The Letter of Aristeas." In *Outside the Bible: Ancient Jewish Writings Related to Scripture*, edited by Louis H. Feldman et al., 3:2711–68. Philadelphia: JPS, 2013.

Habermann, Abraham M. "On Ancient Tefillin." *Eretz-Israel* 3 (1954): 174–77 (Hebrew).

Hendel, Ronald. "2.2.2 Masoretic Texts and Ancient Texts Close to MT." In *Textual History of the Bible*, edited by Armin Lange. Brill, 2020. http://dx.doi.org.ezproxy.tcu.edu/10.1163/2452-4107_thb_COM_0002020501.

Hendel, Ronald. "Assessing the Text-Critical Theories of the Hebrew Bible after Qumran." In *The Oxford Handbook of the Dead Sea Scrolls*, edited by John J. Collins and Timothy H. Lim, 281–302. Oxford: Oxford University Press, 2010.

Hendel, Ronald. *Steps to a New Edition of the Hebrew Bible*. Text-Critical Studies. Atlanta: SBL, 2016.

Himbaza, Innocent. "Le décalogue de Papyrus Nash, Philon, 4QPhyl G, 8QPhyl 3 et 4QMez A." *RevQ* 20 (2002): 411–28.

Ilan, Tal. *Lexicon of Jewish Names in Late Antiquity: Part I: Palestine 330 BCE-200 CE*. TSAJ 91. Tübingen: Mohr Siebeck, 2002.

Jansson, Eva-Maria. "The Magic of the Mezuzah in Rabbinic Literature." *Nordisk Judaistik/ Scandinavian Jewish Studies* 15 (1994): 51–66.
Jansson, Eva-Maria. *The Message of a Mitsvah: The Mezuzah in Rabbinic Literature*. Lund: Novapress, 1999.
Jastram, Nathan. "2.2.5.1 Tefillin and Mezuzot." In *Textual History of the Bible*, edited by Armin Lange. Brill, 2020. http://dx.doi.org.ezproxy.tcu.edu/10.1163/2452-4107_thb_ COM_0002020501.
Jastram, Nathan. "A Comparison of Two 'Proto-Samaritan' Texts from Qumran: 4QpaleoExodM and 4QNumB." *DSD* 5 (1998): 264–89.
Kartveit, Magnar. "2.2.4.2 Exodus." In *Textual History of the Bible*, edited by Armin Lange. Brill, 2020. http://dx.doi.org.ezproxy.tcu.edu/10.1163/2452-4107_thb_COM_ 0002020402.
Kartveit, Magnar. *The Origin of the Samaritans*. Leiden: Brill, 2009.
Kugel, James L. *Traditions of the Bible: A Guide to the Bible as It Was at the Start of the Common Era*. Cambridge: Harvard University Press, 1998.
Kuhn, Karl Georg. *Phylakterien aus der Höhle 4 von Qumran*. Heidelberg: Carl Winter, 1957.
Lange, Armin. "2.2.1 Ancient, Late Ancient, and Early Medieval Manuscript Evidence." In *Textual History of the Bible*, edited by Armin Lange. Brill, 2020. http:// dx.doi.org.ezproxy.tcu.edu/10.1163/2452-4107_thb_COM_0002020100.
Lange, Armin. *Handbuch der Textfunde vom Toten Meer: Band 1: Die Handschriften biblischer Bücher von Qumran und den anderen Fundorten*. Tübingen: Mohr Siebeck, 2009.
Lange, Armin. "The Shema Israel in Second Temple Judaism." *JAJ* 1 (2010): 207–14.
Lange, Armin. "'They Confirmed the Reading' (y. Ta'an. 4.68a): The Textual Standardization of Jewish Scriptures in Second Temple Era." In *From Qumran to Aleppo*, edited by Armin Lange, Matthias Weigold, and József Zsengellér, 29–80. Göttingen: Vandenhoeck & Ruprecht, 2009.
Lapin, Hayim. "The Origins and Development of the Rabbinic Movement in the Land of Israel." In *The Cambridge History of Judaism: Volume 4: The Late Roman-Rabbinic Period*, edited by Steven T. Katz, 4:206–29. The Cambridge History of Judaism. Cambridge: Cambridge University Press, 2006.
Lim, Timothy H. "Deuteronomy in the Judaism of the Second Temple Period." In *Deuteronomy in the New Testament*, edited by Maarten J. J. Menken and Steve Moyise, 6–26. London: T&T Clark, 2007.
Lincicum, David. "St. Paul's Deuteronomy: The End of the Pentateuch and the Apostle to the Gentiles in Second Temple Jewish Context." PhD diss., University of Oxford, 2009.
Longacre, Drew. "A Contextualized Approach to the Hebrew Dead Sea Scrolls Containing Exodus." PhD diss., University of Birmingham, 2014.
Martin, Gary D. *Multiple Originals: New Approaches to Hebrew Bible Textual Criticism*. SBL Text-Critical Studies 7. Leiden: Brill, 2011.
McCarthy, Carmel. *Deuteronomy*. Biblia Hebraica Quinta 5. Stuttgart: Deutsche Bibelgesellschaft, 2005.
Nakman, David. "Tefillin and Mezuzot at Qumran." In *The Qumran Scrolls and Their World*, edited by Menahem Kister, 2:143–55. Between Bible and Mishnah. Jerusalem: Yad Ben-Zvi, 2009 (Hebrew).
Nakman, David. "The Contents and the Order of the Biblical Sections in the Tefillin from Qumran and Rabbinic Halakhah." *Cathedra* 112 (2004): 19–44 (Hebrew).
Parker, Benjamin H. "Fingerprinting the Scribes: Patterns of Scribal Practice in the Biblical Texts from the Judean Desert, with Special Reference to the Tefillin." In *Celebrating the*

Dead Sea Scrolls: A Canadian Contribution, edited by Peter W. Flint, Jean Duhaime, and Kyung S. Baeck, 77–100. Early Judaism and Its Literature 30. Atlanta: SBL, 2011.

Perkins, Larry. "2.4.1.2 Exodus." In *Textual History of the Bible*, edited by Armin Lange. Brill, 2020. http://dx.doi.org.ezproxy.tcu.edu/10.1163/2452-4107_thb_COM_0002040102.

Perkins, Larry. "Deuteronomy." In *T&T Clark Companion to the Septuagint*, edited by James K. Aitken, 68–85. London: T&T Clark, 2015.

Porten, Bezalel, and Ada Yardeni. *Textbook of Aramaic Documents from Ancient Egypt: Volume 3: Literature, Accounts, Lists*. Jerusalem: Hebrew University, 1993.

Puech, Émile. "Identification de nouveaux manuscrits bibliques: Deutéronome et Proverbes dans les debris de la Grotte 4." *RevQ* 20 (2003): 121–26.

Puech, Émile. "Les fragments de Papyrus 7Q6 1–2, 7Q9 et 7Q7 = Pap7QLXXDt." *RevQ* 29 (2017): 119–27.

Pummer, Reinhard. *The Samaritans: A Profile*. Grand Rapids: Eerdmans, 2016.

Qimron, Elisha. *The Hebrew Writings from Qumran: A Composite Edition*. Tel-Aviv: published electronically, 2020 (Hebrew).

Rabinowitz, Louis Isaac. "Mezuzah." In *Encyclopedia Judaica*, edited by Michael Berenbaum and Fred Skolnik, 14:156–57. Detroit: Macmillan, 2007.

Rabinowitz, Louis Isaac. "Tefillin." In *Encyclopedia Judaica*, edited by Michael Berenbaum and Fred Skolnik, 2nd edition., 19:577–80. Detroit: Macmillan, 2007.

Reed, Stephen. "Physical Features of Excerpted Torah Texts." In *Jewish and Christian Scripture as Artifact and Canon*, edited by Craig A. Evans and H. Daniel Zacharias, 82–103. London: T&T Clark, 2009.

Rofé, Alexander. "Deuteronomy 5.28–6.1: Composition and Text in the Light of Deuteronomic Style and Three Tefillin from Qumran (4Q128, 129, 137)." In *Deuteronomy: Issues and Interpretation*, 25–36. London: T&T Clark, 2002.

Rofé, Alexander. "The End of the Song of Moses (Deuteronomy 32.43)." In *Deuteronomy: Issues and Interpretation*, 47–54. London: T&T Clark, 2002.

Rothstein, David. "From Bible to Murabbaʿat: Studies in the Literary, Textual and Scribal Features of Phylacteries and Mezuzot in Ancient Israel and Early Judaism." PhD diss., University of California, Los Angeles, 1992.

Salvesen, Alison. "Exodus." In *T&T Clark Companion to the Septuagint*, edited by James K. Aitken, 29–42. London: T&T Clark, 2015.

Sarna, Nahum. *Exodus*. The JPS Torah Commentary. Philadelphia: JPS, 2003.

Schiffman, Lawrence H. "Phylacteries and Mezuzot." In *Encyclopedia of the Dead Sea Scrolls*, edited by Lawrence H. Schiffman and James C. VanderKam, 2:675–77. Oxford: Oxford University Press, 2000.

Schneider, Heinrich. "Der Dekalog in den Phylakterien von Qumrân." *Biblische Zeitschrift* 3 (1959): 18–31.

Schorch, Stefan. "The Samaritan Version of Deuteronomy and the Origin of Deuteronomy." In *Samaria, Samarians, Samaritans: Studies on Bible, History and Linguistics*, edited by József Zsengellér, 23–37. Studia Samaritana 6. Berlin: De Gruyter, 2011.

Segal, Michael. "4QReworked Pentateuch or 4QPentateuch?" In *The Dead Sea Scrolls: Fifty Years After Their Discovery*, edited by Lawrence H. Schiffman, Emanuel Tov, and James C. VanderKam, 391–99. Jerusalem: Israel Exploration Society, 2000.

Segal, Michael. "Biblical Exegesis in 4Q158: Techniques and Genre." *Textus* 19 (1998): 45–62.

Segal, Michael. "The Text of the Hebrew Bible in Light of the Dead Sea Scrolls." *Materia Giudaica* 12 (2007): 5–20.

Stegemann, Hartmut, and Jürgen Becker. "Zum Text von Fragment 5 Aus Wadi Murabba'at." *RevQ* 3 (1961): 443–48.

Stökl Ben Ezra, Daniel. "Paleographical Observations Regarding 1Q5 – One or Several Scrolls?" In *Qumran Cave 1 Revisited*, edited by Daniel K. Falk, 245–57. STDJ 91. Leiden: Brill, 2010.

Strawn, Brent. "Excerpted Manuscripts at Qumran: Their Significance for the History of the Hebrew Bible and the Socio-Religious History of the Qumran Community and Its Literature." In *The Bible and the Dead Sea Scrolls: Volume 2: The Dead Sea Scrolls and the Qumran Community*, edited by James H. Charlesworth, 107–67. Waco: Baylor University Press, 2006.

Strawn, Brent. "Excerpted Non-Biblical Texts." In *Qumran Studies: New Approaches, New Questions*, edited by Michael Thomas and Brent Strawn, 65–123. Grand Rapids: Eerdmans, 2007.

Strugnell, John. "Notes en marge du volume V des 'Discoveries in the Judaean Desert of Jordan.'" *RevQ* 2 (1970): 163–276.

Teeter, David Andrew. *Scribal Laws: Exegetical Variation in the Textual Transmission of Biblical Law in the Late Second Temple Period*. FAT 92. Tübingen: Mohr Siebeck, 2014.

Tigay, Jeffrey H. "On the Meaning of T(W)TPT." *JBL* 101 (1982): 321–31.

Tigay, Jeffrey H. "On the Term Phylacteries (Matt 23:5)." *HTR* 72 (1979): 45–53.

Tigay, Jeffrey H. "Tefillin." In *Encyclopaedia Biblica*, 8:883–95. Jerusalem: Mosad Bialik, 1982 (Hebrew).

Tigay, Jeffrey H., and Marvin H. Pope. "A Description of Baal." *Ugarit-Forschungen* 3 (1971): 117–30.

Tigchelaar, Eibert. "A Forgotten Qumran Cave 4 'Deuteronomy' Fragment (4Q38D=4QDeut^u)." *RevQ* 23 (2008): 525–28.

Tigchelaar, Eibert. "A Provisional List of Unprovenanced, Twenty-First Century, Dead Sea Scrolls-Like Fragments." *DSD* 24 (2017): 173–88.

Tigchelaar, Eibert. "Assessing Emanuel Tov's Qumran Scribal Practice." In *The Dead Sea Scrolls: Transmission of Traditions and Production of Texts*, edited by Sarianna Metso, Hindy Najman, and Eileen Schuller, 173–207. STDJ 92. Leiden: Brill, 2010.

Tigchelaar, Eibert. "Minuscula Qumranica I." *RevQ* 21 (2004): 643–48.

Tigchelaar, Eibert. "On the Unidentified Fragments of DJD XXXIII and PAM 43.680: A New Manuscript of 4QNarrative and Poetic Composition, and Fragments of 4Q13, 4Q269, 4Q525 and 4QSb(?)." *RevQ* 21 (2004): 477–85.

Tov, Emanuel. "Excerpted and Abbreviated Biblical Texts from Qumran." In *Hebrew Bible, Greek Bible, and Qumran: Collected Essays*, 27–41. TSAJ 121. Tübingen: Mohr Siebeck, 2008.

Tov, Emanuel. "From Popular Jewish LXX-SP Texts to Separate Sectarian Texts: Insights from the Dead Sea Scrolls." In *The Samaritan Pentateuch and the Dead Sea Scrolls*, edited by Michael Langlois, 19–40. CBET 94. Leuven: Peters, 2019.

Tov, Emanuel. "'Proto-Masoretic,' 'Pre-Masoretic,' 'Semi-Masoretic,' and 'Masoretic': A Study in Terminology and Textual Theory." In *Textual Developments: Collected Essays, Volume 4*, 195–213. VTS 181. Leiden: Brill, 2019.

Tov, Emanuel. *Revised Lists of the Texts from the Judaean Desert*. Leiden: Brill, 2009.

Tov, Emanuel. *Scribal Practices and Approaches Reflected in the Texts Found in the Judean Desert*. STDJ 54. Leiden: Brill, 2004.

Tov, Emanuel. "Tefillin of Different Origin from Qumran." In *A Light for Jacob: Study in the Bible and the Dead Sea Scrolls*, edited by Yair Hoffman and Frank H. Pollak, 44*–54*. Jerusalem, Tel-Aviv: Bialik Institute and Tel-Aviv University, 1997.

Tov, Emanuel. *Textual Criticism of the Hebrew Bible*. 3rd ed. Minneapolis: Fortress, 2012.

Tov, Emanuel. "Textual Harmonization in Exodus 1–24." *TC: A Journal of Biblical Textual Criticism* 22 (2017): 1–24.

Tov, Emanuel. "Textual Harmonizations in the Ancient Texts of Deuteronomy." In *Mishneh Toda: Studies in Deuteronomy and Its Cultural Environment in Honor of Jeffrey H. Tigay*, edited by Nili Sacher Fox, David A. Glatt-Gilad, and Michael J. Williams, 15–28. Winona Lake: Eisenbrauns, 2015.

Tov, Emanuel. "The Development of the Text of the Torah in Two Major Text Blocks." *Textus* 26 (2016): 1–27.

Tov, Emanuel. "The Papyrus Nash and the Septuagint." In *A Necessary Task: Essays on Textual Criticism of the Old Testament in Memory of Stephen Pisano*, edited by Dionisio Candido and Leonardo Pessoa de Silva Pinto, 33–50. Biblica 14. Roma: Pontificia Università Gregoriana and Pontificio Istituto Biblico, 2020.

Tov, Emanuel. "The Qumran Scribal Practice: The Evidence from Orthography and Morphology." *Studia Orientalia* 99 (2004): 353–68.

Tov, Emanuel. "The Qumran Tefillin and Their Possible Master Copies." In *On Wings of Prayer*, edited by Nuria Calduch-Benages, Michael W. Duggan, and Dalia Marx, 135–50. Berlin: De Gruyter, 2019.

Tov, Emanuel. "The Socio-Religious Setting of the (Proto-)Masoretic Text." *Textus* 27 (2018): 135–53.

Tov, Emanuel. "The Tefillin from the Judean Desert and the Textual Criticism of the Hebrew Bible." In *Is There a Text in This Cave: Studies in the Textuality of the Dead Sea Scrolls in Honour of George J. Brooke*, edited by Ariel Feldman, Maria Cioată, and Charlotte Hempel, 277–92. STDJ 119. Leiden: Brill, 2017.

Tov, Emanuel, and Eugene Ulrich. "1.1.1.2 Textual Theories." In *Textual History of the Bible*, edited by Armin Lange. Brill, 2020. http://dx.doi.org.ezproxy.tcu.edu/10.1163/2452-4107_thb_COM_0001010102.

Vermes, Geza. "Pre-Mishnaic Jewish Worship and the Phylacteries from the Dead Sea." *VT* 9 (1959): 65–72.

Weinfeld, Moshe. "Grace after Meals in Qumran." *JBL* 111 (1992): 427–40.

Weissenberg, Hanne von. "Deuteronomy at Qumran and in 4QMMT." In *All Good Things: Essays in Memory of Timo Veijola*, edited by Juha Pakkala and Marti Nissinen, 520–37. Helsinki: Finnish Exegetical Society, 2008.

Werman, Cana. "The Two Covenants: An Interpretation of the 4Q158 Fragments." *JSP* 28 (2019): 183–213.

White Crawford, Sidnie. "Exodus in the Dead Sea Scrolls." In *The Book of Exodus: Composition, Reception, and Interpretation*, edited by Thomas Dozeman, Craig A. Evans, and Joel N. Lohr, 305–21. Leiden: Brill, 2014.

White Crawford, Sidnie. "2.4.1.5 Deuteronomy." In *Textual History of the Bible*, edited by Armin Lange. Brill, 2020. http://dx.doi.org.ezproxy.tcu.edu/10.1163/2452-4107_thb_COM_0002040105.

White Crawford, Sidnie. "Reading Deuteronomy in the Second Temple Period." In *Reading the Present in the Qumran Library*, edited by Kristin De Troyer and Armin Lange, 127–40. Atlanta: SBL, 2005.

White Crawford, Sidnie. *Rewriting Scripture in Second Temple Times*. Grand Rapids: Eerdmans, 2008.

White Crawford, Sidnie. "The Excerpted Manuscripts from Qumran, with Special Attention to 4QReworked Pentateuch D and 4QReworked Pentateuch E." In *Scribal Practice, Text and*

Canon in the Dead Sea Scrolls: Essays in Memory of Peter W. Flint, edited by John J. Collins and Ananda Geyser-Fouché, 247–68. STDJ 130. Leiden: Brill, 2019.

White Crawford, Sidnie. "Understanding the Textual History of the Hebrew Bible: A New Proposal." In *The Hebrew Bible in Light of the Dead Sea Scrolls*, 60–69. FRLANT 239. Göttingen: Vandenhoeck & Ruprecht, 2012.

Wise, Michael Owen. *Language and Literacy in Roman Judaea: A Study of the Bar Kokhba Documents*. New Haven: Yale University Press, 2015.

Yadin, Yigael. *Tefillin from Qumran*. Jerusalem: The Israel Exploration Society, 1969.

Yadin, Yigael. "Tefillin (Phylacteries) from Qumran (XQPhyl 1–4)." *Eretz-Israel* 9 (1969): 60–85 (Hebrew).

Yardeni, Ada. *Textbook of Aramaic, Hebrew and Nabataean Documentary Texts from the Judaean Desert and Related Materials*. Jerusalem: The Ben-Zion Dinur Center for Research in Jewish History, 2000.

Young, Ian. "The Stabilization of the Biblical Text in the Light of Qumran and Masada: A Challenge for Conventional Qumran Chronology?" *DSD* 9 (2002): 364–90.

Zahn, Molly. *Genres of Rewriting in Second Temple Judaism: Scribal Composition and Transmission*. Cambridge: Cambridge University Press, 2020.

Zahn, Molly. *Rethinking Rewritten Scripture: Composition and Exegesis in the 4QReworked Pentateuch Manuscripts*. STDJ 95. Leiden: Brill, 2011.

Zahn, Molly. "Reworked Pentateuch." In *T&T Clark Encyclopedia of Second Temple Judaism: Volume 1*, edited by Daniel Gurtner and Loren T. Stuckenbruck, 461–64. London: T&T Clark, 2019.

List of Figures

Figure 1: 4QPhyl S (B–295563).

Figure 2: 4QMez G (PAM 43.458).

Figure 3: 4QPhyl A recto line 17 (PAM 43.454).

Figure 4: 4QPhyl L verso (PAM 43.455).

Figure 5: 4QPhyl L recto. Left: PAM 42.828 (flipped horizontally); right: PAM 42.828.

Figure 6: 4QPhyl L verso (PAM 42.828, flipped horizontally and brightened).

Figure 7: 4QPhyl L verso (PAM 42.828).

Figure 8: Frags. 1 and 2 (PAM 42.604).

Figure 9: PAM 42.829 (left) and PAM 42.828 (right).

Figure 10: Joining semi-folded frags. 1 and 2 (PAM 42.829).

Figure 11: Frags. 1 and 2 (PAM 42.829).

Figure 12: Left: Frags. 2 and 2a recto (PAM 43.456); right: Frags. 2 and 2a verso (PAM 43.457).

Figure 13: Left: Frag. 2a recto (PAM 43.456); right: Frag. 2a verso (PAM 43.457).

Figure 14: Frag. 6. Left: recto (PAM 43.456); right: verso (PAM 43.457).

Figure 15: Placing frag. 6 (PAM 43.456).

Figure 16: A digital unfolding of frag. 2 (PAM 43.456; 43.457).

Figure 17: Frags. 1, 2, 2d, and 6 (PAM 43.456; 43.457).

Figure 18: Frag. 5 (PAM 48.828).

Figure 19: Joining Frag. 5 in the beginning of lines 8–9 of Frag. 1 (PAM 43.456).

Figure 20: Lost scraps? (PAM 48.828).

Figure 21: PAM 42.829 (left; flipped vertically) and PAM 42.828 (right).

Figure 22: Folding 4QPhyl T (PAM 43.456; 43.457).

Figure 23: Horizontal folding (left: PAM 42.828 flipped vertically; right: PAM 42.829).

Figure 24: The last horizontal fold (PAM 42.604).

Figure 25: Reading Deut 11:18–21 in the newly-reconstructed Frag. 1 (PAM 43.456; 43.457).

Figure 26: 4QPhyl U verso (new infrared image).

Figure 27: 4QPhyl U recto (PAM 43.456).

Figure 28: 4QPhyl U recto line 11 (PAM 43.456).

Figure 29: 4QMez C (PAM 43.460).

Figure 30: Frag. 1 (PAM 43.460).

Figure 31: Frag. 2 (PAM 43.460).

Figure 32: The placement of Deut 6:4–9 and 11:13–21 in Group I.

Figure 33: Frag. 16 (PAM 42.494).

Figure 34: Group II, lines 19–21 (Frag. 16; digitally brightened new full-color image).

Figure 35: Frag. 26 (PAM 42.494).

Figure 36: PAM 42.494 (left) and a new infrared image (right; digitally brightened).

Figure 37: Frag. 30 on PAM 42.494 (left) and a new infrared image (right; digitally brightened).

Figure 38: Small scraps of Frag. 30 (digitally brightened new full-color image).

https://doi.org/10.1515/9783110725377-012

Subject Index

Abbreviated (or excerpted) texts 39, 131
– Liturgical use thereof 39, 49, 51, 52
Addition(s), expansion(s) 28, 33, 38–44, 51–
   58, 99, 105, 106, 122, 123, 140
Aggregating thematically related passages
   51, 105, 140, 142
Amulet 2, 6, 8, 9, 59, 80
Angelic names 80, 81
Apotropaic texts and practices 2, 59, 80

Commandments pertaining to tefillin and
   mezuzah 1, 7, 30, 33, 43, 130, 131

Decalogue 20, 26, 28, 30, 39, 41, 42, 49, 51,
   52, 95, 130–32, 140, 141
– Sabbath commandment 30, 105, 106, 130,
   132
Deuteronomy, book of
– Dead Sea Scrolls 44–51
– Masoretic Text 42–43
– Samaritan Pentateuch 43
– Septuagint 43–44
Duplicate passages in tefillin 137–39

Excerpted texts, see *Abbreviated texts*
Exodus, book of
– Dead Sea Scrolls 34–42
– Masoretic Text 32
– Samaritan Pentateuch 33
– Septuagint 33–34

Forgeries, modern 35, 37, 42, 44

Hanani (name) 92, 93
Harmonization 28, 30, 32–34, 43, 44, 50–
   52, 54, 101, 105, 130,
Homoioteleuton 56–58, 60, 123

Karaites 1

Magic 28, 59
Masada 23, 24, 48
Master text 49, 62

Mezuzah
– Cases 25
– Classification 29–30
– Differentiating between mezuzah and
   tefillin 25–28
– Folding 97, 98, 101,
– Morphology 30
– Orthography 30
– Rabbinic halakhah 30
– Scripts 25–26
– Textual profiles 30
Miriam, Song of 40, 124, 140
Moses 32, 42, 43, 54, 55, 131

Non-aligned texts 16, 38, 48, 50, 51

Omission(s) 16, 40, 51, 52, 57–61, 104–106,
   114, 123, 140
Opisthograph 12, 143

Papyrus Nash 26, 44, 49, 51, 79, 106, 125
Paraphrase 50, 51, 105, 123, 130, 140, 142
Pastiche 33, 50, 51, 54
Prayer 1, 5, 49–51, 124
Pre-Samaritan texts 15, 33, 38, 40, 41, 43,
   50, 51

Rabbenu Tam 20, 102
Rashi 20, 102
Rearrangement 42, 55, 138–41
Rewriting 35, 38, 41, 51, 52, 140

Sabbath commandment, see *Decalogue*
Shema 13, 16, 20, 26, 48, 49, 72
Simeon Bar Kokhba 24
Sinai revelation 37, 42, 54
Sukkoth 50, 105, 140

Tefillin
– Arm tefillin 1, 7, 20, 62, 102–104, 139
– Case 6–8, 19–20, 62, 91, 92, 103, 142
– Classification 13–25
– Corrections, scribal 20–21, 47

https://doi.org/10.1515/9783110725377-013

– Fastening 7, 13, 19, 91, 93
– Folding 13, 49, 74, 75, 87–88, 91, 141
– Head tefillin 7, 102, 103, 139
– Layout of the text 19, 59, 104
– Morphology 17–18

– Orthography 17–18
– Rabbinic halakhah 18–21
– Scripts 9, 13
– Textual profile 15–16
Tetragrammaton 130

Index of Ancient Sources

Hebrew Bible

Genesis
Gen 32:25   37

Exodus
Exod 5:6   32
Exod 6:9   33
Exod 7:18   33
Exod 10:2   33
Exod 12:31   135
Exod 12:43–51   20, 72, 102, 105
Exod 12:43–13:7   13
Exod 12:43–13:16   13, 14
Exod 12:44   105
Exod 12:46   105
Exod 12:48   105
Exod 12:49   105
Exod 12:51–13:3   30
Exod 13:1–10   19, 39, 102
Exod 13:1–10, 11–16   103
Exod 13:1–16   26, 39
Exod 13:3   30
Exod 13:5   17, 18, 104
Exod 13:6   16, 17, 141
Exod 13:7   11, 70, 73, 141
Exod 13:8   141
Exod 13:9, 16   1
Exod 13:9   16, 101
Exod 13:11   17
Exod 13:11–16   26, 72
Exod 13:12   15, 104
Exod 13:15   70
Exod 13:15–16   39, 71
Exod 13:16   7, 16, 19, 20, 101
Exod 16:10   35
Exod 16:12   35
Exod 17:4   35
Exod 18:24   33

Exod 19:9   36
Exod 19:17   37
Exod 20:10–11   124
Exod 20:11   30, 106, 131, 132
Exod 20:11–13   125
Exod 20:12–17   41, 42
Exod 20:13–15   44
Exod 20:17   33, 124
Exod 20:18–19a   41
Exod 20:19   41
Exod 20:21   41
Exod 20:22   41, 131
Exod 23:8   50
Exod 24:7   37
Exod 26:35   33
Exod 29:21   33
Exod 30:1–10   33
Exod 36:9–34   34
Exod 37:24–28   34

Leviticus
Lev 19:15   50

Numbers
Num 16:32   50
Num 20:14, 17   43
Num 20:17–18   50
Num 29:14–24   50
Num 29:32–30:1   50
Num 33:31–37   43

Deuteronomy
Deut 1:16–17   50
Deut 2:8–14   50
Deut 2:30–3:2   50
Deut 4:12   131
Deut 4:12–13   54

Note: To facilitate the use of this index, it excludes the sources listed in the tables found on pages 9–12, 28–29, 35–38, and 45–48.

https://doi.org/10.1515/9783110725377-014

Deut 5:1   101, 105
Deut 5:1–2   42, 131
Deut 5:1, 4–5   130
Deut 5:1–14   131
Deut 5:1–21   53
Deut 5:1–22   64, 69
Deut 5:1–6:3   20, 102
Deut 5:1–6:9   13, 14
Deut 5:2   105
Deut 5:3   130, 131
Deut 5:3, 5–6   138
Deut 5:5   105, 124
Deut 5:5, 22   54
Deut 5:6   131
Deut 5:7–24   74, 77
Deut 5:8   94, 95, 105
Deut 5:9   18, 94, 95
Deut 5:11   28, 105, 124, 135, 138
Deut 5:11, 13   124
Deut 5:14   106
Deut 5:15   101, 132, 137
Deut 5:16   79
Deut 5:16–17   94
Deut 5:17   43
Deut 5:17–18   44
Deut 5:20   94, 125
Deut 5:20–21   124, 125, 137
Deut 5:21   95, 124
Deut 5:21–22   136, 138
Deut 5:22   54, 131
Deut 5:22–33   114, 131
Deut 5:22, 5–6, 3, 15–16   137
Deut 5:23–27   64
Deut 5:24   71
Deut 5:24–27   33
Deut 5:24–31   41
Deut 5:27   41
Deut 5:27–33   99
Deut 5:28–29   41, 46
Deut 5:29   54
Deut 5:29, 31   114
Deut 5:29–31   64
Deut 5:29–32   65
Deut 5:29–33   66, 114, 137
Deut 5:29–6:3   59
Deut 5:30–31   41, 42
Deut 5:31   60, 65, 135, 138
Deut 5:32   28, 57

Deut 5:32–33   30, 56–58, 99
Deut 5:32–6:2   55, 59–61, 66, 114
Deut 5:32–6:3   30, 61
Deut 5:33   55, 65, 66, 72
Deut 6:1   57, 106, 111
Deut 6:1–2   44, 58, 60
Deut 6:1–3   106, 114
Deut 6:1–9   72
Deut 6:2   54, 59, 106
Deut 6:3   106, 114
Deut 6:4   44
Deut 6:4–9   1, 13, 14, 19, 20, 26, 102–104
Deut 6:4–11   48
Deut 6:4   16
Deut 6:5   29
Deut 6:6–9   2
Deut 6:7   17
Deut 6:8   7
Deut 6:8–9   1
Deut 6:9   125, 137–39
Deut 7:7   130
Deut 8:5–10   49, 62
Deut 9:20   33
Deut 9:25   44
Deut 10:6–7, 10   50
Deut 10:12   122, 137
Deut 10:12–13   137, 138
Deut 10:12–14   122
Deut 10:12–11:21   13
Deut 10:12–11:10   20
Deut 10:12–11:12   123
Deut 10:12–19   105, 106
Deut 10:13   105, 115, 122, 123, 134, 138
Deut 10:14   122
Deut 10:15   105
Deut 10:15–22   123
Deut 10:17   105
Deut 10:17–18   66, 69
Deut 10:18   106
Deut 10:18–19   105
Deut 10:19   105
Deut 10:20–22   105, 106, 114, 138
Deut 10:20–11:1   123
Deut 10:21–22   123, 137, 138
Deut 10:22   106, 114, 122
Deut 11:1   137, 138
Deut 11:1–12   138
Deut 11:2   116, 123

Deut 11:3   123
Deut 11:4   67, 68, 123
Deut 11:6   50
Deut 11:7   122, 124
Deut 11:8   59, 123
Deut 11:10   123
Deut 11:11   123
Deut 11:12   66, 69, 123
Deut 11:13   17, 122
Deut 11:13–21   20, 62, 69, 72, 102, 104
Deut 11:14   122
Deut 11:17–20   68, 69
Deut 11:18–21   80, 90
Deut 11:19–21   26, 54
Deut 11:21   16, 59, 90
Deut 12:11–14   44
Deut 16:13–14   50
Deut 16:19   50
Deut 18:18–19   41
Deut 23:18   44
Deut 27:4   42, 43, 44
Deut 29:24   45
Deut 32:14–20   49

Joshua
Josh 10:10, 20   124

1 Samuel
1 Sam 4:10   124
1 Sam 6:19   124

1 Sam 19:8   124
1 Sam 23:5   124

1 Kings
1 Kgs 16:1, 7   92

Jeremiah
Jer 10:6   124

Ezekiel
Ezek 14:4, 7   79

Habakkuk
Hab 2:1–3   35

Psalms
Ps 36:9   88
Ps 86:10   124

Ezra
Ezra 10:20   92

Nehemiah
Neh 1:2   92

1 Chronicles
1 Chr 25:4   92

2 Chronicles
2 Chr 19:2   92
2 Chr 20:34   92

Dead Sea Scrolls

Cave 1
1QH^a 12:19   79
1QPhyl (1Q13)   4, 5, 12, 14, 15, 17, 22, 49, 55, 62–73, 81, 101, 141

Cave 4
4QExod^d (4Q15)   39
4QExod^e (4Q16)   39
4QExod^g (4Q18)   30, 40
4QpaleoExod^m (4Q22)   38, 40, 41
4QDeut^j (4Q37)   42, 48, 49, 62
4QDeut^{k1} (4Q38)   48, 49
4QDeut^n (4Q41)   48, 49, 79, 106, 125, 131, 132

4QDeut^q (4Q43)   43, 48, 49
4QMez A (4Q150)   29, 30, 106
4QMez B (4q150)   3, 30, 75
4QMez C (4Q151)   4, 29, 30, 57–60, 66, 96–101, 142
4QMez D (4Q152)   29, 30
4QMez E (4Q153)   30
4QMez F (4Q154)   29, 30, 96
4QMez G (4Q155)   30
4QPhyl A (4Q128)   5, 13–15, 17, 22, 49, 50, 55–56, 58, 66, 72, 114
4QPhyl B (4Q129)   14, 17, 22, 56, 58, 59, 60, 124, 131

4QPhyl C (4Q130)   14, 17, 21, 22, 104
4QPhyl D (4Q131)   4, 13–17, 22, 103
4QPhyl E (4Q132)   4, 13–17, 22, 103
4QPhyl F (4Q133)   4, 13–17, 22, 103
4QPhyl G (4Q134)   14, 15, 17, 22, 42, 51, 53–
   55, 78, 106, 131
4QPhyl H (4Q135)   14, 15, 17, 22, 55, 59–61,
   66
4QPhyl I (4Q136)   14, 15, 17, 22
4QPhyl J (4Q137)   14, 15, 17, 22, 57–59
4QPhyl K (4Q138)   14, 15, 17, 22, 114
4QPhyl L (4Q139)   4, 8, 14, 15, 17, 22, 74–
   79, 141
4QPhyl M (4Q140)   4, 8, 14, 15, 17, 22, 55
4QPhyl N (4Q141)   4, 8, 14, 15, 17, 20–22,
   25, 49, 141
4QPhyl O (4Q142)   14, 15, 17, 22
4QPhyl P (4Q143)   14, 15, 17, 22
4QPhyl Q (4Q144)   14, 15, 17, 22
4QPhyl R (4Q145)   14, 15, 17, 22
4QPhyl S (4Q146)   14–17, 26, 22, 27

4QPhyl T (4Q147)   3, 8, 80–90
4QPhyl U (4Q148)   3, 8, 74, 91–95
4Q158 (4QRPᵃ)   35, 38, 41, 42, 44, 55, 131,
   140
4Q175 (4QTestimonia)   41
4Q364 (4QRPᵇ)   35, 44, 50
4Q365 (4QRPᶜ)   40, 47, 124, 140
4Q366 (4QRPᵈ)   50, 105, 140
4Q377   42

Cave 5
5QPhyl (5Q8)   4, 14, 15, 17

Cave 8
8QMez (8Q4)   3, 5, 26, 30, 96
8QPhyl (8Q3)   4, 5, 14, 15, 17, 18, 21–24, 41,
   42, 51, 54, 55, 59, 61, 63, 102–140, 141,
   142

Cave 11
11Q31   5, 8

Texts from Other Sites in the Judean Desert

Wadi Murabbaʿat
MurPhyl (Mur4)   5, 6, 15, 17, 21, 22, 62
Mur5   3, 5, 28, 29, 141

Naḥal Ṣeʾelim
34ṢePhyl (34Ṣe 1 A-B)   5, 14, 15, 17, 22, 25

Naḥal Ṣeʾelim/Naḥal Ḥever
XḤev/SePhyl (XḤev/Se 5)   5, 14–17, 22, 23

Unknown Provenance
XQPhyl 1   5, 8, 13–15, 17, 21–22, 116
XQPhyl 2   5, 8, 13–15, 17, 21–22, 55, 111,
   116, 131
XQPhyl 3   5, 8, 13–15, 17, 21–22, 116, 125
XQPhyl 4   4, 5, 8, 13, 15, 22, 141, 142

New Testament

Matt 23:5   6

Hellenistic Jewish authors

Letter of Aristeas 158–159   1

Philo
Decal. 52   130
Spec. Laws 4.137–142   2

Josephus
Ant. 3:91   130
Ant. 4:212–213   2

Rabbinic Literature

Mishnah
m. Kelim 18:8   19
m. Megillah 4:8   19
m. Menahot 3:7   19
m. Sanhedrin 11:3   19
m. Tamid 5:1   20, 49

Tosefta
t. Kelim, Bava Bathra 4:1   19

Midrashic collections
Canticles Rabbah 1:2   42
Mek. de Rabbi Ishmael, Bo 18 (Exod 13:16)
     19, 20
Sifre Deut 35   19, 20

Babylonian Talmud
b. Eruvin 98a   21
b. Megillah 18b   19, 30

b. Menahot 32b   19, 30
b. Menahot 33a   30
b. Menahot 34b   20, 102
b. Menahot 35a   19
b. Menahot 35b   20
b. Menahot 36b   5
b. Menahot 47b   31
b. Shabbat 28b   19
b. Shabbat 108a   19
b. Sukkah 28a   5

Jerusalem Talmud
y. Berachot 1:4, 3c   20
y. Megillah 1:9, 71c   19
y. Megillah 4:8, 75c   19